PRAISE FOR
UNDER AND ALONE

"*Under and Alone* is the dangerous and fascinating true story of an undercover ATF agent and the psychological price he was made to pay for his courageous work."

—JOSEPH WAMBAUGH,
bestselling author of *The Onion Field*

"This harrowing, turbocharged account of undercover life is reminiscent of Joseph D. Pistone's *Donnie Brasco*. . . . Queen steers clear of melodrama and captures both sides of his double life. . . . The strength and white-hot intensity of the writing make this read like a movie."

—*Publishers Weekly* (starred review)

"Riveting . . . For two and a half years, undercover federal agent Billy Queen was Billy St. John, a beer-swilling badass biker in the Mongols, an outlaw gang so violent and crazy they make the Hells Angels look like Cub Scouts on Vespas."

—*Maxim* (Book of the Month)

Also by William Queen
Published by Ballantine Books

ARMED AND DANGEROUS

Books published by The Random House Publishing Group
are available at quantity discounts on bulk purchases for
premium, educational, fund-raising, and special sales use.
For details, please call 1-800-733-3000.

UNDER
AND ALONE

THE TRUE STORY OF THE UNDERCOVER AGENT
WHO INFILTRATED AMERICA'S MOST VIOLENT
OUTLAW MOTORCYCLE GANG

WILLIAM QUEEN

FAWCETT

BALLANTINE BOOKS • NEW YORK

2006 Fawcett Books Mass Market Edition

Published in the United States by Fawcett Books, an imprint of The Random House Publishing Group, a division of Random House, Inc., New York.

FAWCETT BOOKS and colophon are trademarks of Random House, Inc.

Originally published in hardcover in the United States by Random House, an imprint of The Random House Publishing Group, a division of Random House, Inc., in 2005.

Grateful acknowledgment is made to the *Los Angeles Times* for permission to reprint an excerpt from "42 Arrested in Motorcycle Gang Raid" by Mitchell Landsberg, published in the May 20, 2000, edition of the *Los Angeles Times*. Reprinted by permission.

ISBN 0-345-48752-4

Printed in the United States of America

www.ballantinebooks.com

OPM 19

To the men and women
who make up
the Thin Blue Line

Author's Note

Except as otherwise noted, the facts recounted in this book, as well as the names of individuals and the places depicted, are real. The government's three-year investigation into the criminal activities of the Mongols Motorcycle Club led to a number of firsts in the efforts of federal law enforcement to curb a growing problem of organized violence in the United States. Criminal acts described in this book are reflected in thousands of hours of covertly recorded conversations as well as thousands of documents generated by law enforcement agencies, along with the United States attorney's office and district attorney offices in numerous jurisdictions.

To the extent that my recounting is less detailed in certain sections of the book than in others, the reader will understand that I have been purposely vague in places where I have felt the need to protect myself and others who may be at risk of retaliation from members of the Mongols Motorcycle Club. Although years have passed since the investigation was concluded, threats continue to surface, making me acutely aware that I will always be looking over my shoulder.

1

"All right, Billy, how long was your fuckin' academy?"

Red Dog pressed his ruddy, windburned face three inches from mine. I smelled that thick mix of Budweiser and crank-fueled sleeplessness on his breath. The words he spat felt hotter than the midday Southern California sun. He cocked his head to one side and pushed closer. "I'm askin' you a fuckin' question, Billy!"

Red Dog, the national sergeant at arms of the Mongols Motorcycle Club, stood six feet tall, with long, stringy hair and a rust-colored handlebar mustache that drooped below his chin. From his pierced forehead, a silver chain swept down ominously past his left eye. His powerfully muscled arms were sleeved out with a web of prison tattoos, and his right hand clutched a loaded 9-mm Glock semiautomatic. Behind him, six other Mongols—Evel, C.J., Domingo, Diablo, Bobby Loco, and Lucifer—all in various states of drunkenness and methamphetamine highs, were slapping magazines into their Glocks and Berettas. More than one had his Mongol colors decorated with the skull-and-crossbones patch, boldly announcing to the world that he had killed for the club.

Here at the end of a long dirt road, in an abandoned orange grove 180 miles north of Los Angeles, what had begun as a typical Southern California day—that perfect golden sun beating down on a ribbon of black highway—had quickly turned into my worst nightmare.

For several months now, working deep undercover on assignment for the Department of the Treasury's Bureau of Alcohol, Tobacco and Firearms (ATF), I'd been posing as a Mongols "prospect"—a probationary member of the club, a position that allowed me to wear my black leather vest with the lower rocker reading CALIFORNIA but not yet the official black-and-white center patch and top rocker that distinguished a full-fledged member.

As a prospect, you're a slave, the property of the club. You have to do everything a member tells you to do, from hauling drugs and guns to wiping a member's ass if he orders you to. Some members were good for simple orders like "Prospect, go get me a beer," or "Light my cigarette," or "Clean my bike." But other members, guys like Red Dog, took inordinate pleasure in making a prospect's life a living hell.

Prospecting inside the Mongols was a dangerous game. According to intel developed by ATF, the Mongols Motorcycle Club had assumed the mantle of the most violent motorcycle gang in America, a tight-knit collective of crazies, unpredictable and unrepentant badasses. With 350 full-patch members, the gang was a small fraction of the size of the Hells Angels, their hated rivals, but the Mongols had wreaked more than their fair share of havoc since they were founded in the early seventies.

Their most significant violent acts in the 1970s and '80s were committed against the Angels, with whom they fought (and ultimately won) a seventeen-year war. But by the mid-nineties, infused by the ruthless Latino gang mentality of East Los Angeles, the Mongols' indiscriminate violence spread outside the biker underworld and began to terrorize the general populace of Southern California. When the Mongols frequented mainstream bars and clubs, where people were not as familiar with the gang's fearsome reputation, the result was a series of vicious assaults, stabbings, and gunfights. In late 1997 the Mongols got into a confrontation in a club in the San Gabriel Valley, just outside of L.A., which resulted in a shoot-out, leaving one man dead. Also in 1997, the Mongols went to two nightclubs in the Los Angeles area and stabbed patrons in plain view of dozens of witnesses, but no one would come forward to testify against them.

Nor was the Mongols' violence limited to the outside world; even within the ranks of the club, the gang had such a reputation for assaulting its prospects that by the late nineties, the membership was dwindling: No one wanted to join a club if it meant that every day and night he had to worry about taking a savage beat-down. In 1998 they adopted a new national policy: No beating on the prospects. And almost everyone stuck by it, except for Red Dog.

Despite the fact that as national sergeant at arms he was supposed to be enforcing the club's rules and constitution—yes, the club had a seventy-page constitution— Red Dog was a loose cannon, riding his Harley through life with a "fuck everyone" attitude. For months he was in my face, smashing his heavy fist into my chest, at times uppercutting me as hard as he could. More than once he'd sucker-punched me in the gut, leaving me doubled over, gasping for air, and ready to puke. But I was a prospect, so I gritted my teeth and sucked it up.

That morning we had all hooked up at C.J.'s house, where the dudes drank hard and I did my prospect thing, fetching beer for the patches (as fully inducted members of the club are called), lighting their cigarettes, watching them do line after line of crank and coke. Then when Red Dog figured everyone was drunk and high enough, he gave an abrupt order: "Let's go shoot."

This was a Mongols membership requirement: Before

any prospect could attain full-patch status in the club, he had to prove that he owned a firearm and was a decent shot. When I got behind the wheel of my bullet-pocked red Mustang, I thought we were heading out to an actual firing range—and so did my ATF backup. We formed a ragged convoy behind Red Dog's burgundy Monte Carlo as we left the Visalia city limits. I kept glancing in my rearview mirror, checking to see that my backup was still there. But as we got farther and farther into the country-side of vineyards and orange groves, eventually turning down a remote dirt driveway, I realized we had com-pletely lost my backup. I also realized this wasn't going to be a standard firearms-qualification exercise. There was nothing ATF could do to help me now. If shit went bad, it just went bad. I was alone.

Now, with a collection of new semiautomatic pistols on the hoods of our cars and the loaded magazines click-ing into place, the mood in the orange grove suddenly turned dark and twisted. One Mongol brother stood loading rounds into a street-sweeper, a high-capacity, drum-fed semiautomatic 12-gauge shotgun that looks similar to the old Thompson submachine gun from the Prohibition era. An awesome assault weapon, beloved by drug dealers and hard-core gangsters, the street-sweeper has since been banned by the feds. I knew that a gun like that was useless for target shooting; like the tommy gun, a street-sweeper is a pure killing machine.

Without warning, Red Dog was up in my face again, head cocked to one side, hollering crazily—accusing me of being an undercover cop. "How long was your fuckin' academy, Billy?"

"What are you talkin' about, Red Dog?"

"You know what I'm talking about, Billy! Who the fuck did you tell you was comin' up here? Who the fuck did you tell you was gonna be with the Mongols today? Who, Billy?"

"I didn't tell nobody. Come on, Red, why you acting like this? I didn't tell nobody I was coming up to Visalia."

He locked his slate blue eyes on mine and, in torturous silence, stared at me for fifteen seconds. "So you're saying if I put a bullet in the back of your fuckin' head right now, ain't *nobody* gonna know where to start looking for you? Is that right, Billy?"

"Yeah, I guess that's right, Red Dog."

He gestured across the dusty, desolate, trash-strewn field, told me to go set up some cans to shoot at. My first thought was of the infamous 1963 Onion Field case, chronicled in Joseph Wambaugh's bestseller and subsequent movie, in which two young LAPD officers, after stopping a vehicle in Hollywood they suspected had been involved in a series of armed robberies, were kidnapped by a pair of ex-convicts and taken to a remote onion field outside Bakersfield. Officer Ian Campbell was shot dead while Officer Karl Hettinger watched in horror before escaping with his life.

When I turned my back to Red Dog and the other armed Mongols, the icy realization hit me: After the firefights in Vietnam, after twenty-five years in law enforcement, this was the way it ended—I was going to die on a gorgeous Southern California day, by a Mongol bullet, in the middle of a godforsaken, abandoned orange grove somewhere outside Visalia.

I closed my eyes and began to walk, waiting for the bullets to start tearing through my back. I couldn't even turn to shoot it out: Red Dog and Domingo had made certain that I was the only one without a gun. It was a simple equation: If they'd made me, I was going to die today. I stumbled across the field in my motorcycle boots and suddenly saw an image of my two sons standing tearfully over my open casket. I'd felt similar eerie premonitions during my tour of duty in Vietnam, but here, without question, there was nothing worth dying for.

Suddenly, I heard a loud pop and felt my boot crunching an empty beer can. My knees buckled, but I bent down and picked up the can. I glanced back toward the Mongols and saw them talking in a tight circle instead of pointing their guns and training their sights on me. No, they weren't going to shoot me, at least not right now . . .

2

"Queen, line one!"

It was a bright morning in late February 1998, and I was sitting in my office on Van Nuys Boulevard, typing up reports, when I got the call that changed my life. Picking up the receiver, I heard the voice of Special Agent John Ciccone, calling from ATF Group II in downtown Los Angeles. "Billy Boy," he said, "how'd you like a shot at riding with the Mongols?"

I stared down at the stream of muscle cars and motorcycles speeding down Van Nuys. Ciccone was known for his bad practical jokes as well as his choice of bad nicknames, but I could tell he was dead serious on this one. "What's going on, Johnny?"

Ciccone knew I'd been hanging out with the Hells Angels for a few weeks, gathering intel for another case agent. At the time, ATF was working an investigation in conjunction with the Internal Revenue Service and the Ventura County Sheriff's Department, trying to make a prosecution against the Angels. Ciccone also knew that the Mongols were the gang responsible for much of the biker-related murder and mayhem in the L.A. area.

"Billy, why don't you forget that Red and White crap and take a look at the Mongols?" The Hells Angels are often called the Red and White because of the colors of their patch. The Mongols are known as the Black and White.

Ciccone, an eleven-year veteran of ATF, wasn't your stereotypical agent: "One-man, one-gun" cases really didn't excite him much. Five feet seven, wiry, clean-cut, Ciccone was the kind of guy you might easily pass on a sidewalk or in a shopping mall and take no notice of. Despite his small stature, he had the fierce determination of a long-distance runner—he ran marathons and pumped weights with fanaticism—and, within ATF, carried himself with tremendous command presence.

Ciccone and I had worked together from 1992 to 1998 in the ATF's Special Response Team, the federal version of SWAT. Over the years I'd developed a deep admiration for John's skills; he could manage complex investigative cases like no one else I had seen at ATF. It's not a talent they can teach at the ATF academy in Glynco, Georgia. John was gifted with the ability to juggle the fragile egos and self-promoting attitudes of ATF management, often a good-ol'-boy network with an ingrained us-versus-them mentality. I had also come to recognize Ciccone as a barracuda who could swim in the shadow of great white sharks and still manage to come away with dinner.

"Talk to me, Johnny," I said. "What you got on the Mongols?"

Over the previous few months Ciccone had been receiving increasingly disturbing reports on the surge in the Mongols' criminal activity across the United States. Those of us who worked the biker underworld for ATF had become alarmed as the Mongols' penchant for assaults, gunfights, and cold-blooded murder spread from the biker scene into the general population.

While this "Mongol Nation," as they refer to themselves, spans the southern and western United States and Mexico, with growing chapters in Oklahoma, Arizona, Colorado, and Georgia, its stronghold is Southern California, in particular the Hispanic communities in and around Los Angeles.

Ciccone told me that he had a confidential informant—or CI—who looked promising. The young woman was willing to make an introduction to the gang. And if I was interested, Ciccone said, he'd deal with the administrative types, handle the paperwork, and we'd be good to go.

I watched the candy-painted Chevy Impalas blasting bass-heavy Latino rap and the roaring Harley-Davidson bikes chewing up the asphalt. "Well, then . . . line it up."

Neither Ciccone nor I realized the extent of the perils we'd be facing or the personal sacrifices we'd be making over the next twenty-eight months; neither one of us dreamed that this routine phone call was about to become the most extensive undercover operation inside an outlaw motorcycle gang in the history of American law enforcement.

In March 1998 I'd gone up to Oakland to trade motorcycles with Special Agent Steve Martin, the group supervisor, also known as the resident agent in charge (RAC), of the Oakland office. I held Martin, a graduate of the U.S. Military Academy at West Point, in high esteem; we'd had a friendly but intense rivalry during our time at the ATF's Special Response Team school. He and I were the two oldest candidates in our class. He'd finished number one and I'd finished a tight number two.

Earlier in his ATF career, Martin had ridden undercover with another outlaw motorcycle gang (or OMG), the Warlocks, out of Florida, and managed to send a well-deserving group of them to prison on federal drug, guns, and explosives charges. He had a soft spot for the bike he'd ridden in that case. When he relocated to Oakland, he'd brought the bike with him as a trophy of his accomplishments. Now I hoped it would bring me a little luck.

It was definitely a biker's bike. A stripped-down version of a Harley-Davidson FLHTC, it was black with leather bags and a badass hot-rod engine that would rival the fastest bike in any gang. With straight drag pipes and a compression ratio well above a stock Harley, this hog could be heard from a mile away. If you were a cop, from two miles. The fact that I would enjoy riding it was simply icing on the cake.

After lining up all the required paperwork, Ciccone called me to say that he'd just talked to his CI and she was going to meet us at the Rose Bowl parking lot in Pasadena at about nine P.M. It was a Thursday night, and we knew that various Mongols would be at The Place.

It had always struck me as appropriate that the Mongols, not the sharpest knives in the drawer, would pick a place called The Place as their watering hole. Reminded me of a little kid's sneakers with *L* and *R* written in Magic Marker on each rubber-tipped toe.

"Okay," I told Ciccone. "I'll be there."

Strangely enough, I didn't really think too much about the plan at the time. It was going to be just another undercover caper. Merely an introduction. No buys, no recordings, no big deal. A basic intelligence-gathering mission.

At this early stage, Ciccone and I, as ATF special agents working out of different offices, answered to different group supervisors. The chain of command in the field looks like this: The special agent (sometimes called a field agent) answers directly to his group supervisor (or resident agent in charge), who oversees six to ten field agents. Directly above the RAC is the assistant special agent in charge (ASAC, pronounced "ay-sack"); for Los Angeles there are two ASACs, each responsible for overseeing half of the groups of special agents. Next in line comes the SAC, or special agent in charge; in L.A. the SAC is responsible for all of Southern California, from the Mexican border to as far north as Paso Robles. Administrators above the rank of special agent seldom leave ATF offices to see action in the field.

I left Van Nuys after informing my RAC that I would be working that night. He ran his standard admin-babble by me. "Be in the office in the morning, and don't forget your duty-agent assignment." "Duty agent" was yet another genius boondoggle dreamed up by ATF administrators wherein they assigned senior investigators to do secretarial work—answering telephones and sorting messages. I doubt this was what Uncle Sam had in mind for his tax dollars when he trained me to be a federal law-enforcement officer.

At about 8:30 P.M. I jumped on my new hot-rod Harley and headed for the Rose Bowl, where I found Ciccone sitting in his black Pontiac Grand Am. John loved that car but drove it like he was going to turn it over to the junkyard tomorrow. I'm not a deeply religious person, but every time I rode anywhere with Ciccone, no matter how short a distance, I said a prayer for myself and any innocent bystanders in his path.

The Rose Bowl, focus of the sports-loving nation every January 1, is a huge venue that holds more than ninety thousand people during college football games. It's located in a narrow pass that separates the San Fernando and San Gabriel valleys. The area is mostly residential, with an affluent, old-money feel. Even during periods with no special events, people come from all over to walk around the area. But on this night the Rose Bowl was dead calm and the parking lot dark. A thousand stars spread out across the clear California sky.

In his Pontiac, Ciccone and I mulled over the upcoming operation while waiting for our CI to show up. Ciccone hadn't said too much to me about the CI. I knew that she'd contacted an LAPD detective and was willing to introduce someone into the Mongols. She claimed, according to this detective, that she was pissed off at the

Mongols because of what she'd seen them do to a friend of hers. Not that the bikers had stolen everything he owned, or beaten him within an inch of his life, or some other god-awful thing. Nope, she was angry because she'd watched as the Mongols scooped up one of her friends and turned him from a good family man into a flaming Mongol asshole. The fact that he was an eager participant in the transformation (or that she herself continued to be a willing Mongol hanger-on) didn't play into her twisted logic. Personally, I didn't care why she was doing what she was doing; I was using her, albeit with her permission, to further our noble cause.

Within the law-enforcement community there is a saying about confidential informants: "You never know when they're gonna piss backward on you." I knew that an introduction into any undercover operation by way of a CI was risky, but I really had no clue how risky until I met Sue* face-to-face.

Within a few minutes a pickup truck rolled into the parking lot. It was old, dirty, banged up, reflecting no pride of ownership. It pulled up under the sole streetlight, where Ciccone and I were sitting in his Pontiac. Although I'd never really given it much thought, I suppose in my own wishful mind I'd envisioned the CI to be a cute little biker chick who'd been turned around by an attack of conscience.

But what rolled out of the truck was two hundred pounds of bleached-blond tweaker that could neither stand still nor shut up. "Tweaker" is cop vernacular for a methamphetamine addict; anyone who knows anything about meth can tell you that its physiological effects are brutal. It can take an attractive young woman and make her look like Medusa in no time. In Sue's case, she had

---

*Not her real name.

probably started from a disadvantaged position, and it had all gone downhill from there.

As Sue rambled on, I glanced over and gave Ciccone a little nod of gratitude for his expert selection. The three of us agreed to split up and meet at a joint called In-N-Out Burger on Foothill Boulevard in Tujunga. Sue would get on my bike, and we would ride over to The Place from there. So that was that. With a loose game plan, we headed out.

Tujunga is a bedroom community within the boundaries of Los Angeles proper, on the northeasternmost edge of the San Fernando Valley. It borders Glendale and Pasadena, nestled quietly into the surrounding mountain range. The residential terrain runs the gamut from beaten-down shacks to palatial custom-built homes on substantial horse property.

Tujunga, per capita, has more than its share of white trash and rednecks as well as an ever-present biker element. In police circles, Tujunga is referred to as The Rock, after Alcatraz's beloved nickname. In my tenure as a criminal investigator, I'd participated in many cases on The Rock, and in this community I began my odyssey.

I rolled into the parking lot of the In-N-Out Burger followed by Sue and Ciccone. Sue parked her truck and got herself ready while Ciccone waited in his car and I sat on my idling bike. Ciccone and I looked at each other across the parking lot and gave a thumbs-up.

Sue walked over to my bike and then, like something out of an old western, hopped onto one of the back passenger foot pegs as if it was Trigger's stirrup. For the uninitiated, any Harley-Davidson could rightfully be called heavy metal, and an FLHTC is heavier still. There was no way I was going to be able to hold up that bike with her big glow-in-the-dark white ass hanging off one side. Though I desperately held on, down we went with a horrific crash in the parking lot—me, my CI, and Steve Martin's revered Harley. It was a less than auspicious start.

From the ground where I lay, I looked up at Ciccone. It's impossible to describe the look on his face. I think he wanted to laugh, wanted to apologize, and was praying to the ATF gods that this was not a harbinger of things to come. I picked up the bike and my ego and prepared for round two. As if I were talking to a six-year-old, I explained to Sue that there was no way I was going to be able to hold up a thousand pounds of motorcycle and her at the same time. She was going to have to use a different technique to get on the bike. She looked at me with a wounded expression but then took a deep breath and carefully got on.

With its reputation for casual violence, The Place was the worst of the many biker bars that dot the Tujunga landscape. There had been frequent assaults and mêlées involving a variety of weapons both inside and outside the bar, and there was no way in hell I would have set foot in there under normal circumstances, at least not without a warrant, a gun, and maybe a backup unit. As we approached, I felt something in the pit of my stomach. Something I'd felt before on other undercover assignments. The edge, I guess. Keeping me sharp, appropriately nervous, greasing the skids for bravado to move front and center, if necessary.

There were six or seven bikes parked at the curb out front. As I got closer I could hear the hard-rock tunes blaring through the front door. A disheveled patron, who had obviously consumed more than his fill of alcohol, stood by a pay phone mounted on the front of the building. I rolled past the bar and turned around in the street to get in a position to park my bike. No one paid us any attention, which was fine by me. Although I carried my

gun, I still felt uneasy. I was about to meet some of the infamous Mongols for the first time.

I stopped the bike just short of the front door so Sue
could get off. With the In-N-Out incident fresh in my
mind, I held on to the bike for dear life. Dropping it in
front of The Place would have made one hell of a first
impression. Sue managed to dismount without pulling
the bike and me down to the ground. I backed the bike
against the curb and killed the engine. As I got off I saw
Ciccone roll by in his black Pontiac. I took off my helmet and put it on one of the rearview mirrors. *Game
time.*

Surprisingly, considering that it's such a dump, The
Place is located in a historic building that was a Pony Express stop in the 1860s. Above the bar were five or six
one-room apartments sharing a common bathroom. The
inside was cramped. Carrena, the owner of The Place,
had managed to squeeze two pool tables in and maintain
an area for throwing darts. The two bathrooms were
filthy. The wood floor looked like it was original construction from the Pony Express era, warped and aged by
the constant soaking of Budweiser, piss, and puke. And
of course there was the requisite jukebox full of Marilyn
Manson, Metallica, and Santana.

The walls were painted black and white, the Mongol
colors, and adorned with biker paraphernalia in honor of
the Mongols. Carrena was a hard-core biker chick, the
"ol' lady" of a Mongol called The Kid, who was away
doing a prison sentence. She had the words PROPERTY OF
THE KID tattooed on her back. Ironically, Carrena's father
was a retired cop.

I strolled in behind Sue. The joint was dimly lit, filled
with stagnant cigarette smoke and unsavory patrons, including two full-patch Mongols huddled together toward the back of the bar, beers in hand. Sue could have
dropped me right in my tracks when she openly pointed

at them in her death-defying effort to identify them for me.

"Jesus Christ!" I hissed. "What the hell's the matter with you? Settle down, before you get both our asses killed."

She was not only a hard-core tweaker but felony stupid on top of it. Luckily, no one saw her blatant move. I moved toward the bar, dragging her in my wake. Of course, I'd known that I was going to have to watch my back, but now I realized that if I wanted to stay alive, I was going to have to keep an eye on Sue also.

The bartender, an older, hard-looking soldier from The Rock, looked my way. I yelled, "Two Buds!" over the guitar-crunching music and passed one of the beers to Sue. I'd planned to stay on top of things and nurse my beer for the entire evening. Apparently Sue had no such intention. In less than thirty seconds, her bottle was empty and she was hollering, "Let's have another!" Jesus, I could see trouble coming. I gave her ten dollars to cover her beer tab for the next few minutes and watched as her beer, and my federal money, quickly vanished.

Sue moved around the bar on her own, hugging and talking with one patron after another until she finally reached the two Mongols. My moment of truth. I watched as she reached out and hugged the first biker, then the other. Neither hugged her back. But they didn't shrug her off either. She turned and motioned for me to come over. "Billy," she said when I got there, "this is Rocky."

He frowned menacingly and tipped his beer bottle my way. I returned the gesture. "Good to meetcha, Rock."

Rocky looked more American Indian than Mexican, with long—almost to his butt—black hair that he wore braided like an Indian warrior. Dressed in all black, he carried a thick length of chain on his belt, along with a large hunting knife. He was on the young side, maybe mid-thirties, and had only been in the gang for about a year and change. He didn't have that real hard-core, badass look yet, but he was working on it.

Sue nodded toward the second Mongol. "This is Rancid," she said.

I tipped my Bud and said, "Good to meetcha, Rancid."

The moniker fit. Rancid had long, black matted hair that hung well past his shoulders. The amount of grease and dirt under his nails was surpassed only by the grease and dirt in his hair, which had turned the top rocker on his patch almost black. He had an array of tattoos that started with an Uzi on his neck. There was a big black MONGOL tattoo across his enormous beer belly, which was displayed for everybody when his T-shirt rode up. He was "sleeved out," meaning that there was no more unmarked skin on his arms for inking. His gruff voice was loud enough to be heard over the Santana guitar riffs blaring from the jukebox he was leaning against. He was wearing black jeans and sported a huge chain and a hunting knife on his belt. I would later learn that the chain and knife were standard equipment for Mongol patches. His black steel-toed boots had chromed metal spikes on the tips—designed for nothing less than ripping open the flesh of whomever he kicked. He was equipped for battle, and made an ominous impression on me.

Sue was talking faster than her brain could function. I knew she was only trying to help, but in her reckless, intoxicated efforts she was digging a hole both of us could fall into. She went on and on about how well she knew me and all that we'd supposedly been through together. This caused me anxiety for more than one reason. First, she was no prize to be seen with. Second, I knew how easy it would be to get caught in the tangled web of bullshit she was weaving. I had to get her out of there, fast.

She'd served her purpose for the night. I turned to her and said, "Look, Sue, we need to go—I got some things to take care of."

She threw back her head and laughed. No way. She was in an alcohol-and-crank-induced party frenzy. She was *home*. This was her niche. She'd dug in for the night with her Mongol buds, and there was no way she was leaving.

After a few more tense minutes, I made my way toward the exit. It was tough, but like dragging an unruly dog on a chain, I managed to pull Sue out to the street with me. I felt like I had walked out of the twilight zone back to reality. No runs, no hits, no errors, and nobody left on. Just like that, our first night of the Mongol undercover investigation was over.

3

To the general public, outlaw motorcycle gangs may seem like a throwback to the 1960s and the freewheeling spirit celebrated in the movie *Easy Rider;* others may associate them with the infamous 1969 murder at Altamont Speedway in which a group of Hells Angels knifed a concertgoer as Mick Jagger danced around singing "Under My Thumb."

But contemporary biker gangs aren't simply hard-charging, heavy-drinking "wild child" Americans, a version of the James Gang on iron horses. Today's biker organizations are sophisticated, calculating, extremely violent—nothing less than the insidious new face of global organized crime.

With written constitutions, bylaws, monthly dues, and a hierarchy of national officers, OMGs are just as organized and dangerous as traditional Cosa Nostra families, and indeed more violent. In fact, their membership now dwarfs that of the Mafia, and they are spreading around the globe, with chapters in far-flung countries like Sweden and New Zealand. They form a closed, impenetrable society like the Italian-American Mob, but the fundamental distinction, from a law-enforcement perspective, is the brazen, in-your-face violence of today's biker organizations. Where the Mafia seeks a pretense of respectability, cloaking its illegal activities in legitimacy, outlaw biker gangs proudly fly their "colors," identifying themselves as Hells Angels, Pagans, Outlaws, Bandidos, or Mongols.

To a biker, these colors—denim or leather sleeveless vests decorated with coded patches that detail a member's sexual and criminal exploits—are absolutely sacred, his most prized possession. Colors are worth fighting for and, if need be, dying for.

A biker wears his colors (or "cut") like a neon sign, announcing to the world precisely who he is. And make no mistake: Outlaw bikers *want* you to know who they are. They *want* to make you tremble when they hit the highways in convoys of a hundred or more deafening Harleys. Bikers feed on the fear that they instill in the mainstream; it's this fear that allows them to control a vast, multibillion-dollar economy of illegal drugs, gunrunning, and prostitution across the United States, Canada, and Europe.

By the late 1990s, when I first began riding undercover to gather intel on the OMGs of Southern California, the biker underworld was in a state of war, an unprecedented international conflict pitting the long-dominant Hells Angels, still the largest outlaw motorcycle club in the United States, against various allied gangs—principally, the Bandidos, Outlaws, Pagans, and Mongols. From Long Island to Montreal to Los Angeles, newspapers were filled with headlines about the widespread knifings, shootings, firebombings—wholesale violence that has resulted in many murders and attempted murders.

Sometimes the violence is the result of sheer machismo. But it also stems from a battle for control of a massive international drug economy. Figures within the OMG drug underworld are difficult to quantify accurately, but a recent Canadian prosecution against the Hells Angels gives a sense of the scope. In March 2001, local and federal law enforcement in Canada brought down a major case called Operation Springtime, during which they seized more than $5.6 million in cash from one apartment safe in Quebec, money described as one day's drug sales. In Quebec alone the Hells Angels controlled an estimated billion-dollar-a-year distribution network, moving hundreds of kilograms of cocaine and hashish each month, with importation tentacles reaching as far as Pakistan, South Africa, the Netherlands, Switzerland, Belgium, and Jamaica. And this was just one law-enforcement operation, focusing on one group of Hells Angels within one province of Canada. The Angels now have chapters in some twenty-seven countries, and they are second to the Bandidos in overall membership.

In many instances outlaw biker groups have begun to resemble international terrorist organizations. In Denmark the Bandidos launched rocket-propelled grenades at a Hells Angels house. In Montreal Maurice "Mom" Boucher, leader of the Quebec Hells Angels, was put on trial—and ultimately sentenced to life in prison—for ordering the murder of two prison guards. The Quebec government had to construct a special courthouse in which to house and protect the sequestered jurors during his trial.

Outlaw biker gangs trace their origins to the years immediately after World War II. Many returning veterans, seeking camaraderie and adventure and having difficulty adjusting to civilian life, formed clubs and took to the highway on their Harley-Davidsons and Indians. They tended to ride hard, drink hard, and fight hard.

The term "1 percenter" was coined in the aftermath of a 1947 mêlée in Hollister, California, the "motorcycle riot" that inspired the film *The Wild One* and sparked the first wave of antibiker hysteria in the United States. Following the unrest, the American Motorcycle Association denounced the small minority of bikers who were sullying the reputation of the "99 percent" of motorcycle enthusiasts who were law-abiding. The outlaw biker groups quickly embraced their characterization as a public menace, and to this day, almost all don a 1%ER patch on their colors.

Among outsiders, the Hells Angels may have the most famous name, but within the world of the 1 percenters, there's no gang more feared than the Mongols. In fact, to those of us in ATF, the Mongols represent a throwback to the anarchic spirit of the early outlaw motorcycle gangs. Their motto is "Respect few, fear none," and they live by those words.

For seventeen years they engaged in a homicidal turf war with the Angels—a furious fight over the right to wear the CALIFORNIA lower rocker on their colors.

When the Mongols first came on the scene in the early 1970s, the Angels gave the new gang an ultimatum: Give up your CALIFORNIA rocker or die. The Hells Angels had never let another gang wear the lower rocker in a state where the Angels had chapters. Everyone expected that the Hells Angels would quickly annihilate the much smaller Mongols. But after seventeen years of war, in which more than two dozen Angels and Mongols were stabbed, machine-gunned, or blown up, the Angels finally backed down. They acknowledged the Mongols' right to wear the CALIFORNIA lower rocker on their colors. And the Mongols acknowledged the right of the Angels to continue to operate in Southern California.*

---

*In 1973 Jesse Ventura, later elected governor of Minnesota, came home from Vietnam a decorated Navy SEAL. Assigned to a naval facility outside San Diego, he began riding with the Mongols and became a member of the club. Just like the SEALs, the Mongols had a reputation for being hard-core and, even when badly outnumbered, would never back down from a brawl or gunfight. However, Ventura maintains that the Mongols shielded him from participating in (or even hearing about) any criminal activity, since he would have been subject to a military court-martial as well as civil prosecution.

* * *

Though much smaller in number than the Hells Angels, Bandidos, or Outlaws,* the Mongols were reputed to have a higher percentage of convicted felons and murderers in their ranks. From the beginning they'd made efforts to recruit from the Chicano criminal culture of East L.A., which had become a feared force within the California prison system, and forged a dangerous alliance with La Eme, or the Mexican Mafia.

All the criminal gangs of California—including the infamous Crips and Bloods—had learned to give the Mongols a wide berth. The Mongols were willing to kill at any time, using murder to resolve even the most trivial disputes and insults. And the intense loyalty and communal focus of the gang made the Mongols a kind of urban commando force. To date, the Mongols have never been beaten in a confrontation with any other outlaw motorcycle gang.

Whereas the Hells Angels today tend to use violence in the pursuit of profit, for the Mongols murder and mayhem have become simply a lifestyle choice. It was no accident that the founding members chose the name Mongols; they take pride in being the scourge of straight society, heirs to the rape-and-pillage terror of Genghis Khan.

Though they'd long been flying beneath the radar of law enforcement, by the late 1990s, the Mongols' penchant for murder, assault, extortion, armed robbery, narcotics dealing, and gunrunning had caught the attention of the Bureau of Alcohol, Tobacco and Firearms. And, more specifically, they'd caught the attention of ATF Special Agent John Ciccone.

---

*According to the most recent law-enforcement estimates, there are approximately 3,000 Hells Angels in 27 countries; 3,000 Bandidos in 13 countries; and 1,100 Outlaws in 11 countries.

Ciccone could see that this had the potential to be a great case; the FBI and plenty of local police departments would have loved to take a crack at the Mongols. But ATF, having a long history of successful investigations into outlaw motorcycle gangs, was the agency best equipped to take on such an investigation.

The groundbreaking ATF undercover operation was the "Widow Makers" case in the early 1970s. The Widow Makers Motorcycle Club was made up of six undercover ATF agents—Ray Ramos, Paul McQuistion, Paul Burke, Dick Newby, Jay Lanning, and Bobby Greenleaf—and targeted actual outlaw bikers in Long Beach, California. The investigation resulted in thirteen arrests for guns and drugs and is considered the first undercover operation on OMGs on the West Coast. Around the same time, ATF, working with the Drug Enforcement Agency, was running an investigation in Northern California, targeting the Hells Angels. Special Agent Douglas Gray went undercover for a couple of months in the Angels, though he didn't actually patch in (that is, become an official member of the club). That case marked the first time that an outlaw biker gang was successfully prosecuted using the federal Title 18 United States Code 1962, the Racketeer Influenced and Corrupt Organizations (RICO) statute.

Over the years a host of ATF investigations continued to chip away at the outlaw clubs' armor. There was my buddy Steve Martin's successful infiltration of the Warlocks Motorcycle Club in Florida, a case in which he managed to bring three other ATF agents into the gang, resulting in a successful weapons-and-narcotics prosecution. And in late 1997, just before I went undercover in the Mongols, ATF agents Blake Boteler and Darrell Edwards infiltrated the Sons of Silence Motorcycle Club, identified by ATF as a major criminal organization in Colorado, which had never had even one of its members arrested and convicted. Boteler and Edwards managed to work two years undercover, earning their full patches as members of the gang's Colorado Springs chapter, finally bringing in a case that resulted in fifty-one arrests, the seizure of more than seventy-five firearms, and a haul of methamphetamine with an estimated street value of more than $250,000.

John Ciccone, in his years targeting the growing OMG problem in Southern California, had developed a "gang" of his own: ATF Special Agents John Carr, Eric Harden, and Darrin Kozlowski, fondly referred to as Koz, were the core. They'd all started with the bureau together and, after a decade, remained the hard chargers they'd been at the beginning of their careers. Having worked together closely, they knew one another's individual styles and had developed a comfort zone—as much as any cop can—with one another. They knew that they could depend on one another if the bullets started flying.

For months Ciccone, Koz, Carr, and Harden strategized about the Mongol problem in Southern California. They threw around the possibility, a long shot, of inserting a federal agent inside the gang.

As they scanned the ranks of potential ATF undercovers, they all agreed on one basic thing: They were going to need an agent who could handle the rigors of going "UC" in the outlaw motorcycle underworld, one who could hold it together under circumstances of extreme deprivation, isolation, and paranoia, and who already had an extensive undercover background—since there really wasn't time to build one from scratch. No one in ATF had as extensive a background in place as I did. Harden is black, and blacks are rarely accepted in the 1 percenter world. Carr had no motorcycle experience. Koz had just come out of a role with the Vagos Motorcycle Gang and could not chance another try. In short, as

Ciccone put it, they were going to need an agent with more balls than good sense.

Over many cups of coffee, John and I assessed the Mongols' current strength: roughly some 350 full-patch members, both in and out of prison. Approximately 300 patches on the street. More than twenty chapters throughout California, Nevada, Colorado, Oklahoma, and Georgia, with a growing presence in Mexico. They were expanding their national presence rapidly, moving up through Northern California into the Pacific Northwest, and had formed alliances with the Outlaws (founded in Chicago and now headquartered in Detroit) and with the Texas-based Bandidos.

While 350 individuals may not sound like a huge criminal organization, such numbers can be misleading; at the present time, according to FBI experts, the Gambino and Genovese crime families, the nation's most powerful Mafia groups, number an estimated 200 to 250 "made members" each. As in the Mafia, each chapter of an outlaw motorcycle gang has its own circle of criminal folowers, called "prospects" and "hang-arounds"—roughly equivalent to the term "Mob associate"—to do the gang's dirty work.

Ciccone and I both knew that prosecutions against outlaw motorcycle gangs are labor-intensive and rarely successful because of the tremendous threat they pose. Outlaw bikers are not run-of-the-mill street criminals. When cases do make it into the criminal-justice system, witnesses, victims—even prosecutors and federal agents—are in extreme danger. In late 1987 members of the Pagans Motorcycle Club in Pennsylvania put out a murder contract on a federal prosecutor and the FBI agent in charge of the Pittsburgh Organized Crime Squad; the plot was uncovered before the murders could be committed, but the intention was clearly to disrupt and terrorize anyone involved in investigating the club. In another chilling incident, two assistant United States attorneys involved in prosecuting the Sons of Silence Motorcycle Club received death threats and had to have remote starters installed in their cars.

It isn't uncommon for prosecutors to be unable to locate key witnesses—or for police to find them murdered. In 1997 I'd worked on a case involving a Southern California outlaw motorcycle gang in which a full-patch member, having been thrown out of the club, became an informant for the federal government. When the gang learned of this betrayal, the informant was murdered in his home in front of his girlfriend.

Ciccone knew that by agreeing to go undercover, I would be giving up much of my regular life, but precisely how much and for how long, we didn't know. We would need massive assistance from other law-enforcement agencies, especially the Los Angeles County Sheriff's Department. And the more outside people who knew about the case, the greater the risk, as even a routine breach in security could prove fatal. As for our ATF bosses, we knew that we'd be fighting an uphill battle to get them to approve all the expenses we'd be incurring while running a long-term undercover investigation, paying bills for an apartment, phone, car, and bike in my undercover alias. Then there was the issue of my personal safety. If we pulled off a successful prosecution of the Mongols, everyone in the ATF hierarchy would happily take the credit, but if things went south—if I got wounded in the line of duty, or worse—I knew that they'd be only too quick to say that the high-risk operation was all Ciccone's and my doing.

But this was the kind of case that was tailor-made for John Ciccone. John loved a good fight with ATF administration even more than I did, and almost as much as he loved putting bad guys in jail.

4

By this point in my law-enforcement career, I'd served seventeen years with ATF, two as a federal border patrol agent, and six as a city cop in North Carolina. I had also been lucky to come home from Vietnam, where I had served throughout I Corps from Da Nang to the DMZ. In my adult life I'd never been anything other than a cop or a soldier, and in that sense I was following in my father's footsteps. My dad was a Treasury officer who chased down moonshiners and worked undercover in the hills of North Carolina and Virginia during the fifties and sixties.

Within ATF, I was known as a "street" agent—everyone knew that I hated paperwork with a passion and had no time for administrative fools, whom I saw as a hindrance to the business of law enforcement. Ciccone had seen me work undercover, buying cocaine from the Crips and the Bloods in South Central Los Angeles and machine guns from neo-Nazis in rural West Virginia as if it was second nature.

The skills of an undercover agent are largely self-taught. Federal agents going deep "UC" get very little training. There's a basic course offered at the Federal Law Enforcement Training Center in Georgia, and after some time on the job, agents who are interested and motivated can request to go to the advanced undercover school. In my experience, the instructors teach the things you should already know, like how to build a believable background and what you can legally do within your role on the street and what you can't. They teach psychological techniques to help you recognize when a situation may be turning bad and how to best use and conceal electronic surveillance equipment. They cover the legal concept of entrapment. An undercover agent can always defend himself but should never instigate violence. Criminal activities need to be initiated by the bad guys themselves.

The ATF rule book explicitly states that there can be no drug use by the agent, with one exception: if he perceives his life to be in grave danger. Having been forced to smoke, ingest, or inject narcotics, the undercover is then treated like any federal agent injured in the line of duty and must be taken to a hospital or doctor at the first possible moment. After recovering, he's responsible for completing an enormous amount of follow-up paperwork to explain and justify the incident. Then, at the discretion of his superior, he may return to his undercover role.

In reality, undercover work can't be taught in a classroom. It's like learning the tailback position in football or learning to play jazz piano. An instructor can give you the basics, but it really comes down to your natural inclination, wit, temperament, and gift for improvisation. Undercover life is more art than science. You eventually learn the tricks of your trade on the street, as I did over some twenty years.

By the time I embarked on my undercover role in the Mongols, I had gone UC on so many operations that I didn't have to fashion a new identity out of whole cloth: Over the past decade I had developed a deep-undercover identity as Billy St. John, an alias I had used when infiltrating various violent far-right groups across the United States—the KKK, neo-Nazis, skinheads, the Aryan Nations, and the National Alliance—making undercover purchases of some serious heavy-duty weaponry, from M-16s to 30mm military cannons. In one investigation I'd gotten so deep inside the National Alliance—the largest and most active neo-Nazi organization in the United States—that I had not only become a member but had been invited to stay and work at the national headquarters in West Virginia. There I befriended the National Alliance's founder and leader, Dr. William Pierce, author of *The Turner Diaries*, the apocalyptic white-supremacist novel later made infamous by Oklahoma City terror bomber Timothy McVeigh, who viewed Pierce as a kind of prophet of the coming racial war. In my personal copy of *The Turner Diaries*, William Pierce himself penned an inscription:

> *Revolutionary regards*
> *To Bill St. John,*
> *A real Comrade*
> *Wm Pierce*
> *7/17/94*

But by January 1998, I was no longer doing neo-Nazi investigations; I was now riding a Harley around the biker underworld of Southern California.

That's the one thing I didn't need to fake about my undercover persona: a genuine love affair with motorcycles. I've ridden bikes my whole adult life. I have a brother who bought a bike before me, when I was sixteen years old, a Triumph 650cc high-compression piece of crap. Somehow we got the thing running, but my brother was almost killed riding it. After I got out of the army and became a police officer in North Carolina, I bought my first Harley-Davidson. I was twenty-four. I've owned Harleys ever since, from hot-rod choppers to straight-off-the-showroom-floor stockers.

Since the beginning of the year, playing my Billy St. John role, I'd been riding an ATF-owned Harley-Davidson and hanging out with some Hells Angels in the San Fernando Valley, trying to gather intelligence for an investigation being run as a joint effort between ATF, the IRS, and the Ventura County Sheriff's Department. Mostly I hung out at a dump of a strip bar called the Candy Cat in Chatsworth. The San Fernando Valley, made nationally famous by the LAPD beating of Rodney King and the Northridge earthquake three years later, was a Hells Angels stronghold.

Working deep undercover requires a tempered adoption of the maxim "When in Rome, do as the Romans do." Hanging with the Angels, I'd grown my hair long and wild. My blond-gray beard was raggedy, and to be perfectly honest, I think a few people were questioning my personal-hygiene habits. The rub, of course, was that my appearance had come to the attention of the ATF group supervisor and had started to piss him off. As the stereotypical paper-pusher, he had his own idea of what an ATF agent should look like—deep undercover or not.

I had the Harley, I had the look, I had the undercover years and background in place. But I had something even more valuable: the benefit of learning from Darrin Kozlowski's experience.

We'd both been assigned to the Van Nuys ATF office, and I'd been able to watch Koz during his undercover operation in the Vagos just a year before. I was amazed that he'd actually been able to patch in. It's no small feat to become a bona fide member of an outlaw motorcycle gang; it entails tests of loyalty, fortitude, stamina, and physical prowess. And that's for people who really *want* to become members. Sometimes gaining the trust of the gang requires engaging in violent criminal activity, including murder. Their background investigations into prospective members rival that of military clearance checks. For an undercover cop, there are tough calls to make when hard drugs are consumed, robberies and rapes are planned, and violent crimes committed. Any undercover in that situation has to know how to act decisively and instinctively, developing a sixth sense about when to bail out of potentially fatal situations. It can be emotionally debilitating to show the gang one side of your personality, while carefully masking who and what you really are, from what you're feeling to what you actually stand for.

I'd watched with admiration and some awe as Koz worked the Vagos. I'd watched his backup agents bust their butts to keep up with him as he flew by the seat of his pants time and again. I'd heard his tales of uncanny, split-second thinking when the Vagos tried to rope him into criminal activity or get him to do drugs. I'd also watched as his investigation turned lethal. First, the CI who'd introduced Koz into the club was killed in a traffic accident on Hollywood Boulevard while riding a motorcycle ATF had provided him. The bike's tag was listed under the CI's name, but the vehicle identification number (VIN) could be traced back to ATF. This was the kind of routine screwup that could quickly lead to homicide. After the fatal accident, the Vagos went to the LAPD to get the accident report and learned that ATF was the true owner of the motorcycle. They went to the deceased CI's wife and threatened her, demanding to know why her husband had been on a bike owned by the federal government. The terrorized woman gave up everything—that her husband was working as an informant for ATF, and that Koz was in fact an undercover agent.

With his cover blown while deep inside an outlaw biker gang, Darrin Kozlowski should be dead today. The fact that he's alive and well is not for lack of various Vagos efforts to see otherwise. When the investigation went south, Koz got a phone call from one Vago, acting as if nothing was amiss and wanting to arrange a meet. The sixth sense that frequently saves a cop's ass served Koz well that day, and he didn't show up for the meet. Nevertheless, the Vagos found out where he lived, began to terrorize his family, and threatened him repeatedly.

But Koz was no one to mess with. A tall, strapping midwestern boy with a quick smile, an easy laugh, and an affable demeanor, Koz refused to relocate or cower. Eventually ATF had to assign members of our crack Special Response Team—armed with assault rifles—to move in with Koz's family for a couple of weeks.

But he was still on the job, and a hell of an ATF agent. As I'd watched him working the Vagos case—despite the ultimate investigative dead end—I made sure to take copious notes.

After my introduction to Rocky and Rancid at The Place, I became a frequent visitor to the Mongols' preferred watering hole in the San Fernando Valley. My CI, having served her purpose, was out of the picture now. I was spending nights on my own in that dingy little bar, shooting pool, talking shit, and draining Buds. The Mongols knew my background as a rough-edged guy named Billy St. John—divorced father, U.S. Army vet, working a legit job in the avionics industry—but I hadn't managed to get past the initial trust issue with them.

I had probably met ten or twelve Mongols by early April 1998, and the pressure was on me to make things happen—and fast. John Torres, the ASAC in the L.A. Division, was already badgering Ciccone and me to show some tangible results for the federal dollars we were spending. Torres simply didn't appreciate or understand an undercover operation this complex. I knew that pushing the Mongols wasn't feasible; the bad guys could feel it when you were trying too hard. And I knew that in a UC operation mistakes only invite suspicion and make for a more difficult and dangerous task. Unfortunately I also knew that, in the L.A. Division, the operation could be jerked right out from under us for no reason at all.

Ciccone and I decided that, in order to push the investigation to the next level, I should try to get an invitation to ride to Laughlin with the Mongols I'd met at The Place.

The Laughlin River Run is the third-biggest annual motorcycle event in the country, ranking just behind Sturgis, South Dakota, and Daytona, Florida. But for Southern California bikers, it's the most important run of the year. The town of Laughlin—sometimes referred to as the "poor man's Vegas"—is situated on the Colorado River near Lake Mohave and Lake Mead, on the Arizona-Nevada border, a relatively easy five-hour drive from Los Angeles proper. A small town with year-round balmy weather, it has a population of around ten thousand. But on the third weekend of April the town swells with law-abiding Harley lovers, wannabes, and outlaws—about twenty-five thousand of them. Along with them come plenty of motorcycle thefts, motorcycle traffic accidents, and outlaw gang rivalry incidents, in addition to the prevailing good-natured fun.

My window of opportunity to get an invitation to Laughlin was narrowing fast. I assessed the personalities of all the Mongols I'd met so far. Rocky was a bad dude, to be sure, but he was nowhere near as hard an outlaw biker as Rancid. Bucket Head, another member of the San Fernando Valley Chapter, struck me as someone I might be able to get next to, but he was unpredictable and wasn't around as much as Rocky. It looked like Rocky was going to be my way in. I did some background work on him and learned that he'd worked a legitimate job for the City of Los Angeles for thirteen years, then joined the Mongols and had been on a downward spiral ever since. He had no convictions, but his arrest record boasted several assaults.

I watched Rocky as he moved around The Place shooting pool and drinking beer. For an outlaw biker, he laughed a lot and seemed to get along with everyone. When I noticed his beer was nearly empty, I knew it was time to make my move.

"Rocky!" I yelled over the jukebox as I passed him another cold Bud. "Listen, you goin' to Laughlin?"

"Sure am. You goin'?"

"I want to. But I haven't found anybody to ride out with yet."

"Shit," Rocky said after a pause, "you oughtta ride out with us."

"I'd love to." I held my beer out as a salute. Rocky clinked his bottle against mine.

"Gonna be a fuckin' good time."

Though I tried my best to mask it, I was beside myself. I wanted to talk to Rocky about the particulars of the trip but didn't dare push it. Tonight I'd settle for the invite. Laughlin was a few days away, and I could get the details straight later. I bought Rocky another beer and shot a few more rounds of pool.

At two in the morning, I high-fived Rocky. He repeated the invitation to ride with him, and I headed for the door. I couldn't wait to hook up with Ciccone. I strapped on my helmet and fired my machine. I let go like someone had just dropped the green flag and disappeared into the night.

For the next couple of days I hung out at The Place, trying to get Rocky to talk about just how we were going to do the Laughlin run. But Rocky was as unreliable as he was unpredictable. His whole attitude had changed, and it seemed like he didn't want to go to Laughlin anymore. Tuesday rolled around to Friday and we still had no plans for the Laughlin trip. Some of the Mongols had already rolled out Friday morning, and I was getting anxious.

Why had his attitude changed? Had he suddenly started to distrust me? I was convinced that if I didn't say something to Rocky, the trip would be off. Shooting pool, I asked him straight out. "Rocky, what time we hitting the road in the morning?"

"Be at my place at about nine."

As I turned and walked out the door, a hard-core Tujunga chick followed me out. She'd obviously been eavesdropping on my conversation with Rocky. "Billy, take me to Laughlin with you," she said.

I turned to look her up and down. She was a tough, typical biker chick (meaning she had a great body but a face that could stop the space shuttle). She asked for a ride home. I smiled at her. Being seen leaving with her on the back of my Harley would do nothing but lend credence to my role as Billy St. John, both tonight and on the Laughlin run. "Jump on. Where ya live?"

"Just head down Foothill Boulevard. I'll show you."

She reached around me and tightened up as I pulled away. As we rolled down Foothill I told her that if she really wanted to go to Laughlin, she should meet me at The Place at about eight-thirty in the morning. In my rearview mirror I saw Ciccone tailing me. I knew that he would be waiting to hear what the plans were for Laughlin. He had a group of agents on standby ready to roll out to Nevada with me.

I dropped the chick off, and Ciccone jumped in behind me. I signaled him to follow me as I turned onto Lowell Avenue, then picked a dark parking lot at a driving range near the 210 for our meet. There wasn't much to discuss besides Rocky's sudden reluctance about the trip. I rolled my bike around in the parking lot and pulled up next to Ciccone's car.

"We still on? What'd he say?"

"I'm gonna meet Rocky at his house at nine in the morning. He didn't say anything else about meeting with other Mongols or anything else about the trip."

"Who's the chick?"

"Just some TJ chick who wants me to take her to Laughlin."

Ciccone smiled knowingly. "It'll be good cover."

"Yeah, it will."

I hadn't yet worn a concealed surveillance device, or wire, at this point in the investigation. I was still too new on the scene, and there was far too great a risk that Rocky or one of the other Mongols might suddenly try to pat me down. Getting caught wearing a wire in a closed criminal society like the Mongols—or any outlaw motorcycle gang, for that matter—is an almost certain death sentence.

Rather, Ciccone and his gang would follow us and I'd make contact through a pay phone if I could. I rode home, uneasy, trying to tell myself everything was going to go according to plan. I couldn't help but feel the whole operation was coming down to tomorrow. My mind played games with me. The night seemed darker and the trip home longer.

I was up before dawn making sure that I had myself together. I still wasn't feeling too confident about the whole situation, but I called Ciccone and told him that I was ready to roll and that I'd be leaving for Tujunga in a few minutes. He told me to be careful.

I turned off Lowell onto Foothill Boulevard and rode down the hill. I was surprised to see the little Tujunga chick waiting for me in front of The Place. I pulled over and she hopped on, wrapping her hands tight around my waist. It was still too early to roll to Rocky's place, so I told her that we'd hit a restaurant down the street before we picked him up. Like Sue, this chick was a hard-core tweaker, but unlike a lot of tweakers, she still had quite an appetite. I watched her shoveling down the pancakes and sausages. I didn't say a thing to her throughout the meal besides "Pass the salt." I was too focused on what would be waiting for me at Rocky's house.

Rocky lived a minute's ride down the road, and we were in front of his place before I could work myself into a more negative mind-set. I backed my bike to the curb. It seemed more like five in the morning than nine; there was nothing to indicate that anyone in the house was alive as I banged my fist against the door. After two minutes, Rocky's "ol' lady" came to the door. Her name was Vicky, and as I was to learn in the coming months, she and Rocky had been childhood sweethearts. Her face was weathered, and her eyes had the vacant look of a long-term dopehead. Vicky let us in, mumbling something about Rocky being still in bed, told us to hang on, and turned and walked back toward the bedroom. In a few minutes Rocky emerged, looking half dead.

"Ah, fuck, Billy, what time is it?"

"Nine."

"Come back about eleven."

I nodded. At least he didn't say the trip was off.

"Okay, Rock—see you in a couple of hours."

The TJ chick and I walked back to my bike. She started complaining, saying that she needed to go back to her place and pick up some dope for the trip. I figured I'd better drop her off, then tell her that I'd changed my mind about going. "Look, baby," I said as I pulled into her driveway. "I don't think I'm going to Laughlin anymore. Think I'm just gonna head home."

She sighed a few times and tried to talk me into making the run, but to no avail. I headed back up Foothill Boulevard to find a phone so I could let Ciccone know what was going on. I told him that Rocky was still asleep and wanted us to come back about eleven. No big deal, Ciccone said, as long as we made the trip.

I tried to put on a good face; Ciccone and a team of ATF agents were fired up for the run to Laughlin, and I didn't want to let them down.

There was no one at The Place at this hour, but the R & J Motorcycle Shop next door was open, and I strolled inside. "R & J" stood for Roy and Johnny. The proprietors were two old-school Harley-Davidson mechanics, disorganized, rough, and dirty, but they knew their way around a Harley like no one else on The Rock.

I made my way back through the jumble of motorcycle parts. "Yo, anybody home?"

"Come on in!" hollered a deep voice from the back.

I found Johnny doing surgery on a Harley engine in his little shop area.

"What's up, Billy?"

"Just fixin' to take off for Laughlin."

"Who you rollin' with?"

"Rocky."

Johnny looked up from the Harley, raised one eyebrow at me. His look spoke volumes. Although not 1 per-centers, Johnny and Roy could hang with the best of them. But they had better sense than to put on a patch. They knew what it meant and wanted nothing to do with it.

One evening after Johnny had seen me hanging with the Mongols, he came up to me, put his arm around my shoulder, and with all the sincerity in the world told me: "Billy, stay away from that brother shit. If you get in-volved with them, you'll come out a loser."

Johnny didn't have a clue who I really was, of course, but after that piece of advice, he held a special place in my heart.

At ten-thirty I decided to head back to Rocky's. If I let too much time pass, it would just give him an excuse to bail out of the trip. As I rolled up to Rocky's place, I tried to be as noisy as hell. "Yo, Rocky!" I shouted, banging repeatedly on the door.

After a long wait, I saw some signs of Mongol life. The lock jiggled. Then the door opened, and Vicky stood staring uncomprehendingly, like I'd just woken her from the deepest sleep of her life. "What're you doin' here, Billy? Rocky's still in bed."

"Can I come in and talk to him?"

I walked straight back to the bedroom where Rocky lay snoring, twisted up in his sheets. "Yo, bud," I said. "We goin'?"

"Yeah, gimme a little longer. Come back in an hour."

I wanted to stay at Rocky's place so that he couldn't change his mind. But I knew better than to push it. I fired up my bike, drove back to The Place, and killed the hour drinking beers with Carrena's father, the retired LAPD officer. I talked to him as if there was no love lost between Billy St. John and the LAPD. He made it clear that he and the LAPD were no mutual-admiration society, either. Over the course of the investigation I had numerous talks with him about his life as a cop, and though he'd retired under favorable circumstances, he just seemed to be one of those guys disgruntled by their whole police career. All of the Mongols treated him as a harmless old man, convinced that he'd never inform on them for any criminal activity that went down in The Place. I sometimes stared at him as I drank my beer and wondered how a guy who'd spent twenty years chasing bad guys could feel so at home in a hornet's nests of outlaw bikers, but he always treated me aboveboard, and I didn't worry much about him. Ciccone, on the other hand, felt I should steer clear of him as much as possible. Who knew if he was still capable of using his LAPD connections to do some background digging on me?

I nursed my beer for that hour, then fired up the bike again, wondering if Rocky was going to give me some new excuse about not making the trip. My heart came alive as I saw him outside his house, working on his bike. I backed my straight pipes to the curb. "You ready to roll?"

Rocky had the side cover off his bike and was sticking an American Arms .22-caliber revolver under it. Things were looking up. Vicky walked out with her leather jacket and helmet.

Rocky kicked and cursed and cursed and kicked until he hit the right combination and the bike cranked up. Then he stood there for a few minutes, breathing heavily, exhausted from the ordeal. He stood there so long I worried that he'd run out of gas. Then he guided the machine through the maze of dogs, toys, broken Harley parts, and assorted Tujunga trash that littered his yard as he made his way to the street. Vicky climbed on the back, and we were on our way to Laughlin.

Soon I'd be partying with a shitload of the black-and-white bad guys for an entire weekend. We stopped a couple of times for gas and burgers. Each time, I'd look around to catch a glimpse of Ciccone or some other ATF agent attempting to surveil us as covertly as possible. Seeing those ATF follow cars made me a bit uneasy. If I could see them watching us, I knew Rocky or Vicky could do the same.

We rolled into Laughlin somewhere around ten that night and made our way to the Riverside Resort Hotel, the Mongol stronghold in Laughlin. Every bike was adorned with black-and-white Mongol stickers, and at least two Mongol prospects were guarding the roped-off parking area. I killed the engine and dropped the kickstand. Two Mongols approached Rocky and greeted him with Mongol handshakes and hugs. He introduced me as a hang-around, telling them that it would be okay for my bike to be parked in the Mongol circle. The two Mongol brothers welcomed me, which helped to ease some tension. Rocky, Vicky, and I made our way to the hotel.

For some reason the atmosphere seemed to grow more businesslike—like we were a combat unit readying ourselves for an attack. I overheard one of the Mongols telling Rocky that there was a meeting in one of the hotel rooms in about a half an hour. Something was up.

Rocky turned to me, whispering: "Billy, there's some kinda fuckin' mixup—we ain't got a room." He turned and walked away. Vicky had hooked up with another Mongol's woman and left me by myself. At least it would be a good chance to put in a call to Ciccone.

Later in the case I had an ATF cell phone I could use in such situations to check in with my backup. But now I had to make do with a pay phone. There was a bank of phones near the hotel entrance, and I quickly made my way there to put in a call. No answer. I called the room where ATF had a small command center. No answer there either. I tried Ciccone's cell again and left a message. "Yo, I'm here at the Riverside. Something's up. Rocky didn't have his shit together, and we don't have a room to stay in."

I glanced around, but no one had seen me talking on the phone. I was tired and I wanted a place to sleep. There was no way I was going to stay up all night. Not being a methamphibian myself, I was going to have to find someplace to lay my head. I went to the check-in line and waited my turn. I got the standard line about the hotel being booked up, then went down to the manager's office and told him I was with the Mongols. He turned on his computer, punched in a few digits, then asked me for my credit card.

So the Mongols' reputation did sling some weight here at the Riverside. With two room keys in hand, I went back to tell Vicky. "Hey, I got us all a room."

"How'd you swing that?"

"Shit, I'm a VIP around here." I smiled at her and told her the room number. "Tell Rocky I'm up there gettin' some sleep."

When I unlocked the door, I saw that the room had only one bed. Oh well. I'd win a few more points and curl up on the floor, leaving the king-size bed for Rocky and his ol' lady. I made myself a pallet of blankets and pillows on the carpet and was so tired I fell into a very deep sleep.

Much later in the night, I heard Rocky and Vicky unlocking the door. I kept my eyes closed, pretending to be asleep while listening to what they had to say.

"This Billy's okay, you know?" Rocky said.

"I can't believe he's sleeping on the floor in his own fuckin' room."

The next morning I was up around nine. Rocky and Vicky were snoring away as I showered, dressed, and headed down for breakfast. I saw a couple of Mongols at the restaurant but didn't say anything to them. In the strict but unspoken etiquette of outlaw bikers, it would have been out of place for me—a nobody—to engage a full patch in conversation. I ate a meal of bacon and eggs, put in a surreptitious phone call to Ciccone, then headed back to the room. Rocky and Vicky were up and moving about. It was uncomfortable trying to make conversation and waiting for them to get ready for the day. The TV helped make the time pass.

Then, just as we were getting ready to leave, Rocky reached into his Mongol vest and retrieved a clear plastic bag containing a white powder that appeared to be either coke or methamphetamine. He held it up in front of my face as he reached for a bowie knife strapped to his side. He pulled the gleaming blade, then turned toward a table, cut a hole at the top of the plastic bag, and let the powder pour out onto the tabletop. He used his bowie to separate out two heavy lines. I watched as he bent over and snorted up one of the lines. I was praying that the other was for Vicky.

No such luck. Rocky turned toward me, raising the knife and holding the blade inches from my face. "Is that line too heavy for you?"

It wasn't an offer; this was a challenge. I hoped Rocky couldn't see my face turning red as I answered. "No, Rock, looks good to me."

I walked around Rocky and his knife to the bathroom, telling him that I had to take a piss first. I stared at myself in the bathroom mirror. What the hell was I going to do? I couldn't stall Rocky for long. If I didn't do the line, there was a good chance he was going to swing that bowie knife. More important, the investigation would be over. On the other hand, if I did snort the meth, I'd have to get out of the hotel as soon as possible, call Ciccone, make my way to the hospital, and start the arduous process of paperwork for an agent who's been forced to use drugs during an undercover operation. And I could tell that Rocky wasn't planning to let me just wander off for a few hours in the middle of the Laughlin run. He'd know something was wrong and never trust me again.

The whole operation was coming down to these next few seconds. I left the bathroom and without any further hesitation asked Rocky for his straw.

"Just roll up a fuckin' dollar bill," he said.

My hand was shaking as I reached in my pocket for the bill. Rocky and Vicky watched closely as I rolled the dollar up into a thin cylinder. I looked at Rocky, then at the white line waiting for me.

Suddenly, I saw my chance. Rocky and Vicky were near the bed. If I moved right now, I could place myself between the meth and them. With my back to them, maybe I could wipe it off the table without them seeing. But if I calculated wrong, Rocky would put his knife right through me.

I moved between Rocky and the dope. Bending over and holding the dollar bill in my right hand, I snorted hard right next to the dope while wiping it off the table with my cupped left hand. I straightened up fast as Rocky looked around me at the table. The dope was gone, and I pretended to snort through my nose a few more times. Rocky grinned at me, staring at my face hard. "Good shit, huh, Billy?"

"*Ooooh-whaaa!*" I let out a loud rebel yell, then shook my head from side to side. "Yeah, Rock. Some good shit."

"Let's go." Rocky, energized by the shot of crank, jumped to his feet.

I looked down to see a small pile of meth on the carpet below the table. Quickly, I put my boot over it, scattering it into the carpet.

"Yeah, let's go."

I turned to follow Rocky and Vicky out the door. Had I really gotten away with this sleight of hand? Maybe they'd seen but were just waiting to call my bluff when there were more Mongols present. I couldn't have pulled off the same stunt if even one more biker had been in the room with me. And I knew I couldn't keep doing it all weekend. I'd have to figure out another way to get around the dope issue, or this investigation wasn't going to last another day.

Downstairs in the lobby, we met up with the San Fernando Valley Chapter president, a frightening-looking guy named Domingo. Domingo was a little younger than Rocky, maybe in his late twenties, with long black hair that he wore in a heavy braid that fell all the way to his belt. A light-skinned Hispanic, he was built like a fire-plug, only five foot eight but at least 225 pounds. His arms were very muscular, and tatted up pretty good.

I later read up on Domingo's criminal history: He'd just come out of prison for his involvement in a nightclub mêlée and running gunfight the Mongols had engaged in just outside of Los Angeles. A victim had been found shot dead at the scene, but the police could never bring a charge of murder and Domingo went to state prison on a conviction of felony assault. I also learned that Domingo had originally been patched in with the L.A. Chapter, but with some recent internal turmoil in the San Fernando Valley, he had been sent by the national president to clean up shop there.

Rocky and Domingo greeted each other with the Mongol handshake, and I heard Rocky tell Domingo in a half whisper: "Yeah, he's okay."

Domingo nodded at me, didn't offer me a handshake. We met up with more Mongols as we made our way to the concession and display area in the hotel parking lot. It was warm outside. Rock music was blaring from a live band on the stage. Cold beer was flowing. Nothing makes Mongols happier than loud music and a plentiful supply of beer—except maybe beating the shit out of an enemy. But for now there was nobody to beat up and plenty of beer to go around.

The Mongols began to circle the wagons. And now I learned the reason that everyone was on high alert: The Vagos were in town, and they had put out the word that they were looking for some Mongol ass. It seemed to me that they weren't looking very hard—the Mongols were gathering en masse, and flying their colors in an awesome public display of force.

Rocky told me to look tough and to stand guard at one of the corners. He said I should do what I was told by other Mongol patches and not ask any questions. "You got that, Billy? Don't ask questions."

Rocky was vouching for me now. I stood in the hot sun looking as serious and tough as I could, keeping lookout for any Vagos. I was a legitimate Mongol hang-around now, the precursor to being an official prospect, and as such I was trusted with guard duty. On an ATF intelligence report, I'd be listed as:

Billy St. John
Known Associate
Mongols M.C.

On Sunday afternoon it was time to head back to L.A.
We had a two-hour delay just outside Laughlin to fix
Rocky's piece-of-shit bike. When we reached the split in
the 10 and 210 freeways, Rocky pulled off at the Fairplex
exit in Pomona; I followed. At this junction we would go
our own ways. Rocky maneuvered his bike into a closed
service station. It was dark, and the ride home had taken
its toll on all of us. Parking his bike, Rocky went to a
phone booth as Vicky and I found an uncomfortable
piece of concrete curb to sit on. I remember watching
Rocky walking away, his fearsome black-and-white
Mongol patch fading into the darkness in front of me.

I reflected on the weekend's progress. I was sitting in
some abandoned service station with a gangster who had
taken me under his wing. If he knew who I really was, he
would kill me right here. He had the gun to do it. The
place was dark and there would be no witnesses. The
noise from the freeway traffic would muffle the sound of
the gunshot.

Rocky walked back after a couple of minutes and sat
down beside me on the curb. "You got any idea what
you're doing?"

The question startled me. "What?" I said, staring at
him.

"You heard me. You're trying to get into something
that might kill you. Do you know that?"

I wasn't sure what my answer should be.

"This ain't no club," Rocky continued. "We're outlaws. I've had to do things that would send me to prison
for years if I got caught. You ready for that? Would you
kill for the Mongols? Because that's what you might have
to do. We're outlaws, Billy. You need to know that. You

need to be sure. You need to understand what you're getting into." Without waiting for an answer, he patted me on the back. "I'm outta here. You think about it, Billy."

I watched as Rocky and Vicky got on their bike and roared away.

The freeway traffic echoed through my head. I was tired. As I fired up my Harley again, I realized that I had no idea what I was really getting into.

5

In the beginning, our investigative goals were relatively modest: We were trying to get next to Rocky, Domingo, and some of the other San Fernando Valley Mongols, buy some methamphetamine and cocaine, and get as many illegal guns off the street as we could. To be honest, if I'd known the way it was going to play out, I'm not sure I would have taken the assignment. Though I'd been through the deep-cover ordeal before, it was usually a matter of days or weeks at a time away from my family. At the start of the operation I'd been divorced for about ten years; my ex-wife and I remained cordial. She lived in Riverside, in a modest suburban community, with our two sons. My boys were then nine and ten years old, and even with the demands of being an ATF agent, I was there almost every weekend, took them to soccer games, went to school plays and parent-teacher conferences. In those months when I began to hang around the Mongols, my sons could see the visible changes in me—my hair and beard growing longer, my unkempt appearance so unlike my usual close-cropped, clean-shaven look. They were just old enough to ask questions but not old enough to understand the sacrifices and demands of a deep-undercover assignment.

Not that I could have told them too much even if I'd wanted to. It's one of the cardinal rules of undercover work: You never know who might blow your cover, what kind of casual remark, even out of the mouth of a child, could have devastating repercussions. The safest thing is to always keep your friends and loved ones in the dark about the specifics of your assignment. Of course, they understand that you're doing some kind of top-secret law-enforcement work, but beyond that, the nature of your job, the specifics of any deep-cover case, can only hurt them in the long run.

On a cool spring night in Los Angeles, where motorcycle riding is a year-round mode of transportation, I was trying to take the investigation to that next level, making my first undercover foray into the Mongols' stronghold in East L.A.

Tony's Hofbrau is a notorious old-time biker bar located in a small enclave just outside downtown Los Angeles. East L.A. is a primarily Hispanic community in the shadows of the city's mirrored skyscrapers, where the smells of cilantro and habanero chili peppers waft through the warm breezes, carried along with mariachi music, rap, and rock. Small, well-maintained houses with gated yards and nurtured gardens commingle with tenement housing projects. The older, honest, hardworking generation lives side by side with the younger, hotheaded criminal element; the God-fearing with the gangbangers. And it was here in East L.A. that the Mongols were most at home.

As I turned onto Valley Boulevard from the Long Beach Freeway I rolled on the throttle of my Harley. It wasn't long before the sea of bikes came into view: truly an awesome sight. There were easily eighty to ninety motorcycles lined up, standing curbside sentry in front of Tony's Hofbrau. Rounding that corner, I felt a sharp pang in my gut, the kind I'd felt in Vietnam. But there was no platoon to back me up, and no one else to look out for. The only ass on the line was mine.

I slowed the Harley down as I approached my target. Slowly, they came into view: dark, shadowy figures that seemed, at first glance, like some mob of grim reapers. With no obvious place to park my motorcycle, I cruised past the hordes of rough, bearded, tattooed, black-leather-clad Hispanic bikers. Predator and prey, eye to eye.

I'd been feeling awkward and nervous to begin with, and now my entire body tensed as I finally reached a break in the asphalt real estate where I could park my hog. Streetlights were either in short supply or purposely rendered inoperative, and the darkness enveloped everything. I could hear the blare of Latino music even from a considerable distance. I backed the bike to the curb, the straight pipes grumbling that famous Harley idle like some mechanical beast. In the space of that moment, I asked myself what I'd gotten into, and told myself that it still wasn't too late to get out. I sat for what seemed like an eternity before I cut the engine. I took a deep breath and repeated my undercover mantra: "Suck it up, Billy, it's game time. You'll come out of this one day and watch all these bad guys parading in handcuffs."

I took my helmet off and placed it over the mirror on my handlebars. I pulled down the bandana I'd been wearing over my mouth like some black-hat gunslinger in a John Wayne movie. I got off the bike hoping my legs wouldn't betray my nerves.

I could feel dozens of Mongols staring at me from a heavy darkness my vision couldn't penetrate. Trying desperately not to be conspicuous, I took a quick look around for Ciccone's Pontiac. He was nowhere in sight, but I knew he was out there somewhere keeping an eye on me. All I could feel was the pounding of my heart and the fear that my T-shirt would show the vibration. I was truly alone. But there was no turning back.

For an undercover agent, fear can be a good thing—when you've got it under control and can make it work in your favor. It keeps your guard up and your edge sharp. However, if you let it control you, fear quickly becomes your worst enemy. With my mission clear but my plan tenuous, I didn't need any more enemies.

As I walked toward the bar, the music got louder and the shadowy figures more distinct. I walked as if pulled by a force I couldn't see, past Mongols in their full regalia of black leather vests with the assortment of patches that can be read like an outlaw's road map. There were small rectangular bars stitched on the left chest, reflecting the various chapters and the club officers' ranks; the "purple heart" patch, meaning that a member had been shot while in combat for the gang; the skull-and-bones patch, signifying that a member had committed murder for the gang; and a multitude of colored wings that I recognized to be club-sanctioned trophies indicating that a member had engaged in acts of group sex and varieties of cunnilingus while being observed by other members of the gang.

I had almost reached the front door when a huge Mongol warrior blocked my path and shouted: "Private party, dude!"

Since my options were few—largely due to his size and my desire to see another day—I stopped in my tracks and looked up at him. Bravado kicked in. "I'm Billy—I'm a guest from San Fernando Valley." The gateway guard took my meaning: I'd been formally invited by the SFV Mongol Chapter.

"Where's Domingo?" he asked.

"I don't know. I thought he was here." I could have been Christ at the Second Coming, but my words would've meant nothing without the validation of the San Fernando Valley Chapter president.

"Wait here," he said as he turned to walk back toward the pack of Mongols I'd passed.

I looked at his colors as he walked away. Worn, dirty.

In a way that only outlaw bikers and those who know them can understand, his colors gave up his secrets. They spoke of who he was and much of what he'd done. In the same way a soldier or cop's uniform can be, his patch was intimidating in its own right. His size and surliness did nothing to temper that effect.

With the mariachi music blaring behind me, I could see him talking to a figure cloaked in the street's darkness. He was looking back and forth between me and whoever he was talking to. The longer he talked, and the more he looked back and forth, the more nervous I became. I steeled myself for whatever came my way. As much as I was hoping he'd just come back and say, "Okay, man, go on in, have a good time," I knew an ass whipping, or worse, was just as likely. Mongols think nothing of hurting people: men or women; friends or foes. Here I was, an unknown, solitary dude claiming to be a guest. For them, kicking my ass would have taken about as much forethought as lighting a cigarette.

He finally turned and walked back toward me. After an agonizing pause, he looked me up and down and said: "Come on, dude. You gotta talk to Red Dog."

Red Dog. Little did I realize that those two words were the beginning of a constant misery that would last for the next two years.

Somewhere between despair and terror, I followed like a hound on a leash back to the group of Budweiser-swilling Mongols I'd been watching a minute before. They were assembled in a semicircle around one figure. He stood out like a neon stop sign on a deserted highway; obviously this was Red Dog. Six feet tall and muscular, he wore his Mongol patch slung over a long black duster. His hair was a fiery red, and his face had that ruddy alcoholic complexion and a thick red mustache that extended well below his chin. He had a bandana around his head and wore sunglasses. That, along with a ton of prison tattoos, made his appearance all the more sinister.

I was ushered forward like a peasant before his king. Knowing this was no time to show any signs of weakness, I extended my hand. "Hey, I'm Billy from San Fernando Valley."

There was no indication that Red Dog even considered returning the gesture. He just stood there and stared at me. This was a tactic, as I would later learn, that he routinely used to intimidate friends and enemies alike. I dropped my hand and waited. The ensuing silence was a good tactic, too. It kept me on edge. After a long wait, Red Dog said: "You know a chick named Sue?"

He might as well have been screwing a gun into my ear. *Shit.*

I'd known from that first glance in the Rose Bowl parking lot that my tweaker-chick CI was going to be trouble down the road. And just a few days earlier Domingo had told me that Sue was shooting off her mouth about being pissed off at the Mongols, that she'd said she was going to pay them back big-time. Domingo thought that she might try to bring an undercover cop into the gang. Domingo had turned to me and said, "Billy, you might be that undercover cop." And then he waited, staring, studying my face for a reaction.

If good news travels fast, bad news travels faster. The Mongol grapevine about Sue's bad intentions had obviously gotten back to Red Dog.

"Yeah, Red Dog, I know Sue, but not any better than anyone else at The Place. Hell, I met her at a funeral. That's all I know about her." It was pretty close to the truth. "Look, if this chick is gonna be a problem—"

Red Dog cut me off. He took a step toward me, got right down in my face so I could smell the stench from his stale beer breath. "Billy, if *you* turn out to be a problem, I'll cut your motherfuckin' throat."

It was like getting hit in the face with a wet squirrel. I wasn't quite sure how to respond, so I didn't say anything. Then, to my relief, Red Dog nodded to his soldier. "Let him in."

"Thanks, Red Dog."

As I turned away, I wondered if I was thanking him for letting me in or for not cutting my throat. Either way it didn't seem to make much difference.

I walked through the door of Tony's. It was standing room only. A live band blared some mongrelized, unrecognizable amateur rock. Mongols were shouting their profane conversations over the blare of Fender guitars. One percenters were everywhere. And there were plenty of ladies who looked willing to become the property of the patches. I couldn't help but notice one chick in particular who was obviously quite proud of her half-covered breasts. They were big, and apparently really hers, but they matched the huge gut that hung over her belt. Both were prominently displayed for all to see. If I was going to be spending much time with this gang, I hoped that they occasionally attracted better-looking women.

I moved toward the bar, being careful not to step in front of any patches. I hollered "Budweiser!" at the bartender. It was becoming painfully obvious, at least to me, just how out of place I was. A white boy in the middle of a hundred Hispanic bikers. I shook off my self-consciousness and decided to try my best to mix in.

I drifted through Tony's, Budweiser in hand. I was picking up pointers quickly. Such as when I patted a Mongol on the back and congratulated him on a good pool shot. He looked at me, grinned his outlaw grin, and politely told me that if I ever touched his patch again, he'd wrap his cue stick around my head. I believed him. Lesson learned—don't touch a Mongol's colors.

Shooting pool is a mainstay of the biker lifestyle. So is getting shitfaced on Jack Daniel's and being an asshole, but I decided to try pool first. It could be either my ride in or my ticket to the intensive care unit. I'd been shooting pool since I was a kid and figured I could handle the competition. But I couldn't help wondering if beating a few Mongols at pool would constitute some kind of disrespect. The first Mongol patch I played was good, but he only got off one shot before I ran the table. After sinking the eight ball, I looked up to see him coming straight for me with his cue stick clenched in his fist like a club. I straightened up and tightened my grip on my own stick. To my shock, he lowered the cue and extended his free hand. He was the first Mongol to do so all night.

"Good shootin'," he said. "Name's Lucifer."

"Billy—from San Fernando Valley. I'm a guest."

He nodded. "Where's Domingo?"

Shit, how many times was I going to have to dance around this question?

"I'm not sure," I told Lucifer.

Luckily, it was only a few minutes before Domingo and Rocky and the rest of the San Fernando Valley Chapter strolled lazily into Tony's. I was never so glad to see a group of Mongols as I was at that moment. Instantaneously, the entire atmosphere changed. Domingo introduced me around, and things settled down, including what was left of my nerves.

I shot pool with Rocky and Domingo, downed beer, told jokes, talked motorcycles, and was actually having a pretty decent time until Red Dog—who, I had by now learned, held the official rank of national sergeant at arms—came in from the street. Things went downhill fast when he showed up at our pool table. Not content to just make me feel uncomfortable, Red Dog was on a campaign to let as many Mongols as possible know that he was going to be taking a personal interest in riding my ass. He loudly told Domingo that if an undercover cop was brought into the club, it wouldn't be just the cop's ass, it would be Domingo's as well. He said it as much for my benefit as Domingo's.

I watched Domingo as he racked up the balls. He was pretty good at letting Red Dog's abuse roll off his back. Although perhaps a little bit suspicious of me, Domingo didn't really believe I was a cop. He patted me on the back as we shot pool. "Relax, Billy. Just have a good time tonight."

Last call in California is two A.M. No Mongol party in a licensed bar winds down before then. I looked at my watch and assessed the evening's progress: I was still in one piece, my body parts hadn't been rearranged, I was convincingly holding my own in conversations with hard-core 1 percenters. People were drifting and staggering through the exit, and I figured it was as good a time as any to do the same. I shook hands with Domingo, Rocky, and the San Fernando Valley guys and headed for the door.

I made it to the sidewalk just in time to see Red Dog standing by my Harley. He wasn't even trying to be discreet: He had a pen and paper out and was copying down the license number on my motorcycle. I had no place to go without looking like I was avoiding him, so I kept walking straight to my hog. Red Dog looked up when he saw me. He gave me a brazen stare; it was like catching a bear rummaging in your trash can. He took a few steps toward me and hissed: "I'm gonna find out who you really are."

As I climbed onto my bike I noticed another Mongol standing in the dark watching me as I prepared to leave. All kinds of thoughts started running through my head. Do they know who I am? Are they going to follow me home? I cranked my bike and headed for the freeway, looking more in my rearview mirror than at the road in front of me. There was no way I could even consider risking a meet with Ciccone. I headed back to my undercover apartment, giving any Mongol who might be following me a run for his money. Seventeen years of working undercover assignments gave me an edge on shaking tails. I wove in and out of traffic, running at over 100 miles per hour every now and then, sure to unnerve even an experienced tail.

By the time I made it to my undercover apartment, I was positive no one had followed me. I cruised on in, parked the bike in the carport, went upstairs, and collapsed onto my sofa, still wearing my leather jacket and motorcycle boots.

At the start of the Memorial Day weekend, Domingo told me to meet them at The Place at nine in the morning. This would be my first official organized outing with the Mongols. At nine sharp, like a well-disciplined soldier, I was standing in front of The Place. My sleeping bag and the accoutrements I'd need for the weekend were tied on my bike. By the time nine-thirty rolled around, there were still no Mongols at The Place. I knew there wasn't anything that the SFV Chapter did punctually, so I killed some time talking to my buddies Roy and Johnny at the R & J Motorcycle Shop.

Sometime after ten, Carrena's dad showed up to open The Place for business. There were already a handful of Tujunga locals craving their morning spirits. The only appropriate thing to do was to go in and join them. I'd been inside for about thirty minutes when I heard the unmistakable roar of mechanical thunder outside. In just a matter of seconds the street in front of The Place was filled with black-clad Mongols on their iron horses.

A loud voice pierced that thunder: "Yo, Billy, let's roll!"

I went straight to my bike, grabbed my helmet off the mirror, put it on, and mounted up all in one motion. I gave the kickstand a nudge with my boot. The blast from my pipes matched those of the pack, and with a roar like that of a squadron of F/A-18s, we were off. The pack moved in unison, and as a lowly hang-around, I assumed my position at the rear, sucking up the requisite amount of burnt motorcycle oil and exhaust. Every now and then I would have to duck out of the way of mirrors and other motorcycle parts that flew off the bikes ahead of me.

I was awed by their stunning display. We made our way across Los Angeles to a cemetery on the southeast side of town, where we met up with what seemed to be the entire Mongol Nation. As we parked amid the rows of bikes, other Mongols welcomed our pack with the traditional loud-clapping Mongol handshakes as well as hugs and kisses. To outsiders, Mongols are as deadly as a pride of lions, but among themselves, they can be remarkably loyal, kind, and affectionate.

After the greetings, everyone moved toward a particular gravesite. They surrounded the headstone of a fallen brother who'd been killed two decades earlier during the original war with the Hells Angels, and with reverence, the Mongols' national vice president conducted roll call for the members of Chapter 13—the brothers who have died and whose memory is revered by club members. Strict military-style decorum was maintained until the ceremony concluded. As a Vietnam vet, I was moved by the respect and sincerity shown by these wild-haired, tattooed, knife-scarred men. The silence was broken when a solitary Mongol screamed: "Who are we?"

Everyone responded with the Mongol fight song:

We are Mongol raiders
We're raiders of the night
We're dirty sons of bitches
We'd rather fuck and fight
    —HOOAH!
We castrate the sheriffs with a dirty piece of glass

And shove our rusty buck knives up their fuckin' ass
    —HOOAH!
Hidy—hidy—Christ Almighty
Who the fuck are we?
Shit—Fuck—Cunt—Suck—
    Mongols M.C.
    —HOOAH!

The memorial ceremony broke up and the Mongol Nation erupted in a frenzy of life. We were headed to Simi Valley for a massive party weekend. Directions were handed out only when Mongols were mounting their bikes. Ever vigilant of being tailed by the law, the Mongol leadership had decided that no one was allowed to know the run's destination prior to this moment. And who but an overeager cop would want to crash a Mongol party?

"Fire 'em up!"

And there was a thunderous roar of Harleys—Panheads, Shovelheads, Evos, Softails, FLHTCs, and so on—as we began to roll out of the cemetery. More than 150 bikes formed into ranks, winding through the streets of Los Angeles like a great anaconda. Under Red Dog's direction, the sergeants at arms from the various chapters blatantly blocked intersections like rent-a-cops as the procession moved through the city. With impunity we blew right past real cops—stunned LAPD officers, overwhelmed California Highway Patrolmen—as well as red lights, stop signs, speed limits. No law had any bearing on this outlaw army. As we rode through one intersection after another at breakneck speed I realized that the Mongol Nation—like those shrieking warriors on horseback terrorizing the known world under Genghis Khan—were in absolute control of any territory they occupied.

* * *

After a trek of some forty miles, the procession rolled into a campground on the west side of Simi Valley, an upscale bedroom community on the easternmost edge of Ventura County, at the border with Los Angeles. After such a well-orchestrated caravan from the cemetery to the campground, I expected something similar in the selection of camping areas. What actually took place, though, was a kind of Chinese fire drill. We rode around the area looking for what we felt would be a good area for the SFV Chapter to set up shop. Like a prognosticator with a divining rod, Domingo stopped and declared a specific territory as ours. We all began to stake out our particular spots. Assuming my rightful position, I had to defer to all the patches and their women before choosing any leftover spot. I laid claim to an area underneath a scrub tree.

While laying out my camping gear, I noticed a black Chevrolet El Camino driving into the SFV area. A woman who looked to be in her late thirties got out and approached the group. She was definitely a typical biker chick. Then I heard Bucket Head, as casual as could be, tell Domingo and Rocky that the guns had arrived.

Bucket Head was our chapter's sergeant at arms. He told Domingo that he was heading for the sergeants' meeting. I would have given my right nut to go with him, but instead I headed to the common area with Rocky.

Music blared and the barbecue was fired up. Mongols were milling around, booze was flowing, and the smell of marijuana filled the air. Domingo, Rocky, and I had moved to the parking lot when a guy named Evel rode up on a black Harley Wide Glide. He smiled as he pulled up next to Domingo.

"Here it is," he said. He shut down the engine as a group of Mongols started to gather around the motorcycle. "Stolen last night—right out in front of the bar. I told the prospect to take it."

What bar and what prospect I didn't know. I was surprised that this frankly criminal conversation was taking place in front of me, since I had no official standing in the gang. They were usually very cryptic around me. I think Rocky had the same thought because he shot a glare in my direction and told me to go away for a while. I did, but not before getting a good look at the stolen motorcycle. I would see it again later at Domingo's house.

The run was shaping up well. I was gathering solid intelligence on the Mongols' firearm and stolen-motorcycle activities—intelligence that would prove valuable to a federal racketeering prosecution down the line.

I filled my plate with carne asada and moved to the common area near the barbecue, where Rancid, a talented tattoo artist, was putting the finishing touches on a full-patch tattoo that covered the entire surface area of Crazy Craig's back. As I watched Rancid work I realized that Crazy Craig would now have to be a Mongol for the rest of his life, because if he went out in bad standing with the club, the Mongols would insist on burning that tattoo off—customary practice for outlaw motorcycle gangs—and a burn that big would surely kill him.

Daylight had given way to night. I was drinking a cold Bud in the common area with six or seven Mongols, exchanging war stories, when a Ventura County Sheriff's unit rolled into the parking lot not fifty feet from where we were standing. No big deal. We'll be cool. He'll be cool. He'll drive away, no trouble. But for the Mongols, a jubilant and carefree atmosphere turned deadly serious. They began to stash their firearms. Drugs were being discarded everywhere. Like a pack of wild dogs, the Mongols had zeroed in on the deputy. But two Mongols didn't hide their guns. I heard one of them whisper that there was no way he could take a shakedown. If he got picked up, he'd be going to prison for a long time. He looked at the other armed Mongol and said something that would rock my night: "If he comes up here, we'll take him."

I was adrift, back on an exploding hill just outside the Cam Lo Valley surrounded by the enemy. How could I possibly warn the deputy? Nightmare scenarios ran through my brain as the two Mongols talked casually about the cold-blooded murder of this unsuspecting officer.

The plan to take out the deputy became more specific. The deputy stopped his car now and looked over in our direction. In my head I was shouting at this officer to keep moving, to hit the gas and, whatever he did, to not step out of that car. I heard one Mongol say, "You talk with him. Keep his attention and I'll take him from behind."

I looked around desperately for an out. There was no way that the deputy and I could win a fight here—we'd both end up dead. I saw a phone booth with a light directly over it near the basketball area. Maybe I could make it to the phone. I could call Ciccone and have him call the sheriff's department. Then they could radio the deputy and tell him to get the hell out of there. I felt the sweat beading up on my forehead. If I was going to make a move, I had to do it now, before the deputy got out of his car.

I had started to move toward the phone when the deputy's car began to roll. *God, make him stay in the car; don't let him get out,* I kept saying to myself.

The patrol car kept moving, continued on out of the park. I just stood there, stunned. I regained my composure and stumbled back to my campsite. The party was over for me. I lay down on my sleeping bag and stared up the black sky, which now matched my mood. I was painfully aware that I was an ATF agent surrounded by outlaws.

I couldn't get the image of the Mongols planning the

murder of a deputy out of my head. I knew that if these guys learned the truth—that I was not Billy St. John but Bill Queen, special agent with the Bureau of Alcohol, Tobacco and Firearms—they wouldn't hesitate one millisecond to put a bullet between my eyes.

6

Deep-undercover assignments are always going to wreak havoc on an agent's nerves. But there are many undercover roles—even working inside such organizations as the Mafia or the Aryan Nations—where violent criminal activity is going to come in spurts. The undercover is inevitably going to have a few days or weeks of downtime, some moments when the criminality takes a backseat. Not with the Mongols. I quickly saw that their entire lives were a blur of potential rapes, beatings, extortion, even murder.

Unlike the Mafia, gangs like the Mongols do not exist for profit. They have various illegal moneymaking activities, ranging from drug dealing to armed robbery to trafficking in illegal guns and stolen motorcycles, but the criminal enterprise is not the glue holding the organization together. For gangsters like the Mongols, membership means a twenty-four-hour-a-day commitment to The Life. They despise legitimacy and have no desire to look like anything other than what they are.

Women play a complex role in these bikers' lives. They're called "mamas" and "sheep" and "ol' ladies" and are designated the sexual "property" either of an individual member or of the gang collectively. Women like Vicky, Rocky's legal wife and the mother of his children, were granted a measure of respect within the gang, meaning no one would dare disrespect her or put a hand on her. Rocky, on the other hand, could beat the hell out of Vicky and no one would think to say a word to him about it.

Probably the most infamous example of this twisted male-female dynamic, reported in *Newsweek* in 1967, was the case of an eighteen-year-old named Christine Deese, the girlfriend of a member of the Outlaws Motorcycle Club named Norman "Spider" Risinger. For violating the rule of not giving her ol' man all her money, Christine was sentenced to a "punishment ceremony." She was publicly crucified by Spider and his Outlaw brothers. According to *Newsweek,* she stood passively and "didn't scream" as the bikers nailed her to a tree and left her there for several hours. When they finally brought her down and dropped her off at a West Palm Beach emergency room, she told the incredulous doctors that she'd fallen on a board with exposed rusty nails. The horrifying incident led to a national manhunt to capture the gang members involved and prompted a dire warning to both the bikers and their women from Florida governor Claude Kirk: "This bunch of bums has got the word they're not welcome in Florida. . . . I hope young, thrill-seeking girls who go with them know they can get their fingers burned—or in this case, their hands nailed." But after recovering from her wounds, Christine not only stayed with Spider, she reputedly wore the nails from the crucifixion on a necklace as some kind of perverse trophy.

It's easy to say that women who are caught up in the biker lifestyle are victims of a dehumanizing codependent relationship. But if you're around them long enough, you quickly see that for many of these women, being "property" of the gang is the one thing that gives their lives meaning. Almost all are there by choice; they're only too happy to put on that PROPERTY patch. For all the sexual abuse and beatings they're subjected to, there's also a sense of belonging, a sense of power. While they are wearing that patch, they are untouchable to the world at large. No one can make trouble for them without bringing down the fury of the whole Mongol Nation.

Hanging out in The Place in the spring of 1998, I quickly saw the kind of women who were pleased to put their bodies at the gang's disposal. One night around twelve, I was wiped out and heading toward the door when one of the Tujunga regulars tapped me on the shoulder. "Better hang out, Billy. Tonight's nude-pool night."

He pointed at a Tujunga barfly. I watched as the young woman sauntered around the pool table. She looked to be in her late twenties and had a great body, but she was rough, to say the least. She carried herself like a man and shot a game of pool like one, too.

I quickly learned just what nude-pool night entailed. This girl would play games of pool with the guys for money. If she lost, rather than pay the money, she would just start taking off clothes, a variation on strip poker. She ended up either with a pocket full of money or, to the applause of the boys, shooting naked. The boys weren't applauding her—they were applauding the guy beating her out of her clothes. She would win a dollar, then lose her blouse. Then she'd win a dollar and lose her pants. She might end up winning ten bucks but have no pockets to put it in.

By the time she was down to her tennis shoes, Rocky walked in. I bought him a beer and we settled in for the show. It didn't take long to realize that the girl enjoyed putting on the show as much as the Tujunga boys enjoyed watching it. She'd line up her shot, bending over the table, making sure that everyone in The Place got a shot of their own. As she bent over in dramatic fashion she made sure that her nipples rubbed against the green felt of the well-worn pool table. Not content to be the floor show, she invited audience participation.

The Place, being a small, crowded joint to begin with, didn't afford pool players enough room for spectators to be kept at a respectable distance. But nothing respectable was going on here tonight. While making her shots (and providing onlookers theirs), she moved her hips to the music that blared from the jukebox. I heard a loud roar from the crowd and looked closer. I saw that one patron had buried his neck between her legs. The neck of his Budweiser bottle, that is. As she moved around the table, it was a beer bottle here, a finger there, it didn't matter— any kind of penetration was okay with her.

The fact that she was someone's daughter, perhaps a sister, maybe even a mother, gnawed at my conscience. But as with many of the people I met during the investigation, the woman really was a willing participant in her own exploitation, and there was little I could do besides wishing that one day she might save herself from herself.

Women were often the catalyst for some of the gang's worst acts of violence. Making trouble for a Mongol's woman, even unintentionally, could have the most violent consequences. I witnessed this early on with a guy called John O. I first heard about John O during the Memorial Day run; several Mongols were standing around casually talking about a fight that had broken out at The Place. Fights at The Place were pretty common, but this sounded like more than just another amateur one-rounder.

John O, a Tujunga barroom slugger, had gotten into a brawl with another local. In an effort to bring the misunderstanding to an early conclusion, he picked up a cue stick to clobber his opponent. But he ended up backstroking a girl standing behind him, breaking her jaw. Ordinarily this wouldn't be any big deal at The Place. But the girl with the broken jaw was the ol' lady of a Mongol who was now away doing prison time. Big problem for John O.

Domingo could have ordered the SFV Chapter to dole out a Mongol boot thumping, but John O was given an alternative. Domingo decreed that he could pay the medical bills and any other expenses incurred by the Mongol's girlfriend. He could also pay the Mongols for pain and suffering, until the Mongols decided things were even. This sounded like a reasonable settlement to John O.

Just a few days after the Memorial Day run, I met John O myself at The Place. He was of average height, with long blond hair falling halfway down his back. He obviously took a lot of pride in that hair; it made him look like the lead singer in some eighties heavy-metal band. He stepped up to me at the bar, asking if I'd seen Rocky or any of the other Mongols. I told him that Domingo would be swinging by in a little while to meet me for a beer.

John O was visibly scared, and he told me why. He had been paid a visit earlier that day by Rocky, who had explained that John O was late on his payment to the club. Rocky explained this to John O while John O stared back at Rocky down the barrel of a .38-caliber revolver.

A few days later, as we drank together at The Place, for some reason—alcohol, drugs, lack of functioning brain cells—John O's payment plan collapsed along with what common sense he possessed. After the trauma of Rocky's threat had worn off, he abruptly decided that he was no longer going to make payments to the Mongols. He must also have decided that he no longer wanted to live, because he made a critical decision to announce to his buddies around The Place that he wasn't afraid of the Mongols. As a matter of fact, according to John O, the Mongols weren't *shit* anyway.

After he left the bar, Carrena—who was property of
The Kid, president of the Riverside County Chapter—
not only informed Rocky and Domingo of John O's dis-
respectful attitude but also agreed to participate in his
reeducation program. Carrena put in a call to John O
and told him that she had a part-time maintenance job
for him at The Place. John O needed whatever work he
could get, so he agreed to come up to the bar. The SFV
Chapter, with behavior-modification tools in hand, was
waiting.

By the time his many misconceptions were straightened out, John O's flowing blond hair had been sliced off
and he was on his way to the hospital for a set of sutures
and some plaster casts.

I never saw John O around the neighborhood after that.
No one else did, either.

But the Mongols SFV Chapter flag—to this day in ATF
custody—still bears John O's bloody hair.

It was Friday night and I was at home putting together
the things I'd need for the weekend trip to Porterville
with the Mongols. I had just gotten off the phone with
my kids. I tried to explain to them that I had to work this
weekend and that I wouldn't get to see them for a few
days. It was very hard for them to understand. My youngest son was going to baseball practice and I wanted to
be there, but this Porterville run was an opportunity to
make serious progress in the investigation—an opportunity I couldn't afford to pass up. My girlfriend was becoming annoyed that my nights and weekends were now
the sole property of the Mongols. She was feeling left out
of my life, and I didn't blame her. My new full-time com-
panion was the investigation.

As I packed, I tried to explain to her how important it
was that I seized the opportunities as they presented
themselves. She really couldn't see it from my perspec-

tive, and I suppose I couldn't see things from hers. "Look, I gotta do what I gotta do," I said, and we didn't say another word to each other the rest of the night.

I was up early Saturday morning, said a terse good-bye, fired up the bike, and headed for Tujunga. It was a gorgeous Southern California day, and as I breezed down the freeway I found myself looking forward to the run.

I met up with the San Fernando Valley Chapter in front of The Place, and we hit the highway. Porterville is a fourteen-square-mile agricultural community about 165 miles north of Los Angeles. It's a little less than the halfway point between Los Angeles and San Francisco, at the base of the Sequoia National Park. The campground there was one of the Mongols' favorite spots for a down-home run.

There was nothing special about it as far as campgrounds go, at least not until 150 outlaw bikers rolled in and took it over. Pulling into the campground, I'd seen a flatbed trailer that had been parked at one end. Domingo grinned, greeted me with a high five, and told me that we were going to have a good time tonight. He left it at that, and I knew better than to ask questions. A little later an uninvited guest came stumbling into the Mongols' camping area. Just your standard, run-of-the-mill, white-trash drunk who was about to learn a lesson in Mongol respect. He was told that he was in an area that belonged to the Mongols. After he refused to leave promptly, several hulking Mongols administered a severe beating and stomping. Sporting a bruised ego and two newly acquired black eyes, the drunk finally realized it was in his best interest to leave the campground.

As the sun went down and the music and barbecue were fired up, I managed to get back into the groove with the assistance of a few beers. Rocky and I walked around visiting several other chapter campsites. Rocky introduced me as a new hang-around. With reserved enthusiasm, others welcomed me.

Some hours after dark, and after we had eaten, the SFV Chapter guys moved over to the flatbed entertainment area where the rest of the Mongol Nation had assembled. Loudspeakers blared rock music, and lights were trained on the flatbed.

Domingo punched me hard to get my attention, his typical Mongol tactic. He pointed to five or six half-naked girls walking up onto the flatbed. Young, sexy, and in good shape. They moved to the music, taking off what little clothes they had on. Unlike the strippers in regulated exotic dance clubs, these girls didn't stop at G-strings. When they were stark naked, they recklessly invited Mongols to participate in the show.

Suddenly, I heard Domingo yell to one of the strippers: "Baby, I want you to sit on my bud's face."

Domingo was waving a five-dollar bill at the stripper, which was like waving a steak at a hungry tiger. She ran over and snatched the five out of his hand. He turned around, grabbed me by my shirt, literally picked me up and threw me onto the stage, where I landed on my back. With one giant step the nude girl stood over me. I heard a loud cheer go up from the Mongol crowd. In that instant I thought about ATF administration, the U.S. Attorney's Office, my already pissed-off girlfriend, my by-the-book case agent, and the possibility of an Internal Affairs beef. The roar of the crowd was the stripper's cue. Shaking and writhing to the music, she bent down on her knees and buried my face in her crotch. As she moved back and forth, I could hear louder cheering from the crowd. After a few seconds she stood up. I took a much-needed breath of air. Domingo pulled me from the stage before I could even stand up. I gathered myself and, like a victorious prizefighter, thrust my fist into the air while still tasting the stripper on my lips.

"Billy!" The Mongols cheered and patted me on the back. Less than a minute went by before the Mongols were again completely fixated on the naked strippers on the stage. I made my way through the crowd looking for a place to spit.

I watched as the Mongols got wilder and more aggressive with the strippers. Inevitably the grabbing and clawing got too much for the girls, who partnered up with their first tricks and the show was over.

When the sun woke me a few hours later, I had a paralyzing headache. Not just an ordinary bad morning-after—this was a world-class hangover. *Holy shit,* I heard myself groaning into the ground, *I'm gonna have to get better just to die.* If this was the pace the investigation was going to take, I wasn't sure I'd live to see the end.

Around eleven, Domingo got up and announced that we would be going up to Visalia to finish partying with our Cen Cal brothers—the Central California Chapter. Jesus, that was not at all what I wanted to hear. I was seriously hurting.

It must have been around two P.M. when the SFV and Cen Cal Chapters headed out for Visalia. There was no way that I could make contact with Ciccone to let him know the change of plan. He would just have to continue his surveillance and follow the pack. I wondered if he was still in the game. It didn't take long to make that determination. At the first stoplight I came to, I looked in my rearview mirror only to see the whites of Ciccone's eyes. He was so close that he could have been a chick sitting on the back of my bike. I wondered who else might be noticing him and his ridiculous proximity. I made a mental note to tell him at a later debrief that he needed to work on some of his surveillance techniques. It was early, though; we'd all learn a few things during this investigation.

We rolled into Visalia and went to the residence of the Cen Cal Chapter president. I was dog tired, but so were

Rocky and Rancid. We found beds, couches, and floor-boards, anything to lie out on and catch some sleep. Only half awake, I observed constant traffic coming in and out of the house. The Cen Cal Chapter president was a pretty prolific cocaine dealer. Another thing that kept me awake was all the talk of gun trafficking that went on until well into the afternoon. I couldn't act like I was listening too closely, so I lay there with my eyes closed, trying to mem-orize the various makes of guns the Mongols were dis-cussing for the ATF report I'd have to type up when I got home.

Finally Domingo and the Cen Cal Chapter president decided it was time to hit a few of the local bars. Among the Mongols, showering and teeth brushing weren't even a consideration. Rocky slapped me on the shoulder. He was good to go. Rancid was altogether another story. Nothing short of a cold bucket of water or Armageddon was going to move him off his lazy, smelly ass. Domingo decided to go with the cold bucket of water, and finally—with a shudder and profane shout—Rancid stirred to life.

I accompanied about a dozen Mongols to a Visalia bar. Domingo began taking some heat about me from the Cen Cal guys. I watched as his demeanor toward me changed. Every little thing I did now became a big problem for Domingo. I went to the bathroom. He questioned me about where I'd been. I went to call my girlfriend. He questioned me about who I'd been talking to. Then he locked me in a mean stare. "I'm keepin' an eye on you, Billy."

At about ten o'clock, after intimidating the bar man-ager out of a few hundred bucks' worth of unpaid-for beer, Domingo approached me and said that we were go-ing over to an associate's place to hook up with some strippers. I could only imagine what this might mean. Was this going to be some kind of new test for the hang-around? Mongols downed their remaining booze and headed for the door. As I made my way outside I looked for Ciccone and the guys; with Domingo hovering over me, I couldn't chance more than a quick glance up and down the street. I didn't see anything remotely resembling a cop car. Reality hit me hard: I'd lost all backup now; it was just my wits against these cranked-up, alcohol-fueled outlaws.

We left the bar and made our way through the streets of Visalia until we arrived at a small house. I had no idea who lived there. Domingo said that the Cen Cal president was going to put in the phone call to the girls and that they would be over in a little bit. I began to wonder just what this was going to turn into.

After a few more beers, Domingo disclosed the real plan for the evening's festivities. He said that the girls had been told that they would be coming over to give a private dance show for the Mongols, for which they would be paid handsomely. He smiled as he told me what was really going to happen. We would tie them up and gang-bang them all before heading back to L.A.

"Great idea," I said, smiling back at Domingo.

Inside, I tried to stifle a retch at the thought of premeditated kidnapping and gang rape. I tried my damnedest to mask the panic in my face. I had to think of a way to get out of this one. I looked around. I had no idea exactly where I was. I had no idea where Ciccone or the backup guys were. I had no gun with me—it was too risky at that point of the investigation to take the chance of the Mongols finding it on me. But I knew that several of the Mongols were carrying firearms. And all the dope the Mongols had consumed wasn't making the situation any better. No one was going to come to their senses.

After about an hour of pacing, frantically wondering what I should do, I was approached by The Kid, Carrena's ol' man and the president of the Riverside County (or RivCo) Chapter. The Kid was a hard-core outlaw, a major-league asshole, and about as predictable as a rabid wolverine. He had gotten out of prison for a felony drug conviction a few months before and was back at the helm of the RivCo Chapter, partying like a man desperate to make up for all those lost years. The Kid clearly didn't trust me. He looked directly into my eyes and said: "You do nose candy, Billy?"

"What?"

"Do you do nose candy?"

I stared at him blankly.

"Cocaine, Billy!" he snapped. "Do you do fuckin' co-caine?"

"Yeah, sometimes. But I ain't doin' *shit* tonight."

"How come?"

"It's hard enough for me to keep up with y'all—Jesus, you're half my fuckin' age. All this beer—and coke, too—that's gonna knock me on my ass."

The Kid began to push methamphetamine as an all-purpose pick-me-up.

"Crank will keep you going, Billy. What you need to do is a few lines of crank."

Domingo walked up, nodding. "Yeah, Billy, you ought to do some crank."

It was unheard of for Domingo to push the dope issue. For one thing, he didn't touch drugs himself. He was still on parole, had only recently come out of prison on an assault charge, and had to pass a weekly piss test with his parole officer. I began to feel the heat of Domingo's stare. A premeditated gang rape and now a dope test. It was going from bad to worse; I looked around to see several other Mongols watching hard for my reaction.

Gangs like the Mongols have been in the cops-and-robbers game for so long they know the signs to look for in someone they suspect of being an undercover. You can't just pull some excuse out of your ass without having your corroboration in place. If I'd gone the Domingo route—"Hey, I gotta take a piss test for my parole officer every week"—then they'd want to know my PO's name, which prison I'd done my time in, and who my cell mate was. The Mongols have plenty of sources in both the federal and state prison systems and could punch holes in that story in short order. If I said I had to take a random drug test for my job, then they'd soon have their private eyes checking out that story. Few real companies are willing to back an undercover operation of this nature, and while we found one that would, they could not withstand intense questioning on the minutiae of drug testing, and I would have been reckless to put them in that position.

The Kid walked a few feet away and laid out a couple of lines of methamphetamine on a car hood. Then, loud enough for everyone to hear, he yelled: "Get yer ass over here, Billy! Do a line or we aren't ever going to believe anything you say!"

I could feel my face getting bright red. I was boxed into a corner, and I knew I had to fight my way off the ropes. But I'd done my homework; I'd studied the way Koz had improvised his way out of similar jams when he was undercover with the Vagos.

Rather than back down, I yelled angrily back at The Kid.

"You don't believe any fucking thing I say anyway, motherfucker! I'm not going to pile my bike into some tree because I did some shit just to make you guys happy. I'll be lucky to get back to L.A. as it is, so fuck you!"

They were all speechless. Hang-arounds don't talk that way to full patches. And they definitely don't talk that way to chapter presidents. I figured the least I'd get away with would be an ass whipping. But it might give me a good excuse to jump on my bike and leave before the strippers got there for the gang rape.

To my astonishment, The Kid laughed. "More for me," he said, and snorted up both lines. Everybody else laughed, too.

The hours crept by, until it was around three in the morning. The strippers still hadn't shown up. Just about all the Mongols were too stoned and drunk to focus on anything. Finally, Domingo said, "Fuck it." He was ready to head back to L.A.

As exhausted as I was, I fully understood that the planned gang rape was meant to be my biggest test yet. If I hadn't participated I would have been out of the Mongols. Of course, as a cop, as a father—as a human being with a conscience—participation wasn't a question. But what could I have done? If I'd tried to stop the rapes, I'd blow my cover and risk getting killed when they realized who I was. Without a gun, without backup, there was no way one cop was going to be able to stop a dozen rapist Mongols flying high on meth and coke.

But Lady Luck smiled on me. And she smiled on those strippers, too.

The Mongols had lost interest in testing me. Without any great fanfare they fired up the bikes. I glanced around the block again—Ciccone and the boys were still nowhere in sight.

I was beyond tired. I'd slept about three hours in the last forty-eight. If I made it home alive, that would be a victory as far as I was concerned. We rode mile after mile until the sun came up. It was about five in the morning when we finally hit the Tujunga area, and my weary head was filled with thoughts of the Mongols luring those unsuspecting dancers into a trap of kidnapping and rape.

7

By the summer of 1998, I'd become an official Mongols prospect. As a probationary member of the gang, a prospect is trusted with more responsibilities than a hang-around, but he also has a lot more at stake. By now I'd been educated in the basic club hierarchy, had begun to master the outlaw traditions and codes. Official club meetings are known as "Church." The club had its by-laws and constitution as well as its own twisted version of the biblical laws of Moses, which I ultimately received from Domingo (and which was vouchered as evidence).

The Five Mongol Commandments
1. A Mongol never lies to another Mongol.
2. A Mongol never steals from another Mongol.
3. A Mongol never messes around with another Mongol's ol' lady.
4. A Mongol never causes another Mongol to get arrested in any way, shape, or form.
5. A Mongol never uses his patch for personal gain.

If you intend to break any of the above commandants [sic], you might as well turn your patch in now or face the consequences.

In order to become a prospect, I had to complete an official Mongols application. I was a little stunned when

Rocky handed it to me one day at his house; it was three pages long, and more intense—and personal—than applications I'd filled out to become a law-enforcement officer. The Mongols wanted to know everything from your Social Security number to how long your dick was.

But I stood there nodding at Rocky, acting unfazed. "No problem, my man. I'll get it back to you in a day or so."

Meanwhile, I could quickly see that we had a major problem; we might even have to deep-six the whole operation. For one thing, Rocky told me that after I filled out the application, it was going to be handed over to a private investigator—quite possibly an ex-cop. I also knew that sometimes the best you can do is not good enough.

I had started building my undercover background as Billy St. John in the mid-eighties, during my work inside the neo-Nazis, the National Alliance, and other antigovernment groups. ATF had the ability to do anything any other federal or local agency could do as far as covering their UC agents, such as creating a bogus arrest record, work history, credit reports, vehicle registration, driver's license, and educational records. In preparing my undercover identity, I had been in touch with other agents and agencies who were in the know about potential pitfalls. I had called on my old friend Steve Campbell, a police department captain in North Carolina, who set up a bogus criminal record for me; it showed several misdemeanor arrests for assault and drug violations. I was one of the few guys in ATF who was able to actually go under with some confidence—at least until I saw that Mongol membership application.

I was scanning the questions and thinking, *How the hell are we going to cover all this shit?* There was no way I could do it alone. If Ciccone wanted his UC agent to stay alive, he was going to have another project dumped in his lap.

Once again, Ciccone saved my skin. He proved himself a genius at navigating the complex and often treacherous administrative waters of ATF. We made a great team that way—John handling the behind-the-scenes machinations of the bureau and me handling the face-to-face stuff with the bad guys on the street.

Within a few hours of seeing my application, Ciccone had a team of ATF agents running from one side of the country to the other, getting things in place to bolster my background. Besides the obvious ID issues—Social Security number, California driver's license, Veterans Administration records—the Mongols wanted telephone numbers and addresses for my relatives. They expected to see high school records, in my case, from North Carolina in the late 1960s. They also wanted to see hard copies of W-2s for five years.

In just a matter of days, Ciccone pulled it all together. He had ATF agents inside the school system in the town where I'd supposedly grown up, doctoring "official" school records for me. He had various agents around the country ready to answer the phone numbers we'd provided, pretending to be my parents, uncles, aunts, cousins.

He got his hands on IRS forms and made some official W-2s "proving" that Billy St. John had worked at a California-based avionics company for the past five years. The avionics industry deals with aircraft instrumentation: radar units, navigational radios, weather scopes, altitude indicators, and speed indicators. My "job" was to buy and sell used equipment. During the day I would pick up equipment in Southern California and take it to a real repair shop. And to give the whole employment cover more credibility, on several occasions I arranged to bring one of the Mongols with me on a pickup. A few times I even took Rocky along to meet with my supposed employer—actually an ATF agent working undercover—so he could pay me in front of Rocky.

We felt like we had covered everything that the Mongols were asking for in the application, and we were sure as fuck betting my life on it. But as thorough as we'd been in preparing my background, I was still a nervous wreck every day I went in to meet the Mongols. And Ciccone was just as wound up and tense as I was.

Following protocol, I turned my application in to our chapter president, Domingo. There was no backing out of it now. Despite my apprehensions, I had to maintain that level of outward confidence, aggression, and surliness that's expected from men in the world of 1 percenters; I couldn't let the possibility of being found out overshadow my performance. If I ever appeared too nervous or jumpy, the Mongols would read it instantly as weakness and sniff me out as a cop or, at least, as a guy pretending to be someone he wasn't.

For weeks as I fired up my Harley, I kept talking to myself: *Hey, Billy, chill out. They like you. If they didn't, they wouldn't have asked you to join the club. If they really thought you were a cop, they'd have fucked you up a long time ago.*

Plus, I didn't have any solid evidence against Domingo or Rocky or Rancid, and therefore, I told myself, they had no reason to kill me even if they did find out who I really was.

Of course, that was the logical analysis, and didn't take into account the irrational, hotheaded, and often psychotic behavior I knew that members of the Mongols were capable of.

I kept up the ritual for the next couple of weeks: I'd get myself good and psyched up, ride into Tujunga on my hog, hang out with the Mongols, buy beer for them, and shoot pool. We would ride to an event or another bar, and Rocky, my designated mentor, would teach me some more time-honored Mongol tradition. I checked the guys' faces and demeanor each time I met with them. I tried to catch any tiny nuances or tics that might signal that I was in trouble.

Then, one lazy midmorning, I was hanging out at my UC pad when I got an unsettling call from Rocky. "Hey, Billy," he said. "Why don't you come on over."

It wasn't a request; it was a command. But it didn't sound like Rocky. His voice was distant, suspicious, spacy.

"What's goin' on, Rock?"

In a long, drawn-out way, completely out of character, he said: "Just come on over here, dude. We're gonna go and pick up your colors. We gotta go see Bobby Loco first. Then we're going to Luna's place and pick up your colors. So come on over."

I didn't know quite what to say. I knew that Bobby Loco was the Mongol who was in charge of checking out the background information in my application. Luna was the Mongols' national secretary-treasurer, a very high ranking officer within the organization. Both men were patched in with the Mother Chapter, which was down in Commerce. Bobby Loco and Leno Luna were old-timers—veterans from the days of the original war with the Hells Angels—and as hard-core as they come.

As a prospect, you are entitled to wear the rudimentary colors of the club; you are allowed to wear the leather vest with PROSPECT on the front and a lower rocker that reads CALIFORNIA on the back. Eventually, having proven yourself by engaging in criminal activities like hauling drugs and guns, and after a unanimous vote by the chapter membership, you can earn the right to a center patch of the club's official logo. But you could never wear the coveted top rocker—the MONGOLS patch—until you were a full-fledged member of the club. When Rocky mentioned getting my colors, I was taken aback; I knew I wasn't scheduled to be picking up any colors and figured Domingo would have mentioned it to me if I had. As Rocky droned on in his spaced-out voice, I began to fear that what I'd really be picking up was a bullet in the back of my head.

Still, I couldn't stall Rocky without raising suspicions. I told him to hang in there; I'd be over in a bit.

"Get on the stick," he said, then abruptly hung up.

I dialed Ciccone right away. "John, I just got a call from Rocky."

"Yeah, what's up with Big Rock?"

"Some weird shit. He's acting really strange. He says he wants me to come over—says we're gonna go pick up my colors. It doesn't sound right to me. It sounds like they may have found out something. I don't like it, John. I don't like this shit at all."

John respected my intuition and knew that the call under these circumstances would be up to me. I went back over the last couple of days in my mind, looking for something that might have given me away. I couldn't think of anything. Neither could John. We kept bouncing scenarios past each other on the phone: What little mistake might I have made? Ciccone was thinking a bit more clearly than I was. "Billy, it might not be anything at all," he said. "We just don't know."

We hadn't gotten any phone calls from any of our background people; we knew the Mongols were looking at me hard—but so far, so good. The club's private investigator had so far turned up only what we'd wanted him to turn up. He had run a credit check and turned up my UC credit report. He'd contacted my supposed relatives with some questions and was satisfied. He'd contacted school officials in North Carolina who were played by ATF agents. He'd contacted my supposed avionics company and verified my employment there. The one hitch occurred when he ran my driver's history with the California Department of Motor Vehicles and, even though my bike and my UC car were registered to Billy St. John, it didn't list a motorcycle endorsement under that name. (The endorsement, meaning I could legally ride a bike, rather than just drive a car, was on my real driver's license.) Luckily, the Mongols figured it to be a typical DMV fuckup.

I wasn't sure what was up with Rocky today, but something was. I didn't have to go see him. I could tell John that this was the end of the road—the case would be over, but I'd still be alive. No one could fault me. The UC always has the last word in these situations. I'd been through some tight places, a lot tighter than this, and come out alive. I could do it.

As a prospect, I didn't carry a gun. I didn't wear a wire—that could have been suicidal given the constant scrutiny I was under. I never wanted too many agents following me around because they could do more harm than good. But this time, I'd put it all on the line. I'd go in armed. I'd wear a wire. I'd get the best backup the L.A. Division had to offer. If it was a setup, I'd be ready for it. I'd take the Mongols on in their own backyard.

I told Ciccone that besides Carr, Koz, and Hardin, I wanted Chuck Pratt and Mike Dawkins there. Pratt and Dawkins were both proven gunfighters and good friends of mine. I had no doubt they would all risk their lives to save mine. Ciccone would roll by Rocky's place on surveillance, and if he saw any of the known Mongol gunslingers there—Red Dog, Woody, Diablo, or Lucifer—we'd call it off. If it looked like no one other than Rocky was there, I would go in. If I was met with a gun, I'd shoot first and ask questions after my backup entered and cleaned up. Ciccone agreed. I even thought about wearing a vest. But that would clearly give me away. I had to calm down.

I had to take the risk and make the best of it. The plan was set. I knew what I had to do.

I picked up my five-shot revolver, wondering if five shots would be enough today. I tucked the gun in the pocket of my jacket where I'd have my hand when I walked into Rocky's place. I thought back to undercover deals that had turned into shoot-outs. I'd seen more than my share of that kind of action, and I had listened to tapes of undercover deals that had gone bad where cops had been shot and you could hear them breathe their last breath. It weighed heavy on me as I fired up and rolled out to meet Ciccone.

John had rallied the troops. Everybody that I wanted was there on backup—guys I had put my life on the line for, guys I trusted, guys who would make this op easier. Ciccone told me they were gathering near Rocky's place and putting together their plan. I felt better as I taped the wire to my leg.

The backup team had checked out the target location. There were no other cars or bikes at Rocky's place. Ciccone and I both understood that we were about to roll the dice on the biggest stakes so far in this investigation.

I climbed on my fire and hit the starter. Soon I rolled up in front of Rocky's place and backed my bike to the curb. Everything looked normal. I glanced down the street and saw the ATF van with my backup team sitting at the ready. Mustering my composure, I walked to Rocky's door, took a deep breath, reached in my pocket, and gripped my revolver. With my left hand I knocked on the door. I could hear footsteps inside. As I had been trained in the ATF National Academy, I got into a modified Weaver stance, turning sideways, feet shoulder width apart, left foot slightly forward for balance, making my body a more narrow target. Adrenaline pumped through me and fired my heart into overdrive. The door began to creak open as I tightened up on my revolver.

It was Vicky, Rocky's wife. *Plan B—plan B—plan B.* She smiled and opened the door.

I smiled back. I knew that Rocky wouldn't be planning a murder in front of her. What the hell was going on?

Rocky came stumbling from the back bedroom, more disheveled than usual, eyes glassy and unfocused. He was stoned out of his mind. He'd been up all night juicing and God knows what else. No wonder he'd been talking like he was pumped full of sodium pentothal. He walked toward me and gave me a big clumsy hug.

"We're gonna go get your patch. I talked with Mother last night and arranged it all," he said, referring to leadership in the Mongols' Mother Chapter. "Luna keeps all the colors, and he lives down in Commerce. We gotta go down there and pick it up. But we gotta go see Bobby Loco first, bro. He's handling your background check now . . ."

From an investigative standpoint, the most valuable aspect of prospecting was the vantage it gave me on Mongol drug-dealing activity. On July 4, 1998, I got my first order from Rocky to pick up an eight ball (one eighth of an ounce) of meth and deliver it to one of his clients. I ended up making several other drug transactions for Rocky that day. Shortly thereafter at an official Mongol meeting the question came up about using prospects to mule drugs for the gang. It was okayed by the club hierarchy and I was positioned to be the full-time drug hauler for the Mongols. That summer I did three more drug runs and one gun run for the club, before Domingo put a stop to it. He said he didn't like the idea that his only prospect was going to be the fall guy for the entire club in the event of a police bust, and he put the kibosh on my days as a drug mule. (From then on, the SFV Mongols tended to rely on their ol' ladies or other hang-arounds to carry out drug-muling duties.)

I remained the SFV Chapter's only prospect until Buster showed up. I have no idea where he came from; I just remember being glad that he was around to take some of the heat off of me. Buster was in his mid-twenties, a bit on the raggedy side with long black hair. No tattoos or tough-guy presence, but he did ride a Harley that needed a little TLC, which fit right in with the busted-up bikes owned by most of the Mongols in our chapter.

Domingo had brought Buster in and planned to sponsor him the way he was sponsoring me. The first big test for Buster would be Domingo's wedding and reception. The wedding was planned for a Saturday, and the prospects' duties would start early that day. There would be a shitload of Mongols there. Which meant a shitload of prospecting to do.

Domingo's wedding was held at the residence of a Mongols associate named Randall. He was a successful businessman but also a bit of a renegade. He had just enough sense to run a business but not enough to know better than to hang out with the Mongols. And the Mongols enjoyed the guy because he always had enough cocaine to share. He lived just outside Tujunga in a sprawling ranch-style home on top of a large hill. It had a separate party house with a full bar, a pool table, a dance area, and a swimming pool. The driveway up the hill was approximately a quarter mile long—a quarter mile that I would become intimately familiar with before the night was out.

By nine in the morning I was running around Tujunga picking up crap for the wedding, carrying tables and chairs and setting up beer stands. I was glad to see Buster, since it would be convenient having another prospect around to share the workload and the abuse.

When evening arrived I checked my Mongol ditty bag

to be sure I had anything and everything a Mongol might hound me for: matches, cigarettes, needle and thread, aspirin, breath mints and gum, rolling papers, condoms, a knife, a comb. I was as ready as I could be for whatever they might throw my way. I wondered if Buster had his shit together.

At approximately six, the first Mongols arrived, and before long Buster and I were running our asses off. Then the peace was shattered, along with my nerves, by the appearance of Red Dog. Now I had to start ducking and dodging. He tracked me down in short order and made sure I knew that he was going to make my night as hellish as he could.

Soon I was assigned to guard duty at the bottom of the hill. My orders from Domingo were: "No one except Mongols gets in without permission." He passed me a small snub-nosed .38, and I hustled down the hill. At the bottom, I found Rocky and Buster. Buster was also given a gun and instructed to use it if anyone, including the cops, tried to crash the party. I knew that I wasn't going to shoot anyone. By the expression on Buster's face, I didn't think he was going to shoot anyone either. He looked like he didn't know what to do with the gun. He finally stuck it in his waistband underneath his prospect patch.

It didn't take long for the Mongols to realize that their only two prospects were standing guard at the bottom of the hill, leaving fifty or sixty of them without slave service. I could hear the call from a quarter mile away: "Prospect!"

I told Buster to hang in, and I hustled back up the hill. Out of breath when I got there, I was directed to the main house, where all the Mongol bigwigs were hanging out. When I walked in, I saw the national officers with presidents from several chapters and a few regular-looking folks I had never seen before. A large silver platter holding lines of cocaine was being passed around. Red Dog had his face buried in it the moment I walked in. Domingo walked up to me and pointed out the two people who were obviously not Mongols.

"Billy, that's our attorney. And you know who the other guy is, right?" Domingo stood shaking his head at my ignorance. "The other guy is our private investigator."

My heart felt like it had burst. So this was the guy who'd been doing background checks on me for the past few months? Had they called me in to let me know that he had found out who I really was? Did I just walk into a fucking Mongol ambush?

Red Dog passed the coke platter and caught a glimpse of me out of the corner of his eye. I knew some snide-assed comment or command would follow, and I got ready. The next thing I heard from him was: "What the fuck you standing around for, Prospect? Go get us some beer!"

That suited me. I wanted to be as far away from Red Dog as I could get. I turned and left the house, making my way toward one of the stashes of beer. All I could hear was simultaneous barks of "Prospect!" "Prospect!" "Prospect!"

I ran my ass off for a couple more hours before I heard Domingo ordering: "Prospect, go down the hill and take guard duty for a while. Send Buster up."

High time. Down the hill I went, considerably more slowly this time. When I reached the bottom, I approached Buster. He looked like an army grunt, a baby-faced kid his first night out on the perimeter in Vietnam.

"Buster, bad news," I said. He stared sheepishly at me like he couldn't possibly handle any more bad news right now. "Relax, bud. They just want you up the hill."

Buster pulled his gun out and started to give it to me.

"Naw, dude," I said, "hang on to it. You might need it."
I was just fucking with him, but Buster nodded solemnly.
He tucked away the revolver and headed up the hill.

An hour later I saw Buster making his slow retreat back
down, looking like he'd been ridden hard and was ready
to crack. But it wasn't anywhere near quitting time. It
was time to take my butt back up the hill for another
round of abuse. The Mongols still had plenty of partying
to do.

I made my way back to the festivities, moving more
slowly each time I had to climb that hill. As I reached the
party, the first Mongol I walked past was Red Dog. Suddenly, I felt a thud from his fist hitting me in the chest. He
grabbed my shirt and pulled me close to him. "I better
see you working your ass off, Billy," he barked.

"You need something, Red Dog?" I asked.

"Yeah. Go get me another beer."

At around four o'clock Domingo told me to hurry
back down the hill. "Billy, go get your car! You're gonna
take me and my new bride home."

Although my legs were rubbery with fatigue, I made
another jog down the hill to my car. Buster looked more
nervous than a kitten in a pit-bull arena. But there was no
time for conversation with my prospect buddy. I blew by
him and jumped into my Mustang. It was a great feeling
not having to run back up that goddamn hill. Domingo
and his drunken ol' lady were waiting when I got there.
They piled into the car and away we went.

It was only a ten-minute drive back to Domingo's
house. I was already seeing visions of my bed when
Domingo turned and said something that hit me like ice
water. "Soon as the ol' lady goes to sleep, we're headed
back to the party."

I lay down on Domingo's couch and just waited for
him to kick me off so I could take him back to the party.
To my relief, I heard a noise that I never thought I'd enjoy

so much. Domingo was snoring his ass off. There'd be no more hill climbing for me that night.

A few days later, I got a frantic call from Buster. He wanted to meet me at The Place as soon as I could get there. After calling Ciccone, I jumped on my bike and headed for Tujunga. When I rolled up, Buster was pacing back and forth like a caged tiger.

"Billy, I can't do it."

"Do what?"

"I just can't do it, Billy. They're going to want me to shoot somebody, and I'm not going to be able to do it. I want out, Billy. Shit. I didn't know what I was getting into."

In his near-frantic state, Buster kept asking me what he should do.

"Look, dude, I don't know. You're gonna have to run it by Domingo. Just go tell him what you told me."

He stared at me for a long minute and then pleaded, "Go with me, Billy, please!"

"Okay."

Buster was scared as hell, and so was I. But he wanted out of the Mongols, and he was going to get out no matter what it cost him.

We got on our bikes and headed for Domingo's. I honestly didn't know how he would react to this news. I couldn't even begin to guess.

We arrived at Domingo's at around one P.M. I knocked on the door several times before I heard our chapter president yelling angrily, "Okay, I'm coming!" When he opened the door, it was obvious we had gotten him out of bed—not a good start. "What's up, guys?"

Buster didn't speak. I stared at him impatiently. Domingo stared at him impatiently. Finally, he found the courage he needed. "I can't do it, Domingo. I want out. I didn't know what I was getting into."

Again there was a long silence. Suddenly, Domingo grabbed my shirt, pulling me close to him and choking me. "Does that shit go for you, too, Billy?"

"No, man, I'm hangin'."

Now Domingo began to vent at Buster. "I brought you in, you fuckin' bastard! I sponsored you. I looked after you, and this is what I get?"

"I'm sorry, man . . . I'm s-s-sorry." Buster was stammering and spitting now. He asked Domingo what he could do to make things right. Domingo shook him off, saying it wasn't going to be that easy, that he'd decide at Church that evening. Then he told us to get the hell out of his house.

When we got back to The Place, we drank a few beers and Buster kept staring at me like a frightened deer, asking me over and over what I thought he should do. I told him that maybe he should pack his bags and leave town tonight. He said he couldn't do that. His whole family lived in the area, and he was afraid the Mongols would go after them. It was a valid concern. I told him that the only thing he could do was face the music. He had about three and a half hours before Church to think about the direction his life was going to take. Three and a half torturous hours.

Church was held at Bucket Head's place in Sunland. I rolled in a few minutes before five, and Buster pulled up in his car shortly thereafter. I stayed outside like a good prospect, talking with Buster, trying to keep him calm.

I told Buster that if the Mongols wanted me to beat him up, I would hit him once and he should go down. He should cover his head and face, and I would kick him in the stomach rather than breaking his nose, loosening his teeth, or giving him a concussion. Buster began to thank me. Somehow orchestrating his beating made us both feel a little better.

At last, Domingo yelled from inside the house for me.

"Prospect Billy!" I looked at Buster, then walked inside. Domingo, Rancid, Bucket Head, and Rocky were all sitting around a table. In the center of the table lay a .38-caliber revolver. Domingo thanked me for hanging in with the Mongols, and so did Rocky. Then Domingo floored me with their decision. If Buster wanted out, he would have to play Russian roulette.

"There's one bullet in the gun," Domingo said. "He's gonna put that gun to his head, pull the trigger, and if he doesn't blow his brains out, then he's out of the club." Domingo told me to send Buster in.

As I turned to walk away, I knew I'd have to tell Buster to run. There wasn't a choice. I couldn't aid and abet in this poor kid's Mongol-ordered suicide. But before I could open my mouth to warn Buster, I saw Domingo following me out.

He pointed at Buster and said one word: "In!"

Buster ambled forward like a tethered cow to the slaughterhouse. Domingo held the door and Buster passed through; I watched the door slam shut behind him. I stood with my back to the wall and heard myself praying for Buster. "Oh God—oh Jesus—oh God . . ." I began pacing, waiting to hear a gunshot from inside.

Suddenly, Buster emerged from inside the house. I wanted to hug him, take him back to The Place, drown him in beer. I smiled at Buster but he didn't look back. He stared straight ahead and walked past. He looked as though he'd just been sitting face-to-face with the Devil himself, gambling over his soul. Without a word he got in his car and drove away. I never saw Buster again.

8

It had been another Mongol all-nighter. I'd watched the sunrise with the SFV Chapter and had just fallen asleep in my UC apartment at around nine A.M. An hour later the phone jolted me half back to life. It was Ciccone. "I need you to come in, Bill. The SAC said he's going to shut down the fucking investigation. We've got a meeting right after lunch."

This news was more ominous to me than to Ciccone. Not because I had been risking my life for the last five months or because we had so much tied up in this investigation, but because I had been through this before with the Los Angeles Division. Ciccone, ever the good soldier, was ready to take on the SAC, the ASAC, or anyone else who threatened the well-being of the investigation. It was just another battle to John, but to me it signified serious trouble. I was aware that this might be not just another run-of-the-mill bureaucratic battle but our Waterloo.

Before getting involved in the Mongols case, I had worked undercover for Special Agent John Jacques in one of the most extensive and complex operations ATF had yet attempted. We'd purchased one fully automatic 30mm cannon from an arms smuggler and had an order in for four more. We desperately needed to jam this guy and his whole operation. He'd already sold one of the cannons to some antigovernment thug up in Washington State. Seeing such armaments in the hands of people willing to sell to the highest bidder was scary enough, but then the smuggler offered to sell me a fully armed Cobra helicopter gunship. This would have been one of the most significant seizures in ATF history. We submitted the plans along with a mountain of paperwork to the SAC and prepared to put the operation into play. But the SAC responded with an absolutely stunning order: *Shut the investigation down.*

I was speechless. I argued with the SAC. I told him that there was already a fully automatic 30mm cannon out there in the hands of some asshole who hated Uncle Sam and everything he stood for. There were smugglers bringing major military armaments into the country; we had U.S. Customs on board with us; as matter of fact, Customs was willing to furnish the money to buy the Cobra. The Los Angeles SAC's response to all our pleading was an unconditional no.

"End of story," he said. "Shut it down."

Against the advice of his RAC, senior Customs officials, and even his own intelligence personnel, the Los Angeles SAC did shut the undercover investigation down. All we could do was walk out of his office in shock and disbelief—letting a once-in-a-lifetime international arms-smuggling investigation wither into just another unremarkable gun buy.

It was a Friday, one P.M. Ciccone and I were in the downtown Los Angeles office, staring at a roomful of suits: Dick Curd, the Los Angeles special agent in charge; John Torres, the assistant special agent in charge; and Tom Brandon, the group resident agent in charge.

Both Curd and Torres had an agenda that was somewhat less than conducive to the success of our complex investigation. Dick Curd was nearing the end of his career with ATF and, from my perspective, wanted to cruise for the remainder of his term as SAC. His young assistant, John Torres, was an administrative climber. And not rocking the boat was the way up in the bureau. Torres knew that deep undercover operations presented potentially career-ending decisions. Operations like this involved laying out large quantities of money, obtaining electronic surveillance, sending vast amounts of paperwork up the chain of command. Our operation, due to its scope and importance, would be monitored in Washington, D.C., by the top officials in ATF and the Treasury Department. There was no way that Curd and Torres wanted any part of a monitored investigation like that.

As we sat down for the meeting, there were smiles and pleasantries all around, but I felt like I was in a used-car salesman's cubicle. Ciccone leaned over and whispered in my ear: "Don't say anything. Not a word."

Tom Brandon, who shared Ciccone's and my ambitions for the case, opened the meeting with a background synopsis of the Mongols investigation. As I watched his presentation, I realized just how remarkable it was that we had gotten as far as we had. We'd accomplished everything that we'd said we were going to accomplish. I'd actually gotten my bottom rocker and was an official prospect for the Mongols Motorcycle Club. Every aspect of the investigation was where it was projected to be at this point; I'd gathered evidence of the Mongols trafficking in methamphetamine and cocaine, witnessed them in possession of stolen motorcycles and assault rifles, and was confident that, given time, I could make some major drug and gun buys from them.

As if he had not heard one word of Brandon's presentation, the SAC said: "I've decided to shut the investigation down."

But Brandon, a former United States Marine, was no pushover. His face turned crimson. He began to argue vehemently with Curd and Torres. The SAC and ASAC were taken aback. If Curd was going to shut down the investigation, Brandon said, he wanted to see it all in writing. He wanted it clearly documented for everyone in the ATF chain of command, from Los Angeles to Washington, D.C. Curd wasn't going to be able to shut this one down for no reason without showing the entire bureau what he'd done and having to answer for it down the line.

There was a long pause. Ciccone and I glanced at each other, unsure how this outburst was going to play.

Then Curd quickly backpedaled. "Well, okay, I'll give it some more thought," he said. "But as of right now the investigation is shut down. Queen's not to go back under until I've made my final decision."

I remembered Ciccone's warning to keep my mouth shut; instead of blowing my cool, I leaned over to John's ear and whispered: "That's not gonna work. I'm prospecting. I gotta be there tonight or I'll be lookin' at a royal Mongol ass-whippin'. At the very least."

Ciccone told Curd that, in the prospect stage, I had to be present to serve the Mongols membership every night of the week. There were no exceptions. The SAC looked at Ciccone and said: "Well, he can just tell the Mongols he was out with some bimbo."

It was obvious that Curd had no clue what outlaw motorcycle gangs were all about, that he couldn't fathom the risk I was placed in or the magnitude of this investigation.

Ciccone and Brandon attempted to explain the gravity of my situation to Curd and Torres. All the while, I sat biting my tongue. At the minimum, Ciccone explained, I'd be physically beaten, quite possibly severely, if I didn't show up this weekend.

"If Queen doesn't have his backstops in place," the SAC said with a shrug, "then shame on him. This meeting is over."

Brandon, Ciccone, and I got up and left the office. Ciccone and I knew what we had to do. Following the SAC's direct order was not an option. *Fuck him*. I left downtown L.A. and went home to my undercover apartment, did a little mechanical work on my Harley, and got ready for another night out with the Mongols. We'd been put in the paradoxical position of disobeying a superior's direct order in order to do our jobs properly. Being a stand-up guy, Tom Brandon paged Dick Curd in an effort to make things right. The SAC didn't return the call. Ciccone and I didn't mention anything to Brandon about what we knew we had to do. We just did it.

To keep the operation alive, I knew I had to start showing some tangible results, get some irrefutable evidence on the Mongols, so that the stream of reports heading to Washington showed our level of progress. We knew that the club was engaged in a variety of violent crimes, but the hard evidence was always hard to come by. As luck would have it, not long after I'd earned my center patch, the Mongols made a run to Phoenix to christen the newly established Arizona Chapter.

The Mother Chapter in Commerce had issued an order that the Arizona run was mandatory for all California Mongols. It was going to be a tough run for the SFV Chapter. Even among bikers, these guys were a bunch of misfits. At the time, I had the only bike in the chapter that actually ran for more than twenty miles at a stretch.

Domingo had just sold his late-model Sportster to keep it from being repossessed by Harley-Davidson. That left him riding a bike taken by force from a member who'd recently been thrown out of the gang. Acquiring an ex-member's motorcycle is common practice in outlaw motorcycle gangs. A member kicked out in "bad standing" loses almost all his worldly possessions to the gang—

sometimes even his woman, who, in the outlaw universe, of course, is just another object in the inventory of his property.

Rocky would be riding his piece-of-shit Harley, which was both stolen and mechanically questionable. Rancid owned an older, rigid-frame Shovelhead, open primary, with ape-hanger handlebars tall enough to make him look like he was damn near standing up while he rode. Bucket Head would be on an equally ragged Panhead that he'd put together in his backyard a couple of hours before the trip. God knows, we were going to need a flatbed truck to pick up the bike remnants falling off our convoy along the way.

Although I was an official Mongol prospect, I was never trusted with any more details than I needed; I vaguely knew we were going to Arizona but wasn't told the specifics of the run. I'd have to be a good, obedient Mongol prospect and fall in at the back of the pack, keep up, hang on. Ciccone and the boys on backup duty would just have to shadow the run. I was to meet up with the SFV Chapter at a McDonald's off the San Bernardino Freeway at the Fairplex exit in Pomona, at seven P.M. As a prospect, you don't dare show up late. I was in the parking lot at twenty to seven. It was dark as I sat there wondering if the SFV Chapter was going to show up at all. It could well have been some prospect hoop they wanted me to jump through simply for their entertainment pleasure. I heard one pack of bikes after another pass by. I knew that they were Mongols from other chapters headed for Arizona. I was just about to call Ciccone to see if he had any word as to the fate of my distinguished SFV brethren when the pitiful bunch rolled into the parking lot, bikes roaring and belching smoke. No one shut down their engines for fear they wouldn't get them started again, plus we were already an hour and a half late. We headed out, and I assumed my assigned position at the rear of the pack.

To my surprise, we made it all the way to the Palm Springs exit without anyone breaking down. Then Rancid went to downshift, only to find that his shift lever had separated from the bike sometime in the last hundred miles. I was certain he'd been too high to remember to tighten it back on. Rancid limped his bike to a service station. No sooner had we parked our motorcycles at the gas station than someone yelled, "Prospect!"

I was ordered to find the nearest 7-Eleven and pick up some Budweiser. First things first under these trying circumstances. When I returned from my beer run, Rancid dropped down to one knee next to my bike. "Prospect," he said, "take the back shift lever off your bike."

Unlike his bike, mine had front and rear shift levers. This allowed me to shift gears using my toe or my heel. My companions had apparently decided that I only needed one. I knelt down and began taking apart my bike. I knew I'd never get the lever back. Everyone carried a sufficient quantity of tools, which was prudent considering the frequent disrepair of the bikes. Getting the lever off was an easy task, and in no time at all, Rancid's bike sported a new shift lever compliments of the ATF.

After downing our beer and gassing up, we left for Arizona. Although it was dark, I had no problem seeing, or smelling, the smoke from the bikes in front of me. Fifty miles flew by. Sixty miles, then seventy, then *boom!* Bucket Head's engine blew like a hand grenade. Off the highway and onto the shoulder we went. It couldn't have happened at a more convenient place—seventy miles from the middle of nowhere, right next to two miles of guardrail. We had only four or five feet to work in, and fifty thousand pounds of speeding eighteen-wheeled tractor trailers were constantly blowing by at eighty-five miles per hour. Bucket Head's rear piston—what was left of it anyway—was sticking completely out of the crankcase. The prognosis was grim, probably terminal.

But how to get the shell of a bike off the highway? We decided Bucket Head would take my bike and ride back to the nearest phone. He'd have his ol' lady come out from the Valley with his pickup truck. That should only take about two or three hours. As a prospect, I had no vote in the proposed plan. So Bucket Head took off on my bike, and the rest of the SFV Chapter settled in for a night of highway camping.

The temperature was dipping below fifty, but it was a beautiful desert night with a star-filled sky. As I lay under a guardrail, I enviously wondered what motel Ciccone and the backup boys were in right now. I had conjured up all kinds of scenarios for what might happen during this Arizona operation, but spending the night on the side of an interstate in the middle of the desert wasn't one of them.

Bucket Head didn't return until about six o'clock the next morning. Domingo was furious and didn't waste any time jumping into Bucket Head's shit. Bucket Head's tale of woe was that by the time he'd actually gotten hold of his ol' lady it was somewhere around two in the morning, so he'd decided to just spend a few hours lying around at the service station where he stopped to call. Domingo was pissed off and decided to leave Bucket Head behind. But someone was going to have to stay with him and help load his bike into the back of the pickup his ol' lady was bringing out. Guess who?

The plan was for Domingo, Rocky, and Rancid to ride to Arizona while I stayed with Bucket Head and helped load the bike. To my surprise, some two hours later, Bucket Head's ol' lady actually showed up. Bucket Head and I wrestled the bike into the back of the truck. I got ready to start up my bike so we could continue our trek, but Bucket Head decided he didn't like the way Domingo had gotten in his face, and he decided to take his ol' lady, his truck, and his dead Panhead motorcycle back to L.A. and pass on Arizona altogether. I would have to ride the rest of the way alone. Bucket Head gave me a map showing the way to the motel in Phoenix where the Mongols would be staying.

Phoenix? I'd never been told our exact destination in Arizona, but Ciccone was sure that we were going to Four Corners. Not only had I wasted a day and spent a night not fit for a desert coyote, but now I was on my own in the middle of nowhere with my ATF backup on their way to a completely different destination. Arizona was Hells Angels territory. A lone biker wearing a Mongol prospect patch here was going to be risky business.

I had to get to the nearest pay phone to let Ciccone know that the run was headed for Phoenix. I stopped at the first service station I came to. Ciccone actually answered his cell phone; it was obvious that my call had awakened him. He and the boys had made it to Flagstaff, Arizona, before they decided to find a motel and call it a night.

"Guess what, ol' buddy? The run's goin' to Phoenix, not Four Corners."

"Shit."

I gave Ciccone directions to the motel in Phoenix and a brief rundown of my night with the guys, and then I headed out.

As I reached the Phoenix city limit I caught up to Domingo and the boys. They were on the side of the road, loading Domingo's broken-down bike in the back of a trailer the Mongols had had to rent as soon as they hit Phoenix. Well, at least I was going to be riding into town with a pack of sorts.

It must have been about ten in the morning when what was left of the SFV Chapter rolled into the parking lot of the Quality Inn. I was dead tired, but there would be no sleep for me. I was immediately assigned guard duty in the hallway where the Mongols' national officers were sleeping. It reminded me of the times when I'd been ordered by ATF to back up the Secret Service, except that when pulling Secret Service duty, you knew you were going to be relieved like clockwork in an hour. Here I was just hoping to be relieved before I fell asleep in my motorcycle boots.

Somewhere around one o'clock that afternoon the national officers decided to get out of bed for something to eat. Finally, Domingo took pity on me and sent me to the room to get some sleep. When I got there, I found Rancid curled up fast asleep on the only bed. He was snoring at the same decibel level at which his hog idled. But I was too tired to see any humor in it. I took my appointed place on the floor and fell right asleep.

Rancid got up around four P.M., agitated that I was sleeping and not out prospecting as he felt I should be. I woke up to find him kicking me in the back and screaming: "Prospect, get your lazy ass up and go across the street and get us a pint of Jack Daniel's."

Like a punch-drunk fighter, I stumbled to my feet. I was feeling way too old for this shit. Fueled by crank, these guys thought nothing of partying for three days straight, catching two hours of sleep, doing more crank, and then running for another three days. It was standard operating procedure for a Mongol on meth. At least I didn't have to worry about taking a shower, changing clothes, or brushing my teeth.

By the time Ciccone and company got a fix on where the Mongols were staying in Phoenix, we had ridden to a Hells Angels watering hole to make a Mongol "statement." It didn't result in any violence, just some tense barroom staring between us and several Arizona-based Angels. But by two in the morning, when headed back to the Quality Inn, the Mongols fully expected retaliation for the incident and were on high alert. A well-armed Mongol contingent was assigned to stand guard all night outside the motel. Around three in the morning, Ciccone, Carr, and Koz drove up to the Quality Inn and saw a parking lot full of Mongol bikes. Although they noticed several black-clad figures in the parking lot and ordinarily would have steered clear, they needed to know if my bike was among them. The welfare of their brother agent outweighed the risk of a Mongol confrontation.

The three backup agents unsnapped their holsters and started to cruise through the parking lot. As they eased forward, scanning the rows of Harley-Davidsons, Ciccone spotted my bike. This was precisely the same time that the Mongols spotted them. The outlaws quickly closed in. Dirty Ernie was the first to step in front of Ciccone's headlights. He had one hand behind his back, no doubt gripping a gun. Two other Mongols blocked their retreat. Rancid approached one side of the car, and two other Mongols approached the opposite side. All three Mongols held their gun hand behind their back. Carr, Koz, and Ciccone readied themselves. They knew the Mongols had them cornered. Each side pretended to hide the fact that they'd gone to "ready-to-shoot" mode, nervous palms tight around the grips, and fingers on the triggers. It was a standoff. In Vietnam, the worst-case scenario for a small operational unit was to get 360'd. That's where Carr, Koz, and Ciccone found themselves. Dirty Ernie circled the car, stuck his head in through the window, and glared at the agents. "That you, Johnny?" he said.

The three ATF agents weren't fooled by Dirty Ernie's ruse—though his random choice of first names was ironic. The verbal jockeying went back and forth until both sides were satisfied that a shoot-out might not be the most prudent course of action. The Mongols let the three agents drive on.

Later on, we were all going to party in Scottsdale, at the residence of the president of the new Arizona Chapter. As I left the Quality Inn, I caught a glimpse of a sight for sore eyes—another prospect. Domingo pointed him out to me. "That's AK," he said (as in AK-47), "a new prospect from the East L.A. Chapter."

More than a hundred strong, we Mongols made our way through the streets of Phoenix until we came to a surprisingly upscale community. We parked our bikes in the driveway, in the yard, and up and down the street. Then everyone adjourned to the backyard for the festivities. I hadn't even gotten my kickstand down when I heard "Prospect!" As if just the word wasn't bad enough, I realized the call was coming from Red Dog. Then he got right in my face. "I better see you running your ass off all day, Prospect. You got that?"

What I wanted to say was, *You've got the right to remain silent, you piece of shit. You got that?* But I replied with the required deference. "Sure, what do you need, Red Dog?"

"You know what I fuckin' need, Prospect."

I fetched Red Dog a Budweiser and continued doing my prospect duties for another hour until Domingo told me to take a break and fix myself a plate. As I moved to a picnic table, I got my first glimpse of the stuff from which an ATF agent's dreams are made. A group of Mongols were sitting in a semicircle admiring an open lockbox and briefcase. Both were full of firearms, including a MAC-10 submachine gun. I'd been sitting there for only a minute, trying as inconspicuously as possible to eavesdrop, when I heard Red Dog yelling at me again.

"What the fuck you sittin' down for, Prospect? You better move your ass!"

I got back to my feet. Seeing those guns, the reason I was putting up with this abuse, fueled my resolve. How could I get word to Ciccone? Jamming a group of Mongols with a cache of high-powered guns, including a MAC-10 submachine gun, would be a home run for our side.

Red Dog walked up and punched me hard in the chest. "Go out front and see if the guys standing guard need anything."

In silence and a bit out of breath, I turned and walked away. I was, however, keeping score, confident that Red Dog would get his due in a court of law one day.

I ran hard for the rest of the day. But as I answered one Mongol call after another, in my mind I was already starting to list and describe the makes of those guns for my 3270 ROIs (Report of Incident), paperwork that would certainly counter any move by the SAC and ASAC to shut the investigation down.

Around six in the evening, the party began to break up. Mongols began to head out, ten or twenty to a pack. I wanted to be in the first group that left, but I soon found myself flat on my back, tools in hand, fixing Rocky's bike. His headlight was out, and it would be dark soon.

We caught a break when Domingo said that we would all be riding back with the Mother Chapter. Since the Mother Chapter had its shit infinitely more together than the SFV Chapter, this was welcome news.

We could see black thunderheads building on the horizon. The rain began to pelt down hard on us, beating a frenzied drumbeat on my helmet. But riding in the heavy rain, though dangerous, was a hell of a lot better than hanging around and taking a Mongol prospect beating from Red Dog. A dozen Mongols, including a guy named Mansion Mike, waited out the rain in Phoenix and left after dark.

Somewhere in the desert between Phoenix and the California line, a truck driver came up too fast behind a pack of Mongols, plowing his eighteen-wheeler straight into the pack of Harleys. Mansion Mike was pulling up the rear and didn't even see the truck coming. The eighteen-wheeler smashed into his bike, dragging him and his Harley down the highway. Sometime before the truck was able to stop Mike had lost one of his legs. The Mongols' follow truck—driven by AK and Cowboy and filled with the stash of illegal guns I'd observed at the campsite—stopped and pulled Mike from the wreck.

After the paramedics had stabilized Mike at the scene, Cowboy and AK threw his bloody clothes—which the paramedics had been forced to cut off his body—in the back of the truck and headed for the hospital along with ten or twelve other Mongols. Later, assured that Mike would live, AK and Cowboy took the truck with the guns and continued toward L.A. It was early in the morning when they reached West Covina, east of L.A. Cowboy pulled over to take a leak. They weren't parked for more than a minute when a West Covina patrol car pulled up. Two outlaw bikers driving a beat-up pickup truck warranted a closer look. The first thing the cops saw was a blood-soaked shirt in the back of the truck. The explanation about Mansion Mike's tragic accident didn't make any difference; the cops treated the truck like a crime scene.

It wasn't a good night for the Mongols. Mansion Mike lost his leg, and the cops nabbed AK and Cowboy along with that lockbox full of high-powered guns, including the MAC-10.

Unfortunately, the DA's office had a big problem with the search. The Mongols retained some pretty sharp defense attorneys for Cowboy and AK, and they managed to get the seizure thrown out of court as an illegal search. Behind the scenes, Ciccone went to talk to the DA as well as the West Covina Police Department and, without divulging my role as a deep-cover agent, told them that ATF had a strong interest in making this case stick. The DA dropped the state charges against Cowboy and AK so that we had a green light to charge them in a federal prosecution.

The problem, from our point of view, was that we couldn't make the local cops' gun seizure any more admissible in a federal court—not without me getting some incriminating statements on tape.

It took me a few months to find the appropriate way to approach Cowboy and AK. I didn't see them on a regular basis in the San Fernando Valley, and there was no plausible way to seek them out and try to get them to make blatant criminal admissions while I was wearing a wire. This is part of the improvisational nature of undercover work; you can strategize all you want with your case agent, but sometimes you just have to have a gut feeling for when the time is right to make a move. In this case, I waited a few months until the greater Mongol Nation was making a run to Palm Springs.

By this point, I had become comfortable enough in the gang to carry a concealed recording device if I thought I'd have a chance to gather pertinent information. I was still extremely anxious about carrying a wire, but at least I had access to the best digital technology the federal government had to offer in the late 1990s. When I began my career, undercover agents used to have to tape clunky old Nagra recorders and microphones to their groins and their shaved chests. I could never have risked doing that with the Mongols, as we were often together for days at a time, camping out and sleeping in tight quarters.

With the Mongols, I would carry a tiny, sophisticated NT microcassette recording device that I could easily hide in my coat pocket or inside my motorcycle boot. The NT made a crystal-clear recording, but it had a somewhat complicated activation procedure. Another device I used was a standard Motorola pager that had been fitted with a digital recorder, which I could wear in plain view. It functioned as a working pager—the Mongols believed that I had to wear a beeper for my avionics job—and had a capability of recording up to six hours on a computer chip.

We were all relaxing at a big outdoor party in Palm Springs; the music was loud and the beer was flowing freely when I saw my opening. As nonchalantly as possible, I sat down with Cowboy and a few other Mongols.

We bullshitted for a while, and then I leaned over and asked Cowboy how in hell he had beaten that machine-gun rap in West Covina. Without any hesitation, Cowboy said the search was bad because the cops couldn't put the box of guns to anyone. He added that the cops were idiots, and if they would have searched him better, they would have found the key for the lockbox in the little front pocket of his Levi's. After they had transported him to the police jail, when the cops weren't looking, he'd pulled the key from his pants and swallowed it.

I was carrying my tiny hidden NT digital recorder during this Palm Springs party, and Cowboy's incriminating conversation was on tape. In spite of the blaring rock music, the conversation was clear and irrefutable. It was just what the U.S. Attorney's Office was hoping for. Coupled with my eyewitness testimony, we were confident of sending Cowboy and AK away to federal prison on illegal-firearms charges.

It also helped Ciccone and me placate the brass in ATF. Getting proof of this kind of gun violation satisfied the bosses that when we eventually broke through to daylight—if I could make it to daylight—we'd be bringing down a massive racketeering case against one of the most dangerous outlaw motorcycle gangs in the country.

Even among outlaw clubs, the Mongols were known as a gun-crazy bunch. Before you could become a full patch, they wanted proof that you owned at least one firearm and that you knew how to use it. Part of the application process stipulated that you had qualified with firearms under the supervision of the national sergeant at arms.

Domingo had called me and told me to pick him up that afternoon and bring my handgun with me. Ciccone and I assumed they were going to take me to a legitimate firing range somewhere north of L.A.

My undercover car was a dull red, oxidized, four-speed Mustang convertible. It was fast as hell, had a half dozen bullet holes in the hood and doors from a previous ATF investigation—the chassis perforated by semiautomatic gunfire in the gang heartland of South Central L.A. Like war wounds, these pockmarks lent real credibility to my supposed badass background. The Mustang was also wired for audio, with a secret little switch I could activate under my seat. I would end up with some very incriminating conversations taped in the car before the end of this case.

It was before eleven A.M. when I eased my Mustang off the Ventura Freeway and made my way to Ciccone's house. The more I talked to myself about what the day might bring, the more nervous I became. I was trying hard to shake the fear and reluctance I felt about wearing a wire.

It was a tough call, balancing the risk of carrying a recorder against the unmistakable value of the hard evidence it could provide. Especially today, knowing that I'd be with a group of Mongols who were all convicted felons and who would all be in possession of firearms. Of course, Ciccone and the U.S. Attorney's Office wanted me to get the evidence on tape.

I sat in front of Ciccone's house in a daze.

"Billy Boy, talk to me," he said.

"Hey, bud, I need to gas up. I'll meet you at the gas station down the street."

In the short distance between Ciccone's place and the gas station, something hit me in the pit of my stomach. I don't know if it was cop intuition, plain fear, or a real guardian angel, but it came to me nonetheless—and without ambiguity: *Don't carry a fucking tape recorder today, Billy.*

I knew Ciccone and the U.S. Attorney's Office would be disappointed. Hell, I wanted to get the whole day's activities on tape myself. But I wanted to stay alive more. At the gas station I got out of the car, bent down, and removed the tiny recording device from my boot. Ciccone screeched to a stop in his Pontiac.

"I don't have a good feeling about the recorder, dude. I'm not gonna carry it."

I braced myself for the company line, but to my relief Ciccone looked at me and nodded. "Go with your gut," he said. "Tell you the truth, I don't have a good feeling about it either."

The plan was to pick up Domingo at his house and then he and I would ride up to Visalia in my car. We'd meet Red Dog and the rest of the boys when we got up there. I tossed the tape recorder to Ciccone like it was a live hand grenade and sped off to Domingo's place.

Ciccone followed close behind me. I watched my speedometer passing 85, 90, then 100 miles per hour. I switched lanes repeatedly, but Johnny was keeping right up. Ciccone and I had a thing about following each other on freeways. It wasn't exactly how you'd expect two on-duty feds to drive. It was more like a NASCAR race than an official ATF trip to an undercover operation. Again, I had to say a silent prayer for all the hapless civilians caught in the crossfire of our driving. But it was worth the potential risk of the speeding tickets. Running at 110 miles per hour with Ciccone on my tail always helped to take my mind off things.

As I pulled into Domingo's driveway, I looked in my rearview mirror to see if Ciccone would pass by, but he didn't. I smiled to myself. He was finally learning how to play the surveillance game.

I was feeling better about the day now. I didn't have the added mental baggage of the wire in my boot, and I followed the driveway into the backyard, which was protocol for Mongol doings at Domingo's place. Domingo came out of his house, happy to see me. "Yo, Billy, what's happenin', dude?"

"I'm ready, Pres. Let's do it."

Then my good feeling took a quick and decisive dump. Out of nowhere, Domingo said: "Raise the hood on your car, Billy."

As a Mongol prospect, I was well indoctrinated not to ask questions. A chill came over me. The car was hardwired for a recorder. Was there anything under the hood that would give me away? I was taking a mental inventory of the Mustang. What possible reason could Domingo have for wanting to check under my hood? He had to be looking for evidence of police recording equipment. Did something happen last night? Did they find something in their background checks? Was this whole day going to be a ruse to ambush and kill a federal agent?

"Where's your gun, Billy?" Domingo asked.

I thought for a moment before replying. "Under the seat."

"Give it to me."

I stopped dead. For the first time that day, I thought back to that Onion Field case, in which both cops had complied with an order to surrender their handguns.

Should I give up my piece to Domingo? Should I at least ask why? Should I take the bullets out first? Why the hell would he want my gun?

I watched as Domingo, head under the hood, took the Mustang's air filter apart. With all the pride of a master criminal, he grinned up at me. "Great hiding place, huh?"

"Right."

I pulled my snub-nosed blue-steel .38-caliber revolver from under the car seat. I handed Domingo the gun, bullets and all. Domingo took the air filter out and replaced it with our two guns. I'd never seen this trick, and I stood there wondering how many hidden guns I had missed during my twenty-five years in law enforcement.

But then Domingo proceeded to throw the air filter into the trunk of the car, reinforcing my opinion that most criminals are inherently stupid. "Let's go, dude."

Domingo was no ball of fire, and being the only guy in the chapter besides me who didn't snort meth or coke, he lasted about five minutes on the road before he was sleeping like a newborn baby. He snored the entire 160-mile trip from The Rock to Visalia. I gave him a punch when we got there, and he directed me to a house just outside of town. I had no idea whose house it was, but I immediately recognized the characters sitting out front.

I could spot Red Dog's ugly mug a mile away. Lucifer was there along with an older, dark-skinned Mongol called C.J. I parked the car and got ready for the inevitable pile of shit Red Dog was going to shovel at me.

I walked up to him to extend the traditional Mongol greeting. Red Dog held out his hand. As a Mongol prospect, I acknowledged with the official verbal response: "Order."

Red Dog didn't say anything.

"Order," I repeated.

Red Dog again said nothing. At that point I dropped my hand. Only now did Red Dog respond. He landed a sucker punch dead center to my solar plexus. I heard the thud and felt the air leave my chest as I doubled over, making sure I didn't give the impression that it hurt as much as it really did. Red Dog turned and walked away, laughing. I caught my breath. I told myself, *Payback is a bitch, brother*.

I began to do the prospect slave chores—lighting smokes, fetching brews for the patches. I watched as lines of meth and coke were consumed along with an endless supply of beer.

When Red Dog figured everyone was drunk and high enough, he gave an abrupt order: "Let's go shoot."

He walked up to me, looked me in the eye, and said, "Follow me, Prospect."

Domingo and I got back in my Mustang and followed behind Red Dog, who was driving an old burgundy Chevy Monte Carlo. It was a trashy car and suited him well.

I knew from Ciccone that there were only two legal shooting ranges in the Visalia area. It would be a short ride to either one. One mile went by, then two, three, four, and five—until it was clear we weren't going to any licensed shooting range.

I began to look in my rearview mirror to see if I could spot my backup. To my relief I caught a split-second glimpse of Special Agent John Carr trailing our small convoy. We worked our way out of town, turning down one back road after another. Mile after mile of California countryside went by, my curiosity about where the hell we were going increasing with each one. Then we made an abrupt turn onto a dirt road.

It wasn't really a road at all, more like a path. I didn't know where it would lead, but I did know my backup wouldn't be able to follow. My heart pounded. I was on my own with a bunch of armed, stoned criminals, and it was starting to look bad.

The dirt path ran for maybe a quarter mile before opening up to an orange grove. At the far end of the grove was a small house next to an open field. The cars stopped, and all nine of us got out. I cut the motor on my car and was painfully cognizant of the fact that I might well be walking into my own death trap. What could I do? I got out along with everyone else. Domingo didn't say anything about getting our guns out from under the hood of the Mustang.

I watched the scene unfolding around me with an almost surreal detachment. Red Dog was higher than a Georgia pine, clutching a loaded 9mm handgun. Crazy Craig, C.J., Domingo, Diablo, Bobby Loco, and Lucifer were all slapping magazines into their Glocks and Berettas. With the guns all loaded, the Mongols walked toward me, circling me. Red Dog held his Glock loosely at his side. "All right, Billy," he demanded, "how long was your fuckin' academy?"

I was too stunned to open my mouth. Red Dog cocked his head to one side and moved even closer, hollering crazily. "I'm askin' you a fuckin' question, Billy!"

"Huh?"

"How long was your fuckin' academy, Billy?" He was yelling as if I was deaf, stupid, or both.

"What are you talkin' about, Red Dog?"

"You know what I'm talking about, Billy! Who the fuck did you tell you was comin' up here? Who the fuck did you tell you was gonna be with the Mongols today? Who, Billy?"

"I didn't tell nobody. Come on, Red, why you acting like this? I didn't tell nobody I was coming up to Visalia."

He locked his slate blue eyes on mine. "So you're saying if I put a bullet in the back of your fuckin' head right now, ain't *nobody* gonna know where to start looking for you? Is that right, Billy?"

"Yeah, I guess that's right, Red Dog."

He gestured across the dusty, desolate, trash-strewn field and said, "All right, Billy, go out there and set up some targets."

I looked off in the distance for Ciccone or Carr or any other backup, wondering if they would see or at least hear what I was sure was about to happen. If the shit went bad, I knew they would come in and get me. In Vietnam, we had a pact: We all come out or none of us come out. I felt the same loyalty from my ATF brothers Carr, Koz, and Ciccone. Law enforcement, in many ways, was really just a civilian variation of the military, replete with honor and integrity and selfless sacrifices. If my sacrifice turned out to be my life, I knew my brother agents would come in and shoot it out with my killers. Small consolation.

I glanced back toward the Mongols and saw them talking in a tight circle instead of pointing their guns and training their sights on me. Doing my best to collect myself, I set up a couple of beer cans, an empty milk jug, and some other trash left in the field by some previous gun-wielding outlaws.

"That's enough, Billy, come on back!" Red Dog yelled.

I wished he'd just tell me to keep walking down the dirt road.

As I walked back toward them, I could hear the group laughing. I wasn't able to share in their levity. I knew that I was in for a long night.

Before I reached the group, Red Dog raised his gun and capped off a round. I saw the flash and heard the deafening blast. I actually felt the wind from the bullet as it whizzed by me. Everybody laughed. Everybody but me. Then I heard someone give the order: "Fire at will!"

Eight drunk, cranked-up Mongols opened up for all they were worth, emptying one clip after another.

The hit ratio in Vietnam was not all that admirable, but here, among the Mongols, it was downright pitiful. Maybe it was the alcohol and the meth, I don't know, but the end result was that I certainly didn't have to run out into the field to reset the targets.

It was starting to get dark when Red Dog again turned his attention to me.

He passed me his Glock, fully loaded. "Here, Billy, let's see what you can do."

Behind me, I heard Mongols murmuring. One of them said, "If he hits all the fuckin' targets, he's a cop." Another Mongol said, "If he misses all the fuckin' targets, he's a cop."

With my Vietnam training and decades in law enforcement, I was an excellent shot. I'd put in hundreds of hours at the firing range and knew I could accurately hit all the targets in short order. I assumed an old-time military stance and cranked off a few rounds, hitting a few beer cans and intentionally missing a few others.

After I'd emptied a magazine, I heard Lucifer say: "See, I told you he was a fuckin' cop."

I couldn't help but laugh at him. "Yeah, why, Lucifer? Just because you guys can't hit shit?"

Red Dog reclaimed his gun, reloaded it, and turned back toward the field. He raised the Glock, and I saw that his hand was riding too high on the grip. He fired and the slide recoiled, slicing open his hand between his thumb and index finger. "Fuck!"

He'd get no sympathy from me. Shouting and bleeding profusely, he dropped the gun. The shooting party was over. At least that's what I thought.

I was finally starting to relax. Maybe today wasn't my day to die after all. I told myself that since Red Dog was hurt—probably needed a few stitches in his hand—and it was getting dark, we'd be out of there in no time.

Then reality bit me on the ass. Red Dog strutted up to me, wiping the blood from one hand with the other. He dropped down on one knee and began to wipe his bloody hands on my pants. I wasn't sure if this was some Mongol ritual. Then, to my shock, Red Dog grabbed one of the legs of my dirty jeans and jerked it up violently. With a small flashlight in hand, he began looking down into my boot, searching for a hidden recording device. I froze.

Then he did the same with the other pant leg and boot. I alternated between mild panic and astonishment at Red Dog's actions. Finally, momentarily placated, Red Dog stood up, and in a voice loud enough for everyone to hear he announced: "I'll find out if you're a cop." He turned and walked away.

Day turned to night. We were still gathered behind the dilapidated house. From behind me I could hear Mongol Eddie blurting out: "Shit, you ain't seen nothin' yet."

He ran off to the house and emerged with a street-sweeper. He was grinning, like a kid showing off his latest toy. We were all standing in a semicircle, and suddenly, like a maniac, Eddie fired off twelve rounds of 12-gauge buckshot into the ground, dead center in the circle of Mongols, inches from our feet. With an instinctive reaction, I covered my eyes and turned my head to keep from getting hit by flying debris.

What a fuckin' idiot! I looked around to see if anyone had been hit. Somehow, despite Eddie's insane stunt, everybody came through unscathed.

"Yo dude, lemme see that thing!" Bobby Loco shouted.

Mongols passed the massive gun back and forth like a good joint. For the moment, at least, they weren't paying any attention to me.

But soon the novelty of the street-sweeper wore off.

Out of the blue, Red Dog got up in my face with a new

line of questioning. "Yo, Billy, where'd ya go to high school?"

"In North Carolina. Why?"

"'Cause I wanna see your fuckin' yearbook."

"Jesus, Red, that was twenty-some years ago. I haven't seen my yearbook in I don't know how long."

"You better see it pretty fuckin' soon."

And now, with darkness fully descended on the orange grove, Red Dog decided it was time to sic one of the most dangerous Mongols on me.

C.J. was a deep brown Indian, so dark-skinned that his many tattoos were barely visible on his arms. Within the biker underworld, C.J. could function and gain a measure of acceptance, though he was clearly mentally challenged. I'd seen it before: When drinking hard and snorting meth, he would do whatever Red Dog told him to do, like some psychopathic robot. As Red Dog interrogated me about my school years, C.J. suddenly approached, put his arm on my shoulder, partly for effect, partly for balance, then slurred his sour beer breath into my face. "Billy, I love you, brother," he said, "but if you turn out to be a cop, I'll fuckin' kill you."

Everyone laughed loudly, and like a sponge, C.J. soaked up his newfound attention. He was now clutching his knife in one hand, and he grabbed my neck in a hammerlock and glared at me with his coal black eyes. "If you hurt any of my brothers, Billy, I'll track you down. I'll put a piece of piano wire around your neck, and I'll cut your fuckin' head off. I don't care where you go. If you are a cop, I'm gonna find you—"

"Come on, C.J., lighten up. I'm not a cop."

Not many things stuck with C.J., but the cop business did. The spotlight seemed to energize him. He was right in my face. "I don't care where you go, Billy, I'll track you down and I'll fuckin' kill you."

Red Dog chimed in. "Shit, Billy," he said, "if I tell him to, C.J. will kill you right *now*."

I felt C.J.'s grip tighten and tense up. His hand went to his knife again. I could sense him readying himself for the order to kill.

I knew I had to make a move quickly or this moron was going to act on his own and cut my throat. He was a dim-wit, blind drunk, and just itching for some knife play.

"Jesus, Red, tell him not to kill me now." I tried to say it calmly, almost flippantly. Red Dog knew what everyone else knew—C.J. was indeed about to act.

"C.J., don't kill him right now," Red Dog said.

I watched C.J. relax, take his hand off his knife.

C.J. would stay on me the rest of the night. He made sure I had a visual image of all the different ways that he was going to track me down and kill me. Hour after hour passed with him following me around, putting his arm around my shoulder, telling me how much he loved me but how much he'd love to kill me if I turned out to be a cop.

We still had a three-hour trip back to L.A., and luckily, Domingo was ready to leave. As we got in my Mustang, Red Dog made his final demands. "Here's the deal," he said. "I want to see your high school yearbook before you can patch in."

Like I gave two shits about trying to patch in now! I'd nearly been executed by these gun-crazed maniacs, and had spent the last several hours listening to a deranged criminal psychopath telling me in excruciating detail all the different ways he was going to hunt me down and kill me. *Fuck patching in, and fuck this investigation.*

I don't even remember saying good-bye to anyone. I only remember getting in the car to leave with Domingo, and the terrible feeling of being alone.

9

I vowed that I wouldn't be spending another night with Red Dog. I was so fed up with my prospect life, running around all over the place for the Mongols, following the commands of a group of criminals whose collective IQ didn't add up to the median temperature, and being in constant fear for my life, that I was ready to phone Ciccone first thing in the morning and tell him the investigation was over. The ATF brass had wanted to shut the case down anyway. Why not let them?

The call was solely mine to make; no case agent can talk an undercover into continuing an investigation if he feels it's become too dangerous.

But after my head cleared and my fury at Red Dog's abuse had subsided, I felt I had a better handle on the night's events. It was probably just another of Red Dog's mind games, another sadistic attempt to fuck with my sanity; if he'd truly known something, or had some solid reason to believe I was a cop, he would have had C.J. kill me right there with no witnesses besides those Mongols.

The week following Visalia, I was staring at myself in the full-length living room mirror. *Hang in there, Billy. You can't be too far from becoming a full patch.*

But hang in there for what? So Red Dog could finally dig up some dirt on me? So the Mongols could leave me in a deserted ditch somewhere with a bullet in my head? My ATF bosses had made it abundantly clear that they didn't give a shit about either Billy St. John or Bill Queen. I could so easily go back to my desk job in the Van Nuys office, making routine one-man, one-gun cases until my retirement day.

But I prided myself on being more than a typical agent. I prided myself on following in the footsteps of ATF men who put their lives on the line doing undercover work, men like Steve Martin, Darrin Kozlowski, Darrell Edwards, and Blake Boteler. The list was long and distinguished, and it kept rolling through my head, along with images of John Ciccone having to eat a teaspoon of administrative shit every day in the L.A. office and then hanging out on the streets watching my back until all hours of the morning. Images of my brother coming back from Vietnam on a stretcher. Images of some fifty-eight thousand soldiers who didn't come back at all. I saw my work as part of a tradition of service to this country, and as I fastened my black bandana around my neck, that sense of tradition began to overwhelm the thought of Red Dog or C.J. shooting me. Yes, I'd hang in there, and I'd beat Red Dog and the rest of the Mongols.

As I sat in the passenger seat of Ciccone's Pontiac after Visalia, John came at me straight out: "You think you can go forward, Billy? You think you can go back in there?"

"Yeah, I do. If I can steer clear of Red Dog, I think I can patch in. We've put too much time into the case, and I think I'm maybe a month or two away from that top rocker." By this point, I had been riding with the Mongols for about six months.

Ciccone and I were both surprised that we had gotten this far, given the gang's erratic behavior and propensity for hair-trigger violence. We had been able to skirt all the case-ending events that had arisen during the investigation, some thanks to correct decisions on our part, and some—like the target practice in the orange grove— thanks to pure luck.

*   *   *

On a hot Thursday night in August, Rocky, Domingo, and I planned to do the bar scene in the Valley. Rocky and Domingo were bringing their wives, and I was a fifth wheel, tagging along to do security for the chapter president. We weren't riding our bikes, and we weren't wearing any patches.

Domingo, despite his tough-guy persona, was quite the lively entertainer. He had a good baritone voice and enjoyed singing at several karaoke bars in the Valley. Many bar owners were justifiably nervous about Mongols being in their establishments, but I suppose some enjoyed the mystique of having outlaws as patrons.

Despite being chronically unemployed, Rocky's wife, Vicky, had managed to buy a new car on credit, and Rocky wanted to show it off.

I had called Ciccone and told him that it was going to be an uneventful night of karaoke singing. "Just me, Domingo, and Rocky with their ol' ladies hitting a few bars in the Valley. No bikes, no patches."

"So none of the other backup guys needed?"

"No backup. Tell the boys to take the night off."

Ciccone would be following me on solo surveillance duty in his Pontiac. The plan was for me to park my bike over at Domingo's, and we would all drive in Vicky's new car. I left the UC apartment at six P.M. I rolled into Domingo's place and parked my bike in the back. Domingo's wife, Terry, met me at the door, sporting a fresh black eye. "Come on in, Billy. Domingo's taking a shower. You want a beer?"

"You bet." As usual, I helped myself. They had nothing but beer in the fridge anyway.

I had never seen Domingo beat Terry before, and it was a bit of a surprise to see her with a black eye. Like a lot of biker women, Terry was an embodiment of the battered woman syndrome, and on some level, I suppose, she had confused that kind of negative attention from Domingo with genuine love. Maybe she'd never known any other kind in her life. It sickened me to see any woman get beaten up by a man, but I was in no position to moralize on the subject. I was living the life of an outlaw, and in their world, there were very few ol' ladies who I didn't see regularly sporting the signs of domestic abuse.

Domingo now bounded from the bathroom, a towel wrapped around him. Still dripping, he walked up to me and did the Mongol handshake. I hugged him tight, and the water from his chest soaked through my shirt.

It was the first time I had seen Domingo without all his biker gear on. Not only were his arms tatted up, but his legs sported a couple of barrio tattoos as well.

Rocky and Vicky arrived with their newly financed car. Domingo finished getting dressed and told Terry to hurry up, then we all headed out for our night on the town.

As he got in the car, Rocky pulled a revolver from his waist and tucked it under the front seat. I had never seen this gun before. It was a blue-steel revolver that looked— from the quick glimpse I caught—to be a .38-caliber. I made note of that detail for the ROI I'd be typing up in my UC apartment sometime before sunrise.

We hit a couple of karaoke bars in the Valley until ten P.M., when Domingo, bored with belting out Santana tunes, changed the plan.

"Let's head back over the hill and hit the Sundowner."

The Sundowner was a semiregular hangout for us. The parking lot was dark except for one small area lit up enough for a security camera to keep a keen eye on the motorcycles. Loud music was blaring from the back door. Several bikes were parked out back, including two adorned with black-and-white stickers.

For me, this meant that I'd be prospecting and fetching beers for at least two more full-patch Mongols. My relaxed mood faded as we walked through the back door. It was dark in the narrow hallway, and the bar was standing room only. I assessed the potential for trouble. A battle-scarred barroom brawler leaned against an ice machine to the left. He had a Budweiser in hand, and judging from his stare he was probably into his second or third six-pack of the evening. He was looking too hard in the direction of Domingo's wife.

He started to say something to her, but I couldn't hear it clearly over the blasting jukebox. Domingo picked up on the comment, though. Rocky pushed forward through the crowd. I stood shoulder-to-shoulder with my president.

The drunk had stopped staring at Terry. His angry glare was now fixed on Domingo. Domingo squared off in front of him. "What the fuck you lookin' at?" he shouted in the drunk's face.

"You!" the drunk spat back defiantly.

Domingo's fist landed dead center on the drunk's chin. His beer flew straight up from his hand and hit the ceiling as he fell backward onto the ice machine. The bouncer was standing close by and grabbed Domingo in a bear hug. "Easy, big boy!" he said.

With Domingo's arms pinned, the drunk made a remarkable recovery and drew back to unload on Domingo. Neither the bouncer nor Domingo saw the punch coming. But I knew what I had to do. Before the drunk could land his punch, I caught him with a hard right hand to the head and knocked him to the floor.

Before I could throw another fist, though, images from the United States Attorney's Office began to flash through my mind. This exact scenario had been run past me. Sitting in the offices of assistant United States attorneys Sally Meloch and Jerry Friedberg, two of the most respected prosecutors in the district, I had asked: "What do I do when confronted with a violent situation like a barroom fight?" Jerry's response was to stick his fingers in his ears and begin chanting, "La-la-la-la-la." I said, "Look, I don't have to let someone hurt me, do I?" "Of course not," Jerry answered. Meloch and Friedberg both knew that the Mongols would expect nothing less from me than they would from any other Mongol prospect. I had to use my best judgment, but as far as the U.S. Attorney's Office was concerned, I could vigorously defend myself or my fellow Mongols, as long as I didn't instigate any fights.

The drunk was now on his hands and knees. I grabbed him from behind and, wanting to put on a good display without really hurting him, I began a series of blows to the back of his head with only a semiclosed fist. In truth, it was hurting my hand more than it was his head.

But I had to look like I was beating this guy's ass, in order to save his life. I needed to get him out of the club before we saw any knives or Rocky's snub-nosed .38. As I punched his head, I began pulling him toward the back door.

But now Easy, one of the other Mongol patches in the Sundowner, came flying over to help out. Easy was a lunatic, ready to kill for the club at any moment. I'd only pulled the drunk a couple of steps toward the door when Easy caught him square in the face with his steel-toed boot. The kick was so high and vicious it looked like Easy was trying to kick a fifty-yard field goal.

Boom! The blood went splattering as the drunk's head recoiled toward me. I cringed at the sight. I knew I had to get him out of the bar before he was stomped to death right before my eyes.

Easy landed another steel toe to his face. I began to drag him faster toward the door. Another savage kick landed, and another. I pulled him into the narrow hallway where there was not enough room for Easy to kick him anymore. I landed a couple more show punches to the back of his head, yanking him harder toward the back door.

Finally, he was outside, but Easy was out in the parking lot with us and landed another devastating boot to the drunk's face. He collapsed on the ground. I let go of the back of his shirt.

Then, like a stunned deer on the highway, the drunk rolled over once, sprang to his feet, and sprinted out of the parking lot.

By this time more than half the Sundowner had emptied into the parking lot. The owner and the manager were attempting to calm everybody down and restore some order. Domingo and I joined the line walking back inside. We had made it to the hallway when round two began.

Another inebriated patron, even bigger than the last one, was walking our way. He caught Domingo with an intentional elbow, knocking him into the wall. My adrenaline was still pumping from the first fight, and I reacted on instinct, grabbing his shirt, forcing him against the wall. The guy's fist seemingly came from nowhere, catching me upside the head.

I reeled back. Although stunned, I didn't let go of his shirt, and I responded with a fast shot to his face. I saw his hand go to his back belt area, then a very shiny bowie knife coming up fast.

I let go of his shirt and sprang backward toward the other side of the hall. He swiped the knife across the front of my jacket, slicing it clean open across the front. I jumped back again as he lunged forward repeatedly, trying to stab me, until I was outside in the parking lot.

He kept coming at me. He wasn't trying to slash me now; he was trying to run me right through with that eight-inch blade. Suddenly, I saw Rocky out of the corner of my eye. I hoped that he'd been to the car to retrieve that .38-caliber revolver. "Shoot him! Shoot him, Rocky!"

Just like that, I knew that this investigation was over. I was in pure survival mode. Rocky would kill him. I could see myself on the witness stand, testifying that I'd begged my chapter's sergeant at arms to shoot this crazed, knife-wielding attacker.

He swiped the knife at me again, nearly splitting open my face. "Shoot him, Rocky! For fuck's sake, shoot him!"

But as it turned out, Rocky knew this drunk. I heard Rocky hollering his name. Before he could take another swipe at me, he looked at Rocky and lowered the knife. Everything stopped except the pounding in my heart. Rocky ran up to him, screaming, "What the fuck's the matter with you, you fuckin' idiot?"

Easy had made his way back out with another patched Mongol and moved toward the blade-wielding drunk. He was now holding the bowie knife down by his side. I stood there shaking with rage. The Mongols demanded the knife. I figured once they had the guy's knife, we'd square off in a fistfight and I'd clean his fucking clock. My heart was racing a mile a minute.

Not in this life—cop or no cop—had I ever let anyone attack me like this without serious retaliation. I shook with rage as I waited for the Mongols to get his knife.

Then he handed the knife over to Rocky. I moved forward to finish this guy off, but my path was blocked by Easy. "Hold on, Billy, we're gonna take care of this."

I bit my lip, waiting to see what was going to happen. To my disbelief, the Mongols let the drunk off the hook.

"What the fuck?" I said.

Domingo, Rocky, and Easy huddled for a minute, talking to the guy, then I watched my attacker walk away.

Domingo turned and explained the situation to me. "Don't worry about this shit, Billy. We got his knife. I told him that he would have to come up to The Place next Tuesday to get it back. When he shows up, you're gonna stab him with it."

My heart stopped pounding. "Hell, yeah. Be my pleasure."

He'd insulted the club. No one *ever* did that to a Mongol. No one ever attempted to hit a Mongol, stab a Mongol, or insult a Mongol without bringing down the most violent form of retribution.

Domingo knew that too many eyewitnesses had seen our faces in the Sundowner, and that if we killed the guy here, we'd all be getting locked up for it. But next week at The Place would be a different story.

I looked at the bowie knife in Domingo's hand, and pictured myself cutting the guy open in the dark alley behind The Place.

But sanity quickly returned. Although I really wanted to throw a few fists at the guy, there was no way I was going to stab him. I'd been a cop for twenty-five years, and it wasn't likely that ATF or the U.S. Attorney's Office would authorize me gutting a guy with his own eight-inch bowie knife no matter how much he deserved it.

We were all watching for the cops to show up at any moment. Domingo gave the order to split, and we loaded up in Rocky's car.

Now I had another problem: How was I going to get out of stabbing the guy? There needed to be some kind of answer to the question or this case was over. The next Church was held on Saturday at Bucket Head's place. Everything had gone back to normal since Thursday night's mêlée at the Sundowner. As I stood outside Bucket Head's house doing my prospect duty I heard a loud voice calling from inside. "Prospect Billy! Get in here!"

I hustled in to a group of Mongols sitting around a kitchen table.

"Listen, Prospect," Rocky said. "We got just one question for you."

"Yeah, Rock?"

"What the hell was with all those haymakers you were throwing the other night? Dude, you gotta stay tucked in. Make shorter punches when you're on top of a motherfucker like that."

I laughed. "Yeah, I'll try to do better the next time round." They all laughed along with me.

"Okay," Domingo said. "Get out of here."

I was halfway out the door when Domingo called me back in.

"Oh, by the way, that fuckhead that tried to stab you the other night, he found out that you were a Mongol and took off for fuckin' Florida. I guess you're not gonna get to stab him, Prospect."

"Shit."

"Yeah, too bad, huh?"

Back in February 1998, when Ciccone called me up to ask if I wanted a shot at riding UC with the Mongols, neither he nor I thought that I'd be able to actually patch into the gang. Rumors flew about the secretive initiation rites of various clubs. In some cases, a prospective member had to commit a serious felony. Often he had to commit murder for the club. The outlaws had long ago figured out the lines that a law-enforcement officer, no matter how deep undercover, could not legally cross. Initiations could be brutal, degrading, and downright filthy. You might be required to take hard drugs and participate in sexual acts with women. Back in the 1960s, prospects were beaten and covered in human feces before gaining that coveted top rocker.

The fact is, neither Ciccone nor I knew what I might have to do while riding with the Mongols. I had my own line in the sand, but I was worried I'd find myself in a situation when I'd unexpectedly have to leap across it. But I had now become the best prospect the Mongols M.C. had ever seen. I'd hauled drugs for them, stood guard for them, and now I'd shed my blood fighting for the club. What more could they want from me?

It was mid-October, somewhere around six in the evening, when I left my place and headed for The Rock. I had talked with Ciccone earlier, and he was planning to tail me in his Pontiac for what we assumed would be another routine night of prospecting.

We had gathered enough information and evidence by this time that criminal cases were starting to come together, and the U.S. Attorney's Office was thrilled with our progress. Besides that, on the personal level, Red Dog was on my list. If it was the last thing I ever did in my life, I was determined to see that Red Dog was going to prison. I'd taken more shit off him than from anyone else in my law-enforcement career, and he was going to pay for it. Red Dog's windburned face became a kind of beacon to me, driving me forward to get to the finish line. As I rode through Tujunga, I could see his image in my mind, his snarling, taunting face inches from my own.

"Billy, did your president tell you that you ain't ever gonna get your Mongol patch?" he'd said one afternoon when we were all down in Venice Beach.

"No, Red, nobody ever told me that."

"Well, you ain't! And you wanna know why, Billy?"

"Yeah, Red Dog. I wanna know why."

He smiled his nasty, yellow-toothed smile. "'Cause you ain't *Chicón*, Billy. This is a Chicano club. And, Billy, you ain't *Chicón*."

Everybody laughed at me. I stared at Red Dog.

"Check me if I'm wrong, Red, but you ain't *Chicón,* either."

Everybody laughed again. Except Red Dog.

Now as I rode, I thought about the orange grove and Red Dog holding his Glock. I rolled on until I found myself turning onto Foothill Boulevard. I always held my breath to see what bikes were sitting out front or who might be standing next to them. As The Place came into sight I could see three or four bikes.

I rolled up in front and backed my straight pipes to the curb.

"You need to be on your toes tonight, Billy," Domingo said when I walked inside. "The national president's going to be here."

With Little Dave, the top dog from the Mother Chapter, coming to The Place, I'd be running my ass off all night.

A couple more bikes rolled up out front. I glanced out to see who it was. Two Mongol patches backed to the curb. I saw Stinky, one of the regular biker chicks, and a couple of others like her milling about. I heard that familiar spine-tingling call—*"Prospect!"*—and turned to see Rancid offering me a hit off his JD bottle. I grabbed it and downed a gulp. Rancid looked at me with a strange expression. "I like you, Billy," he said.

Rancid hardly ever called me anything but Prospect. His using my first name made me a little uneasy. I was always studying these guys for the most subtle changes in their demeanor, any little tic that would indicate some change in their attitude toward me.

The national president, Little Dave, rolled up. Now the whole SFV Chapter was at The Place, along with a few Mongols from other chapters. It was truly going to be a long work night for Prospect Billy.

Evel walked up to me and said, "Take your colors off a minute, Billy. I wanna see the inside of them."

The request was a bit strange, but I knew better than to challenge a patch. I slipped my colors off, turned them inside out, then held them up for Evel to see. Before I could react, he snatched my colors from my hand, then started yelling at me like a maniac. "I got your colors, Prospect! What the fuck's up with that?"

I didn't know how to react.

Evel threw my colors back in my face. "You *never* let anyone take your colors, Prospect. Never!" He turned and walked out.

Domingo stormed across the bar to me. He looked pissed. "Billy, did Evel get your colors?"

I was taken aback. "Yeah . . . but he set me up, Domingo. He told me to take 'em off, then he snatched 'em from me."

Domingo stared, angry and thick-necked as a pit pull. "Billy, don't ever let anyone get your colors, you son of a bitch." He turned and walked out.

Everything was going straight to hell. Here I thought Evel liked me. There was no reason for him to make me look bad, especially in front of the national president. Rocky came in now and gave me the same treatment as Domingo. "Billy, did you let Evel get your colors?" he asked.

"Yeah, Rock, but I mean, he set me up."

Rocky looked very disappointed in me. "Look, man, Domingo wants to see you out back."

Out back? I didn't dare ask what was going on. Several other patrons had overheard and seen what had happened with me and Evel. Despite the happy clinking of beer bottles and the hard rock blasting from the jukebox, the atmosphere in the bar was now tense, as if something terrible was about to go down. I turned and walked out. Rocky walked close behind me as if he was escorting me.

All the Mongols had now assembled behind The Place. It was dark outside and everyone was quiet as I walked

John Ciccone and Bill Queen when they worked together on the ATF Special Response Team.

A few of the many undercover documents and credentials used by Bill Queen in his role as Billy St. John.

Billy in front of The Place at the beginning of the investigation. A Mongol finally told him to trim his beard.

A group gathering at the Simi Valley run. Here, Billy listened in horror as Mongols planned the ambush and murder of a Ventura County deputy.

Where there are Mongols, there are guns.

John-O's scalp and hair hung on a tree, underneath the San Fernando Valley Chapter flag.

Billy and Buster outside The Place. Buster was forced to play Russian roulette to get out of the club.

Red Dog, né Donald Jarvis, a Mongol who was a constant source of grief for Billy during the entire investigation.

A Mongol from the Mexico Chapter, Red Dog, an unknown Mongol, and Little Dave, the national president.

Rocky and Bucket Head (right) at Tony's Hofbrau.

Unknown woman with Rocky (center) and Rancid (right) at a funeral.

Bill Queen celebrating his achievement of full-patch status with John Ciccone (center) and Darrin Kozlowski (right, in his Vago regalia). *(Courtesy of C. M. Pratt)*

Full-patch Mongol Billy St. John, astride his stolen Harley Davidson motorcycle. *(Courtesy of John Ciccone)*

Billy and Easy, who told Billy, in detail, how he planned to kill his own sister and her children.

Billy in a sea of outlaw Mongols.

Billy, Domingo, and Evel in Florida at Daytona Bike Week.

Billy St. John (left) at Daytona Bike Week, where the Mongols were hosted by the Outlaws motorcycle gang. Like the Mongols, the Outlaws are also enemies of the Hells Angels.

One of many times Billy St. John was stopped by the police.

Panhead (right, standing with the Pico Chapter president) was convicted of a murder that was committed while Bill Queen was undercover with the gang.

Billy, near the end of the investigation. *(Courtesy of the Los Angeles County Sheriff's Department)*

up. Little Dave, the national president, looked at me and said sharply: "Get in the circle and face your president, Prospect."

What the hell had I stepped into? My supposed offense, letting Evel snatch my colors, didn't seem egregious enough for all this drama. I couldn't make sense of it. Still, I had my colors on now, and they damn sure weren't going to shoot me with my colors on.

Domingo leaned in and gave me another direct command. "Take your colors off, Prospect."

What kind of setup was this? Did I dare take my colors off again and have Domingo, or one of the other patches, snatch them from me? Slowly I took my colors off, but clenched them tightly in my hand. Domingo got right in my face now but didn't make a grab for my colors. "You never let anybody get your colors, Billy. Never. Why was Evel able to get your colors, Billy? Why?"

"He set me up, Domingo. He said he wanted to see the inside of them, so I took 'em off for him. He set me up—"

Evel had jumped up and was hollering in my face. "You better watch what you say, Prospect!"

"Come on, Evel," I said. "What's this all about?"

"This is all about you letting somebody snatch your colors," Domingo snarled.

I thought that maybe I had embarrassed Domingo in front of the national president. Maybe it was all about some perceived act of disrespect and they were getting ready to sentence me to an ass-whipping back here.

But then Domingo's face softened a bit. "Well, anyway, ain't nobody in the SFV Chapter ever got their full patch without fuckin' up along the way. I guess tonight was your fuckup, Billy. You wanna lose that center patch, Billy?"

Okay, losing my center patch was better than getting shot. But then I thought about prospecting for another month or two, running my ass ragged trying to keep a bunch of crank-and-beer-fueled Mongols happy and fully satisfied. "Hell no! I worked my fuckin' ass off for this."

"No, don't feel bad, Billy," Domingo said. "Everybody seems to lose their center before they get their top."

"No way, Domingo. Come on, I was set up."

"You wanna keep that center patch, Billy?"

"Shit, yeah, I wanna keep it."

Suddenly, Domingo reached under his colors as if drawing a gun. "If you wanna keep that center," he said, "then sew *this* on." He pulled out a Mongol top rocker and threw it to me.

A massive cheer swept through from the crowd of Mongols.

Beer cans were raised, shaken, sprayed open, and dumped on my head. I was screaming, along with the rest of the Mongols: "Yeah! Yeah! Yeah! Yeah!"

I grabbed the Mongol top rocker and waved it like a precious flag. A genuine sense of pride welled up inside of me. I was being pulled back and forth, hugged and backslapped, as the beer ran down me, drenching my hair and clothes, streaming in my eyes until I was blind. I wanted that patch for real—Jesus, I had *made* it! I wanted Ciccone there. I wanted Koz, Carr, Pratt, and Harden, all my ATF brethren, there to see that I'd made it: I was a fully patched-in member of the most violent outlaw motorcycle gang in America!

Shit, I was grinning and howling as I reached up to wipe the beer away, except that now the liquid I was half drowning in didn't feel like beer at all. It was thick as molasses and sticking in my hair and beard. Squinting through the foam and syrupy mess, I saw one Mongol holding a can over my head. There were baptizing me in a mix of Budweiser and fifty-weight motor oil. Everybody was laughing and whooping it up. Domingo handed me a full-patch T-shirt, black and white, with the fierce-looking Mongol logo.

"Here ya go, Billy. I've been saving this for you."

I wiped my eyes so I could see more clearly. I'd actually made it. I'd done what I never thought we would really be able to do.

I was a Mongol. I was an ATF agent. Well, what the hell was I?

We all walked back to the front of The Place. Carrena met me, giving me a hug and congratulations. She handed me a towel, laughing at me as I went to work trying to wipe my face. "It's gonna take a while to clean you up," she said.

I reached into my jeans and pulled out a wad of cash, bought rounds for the whole house, high-fiving, back-slapping, doing the Mongol handshake everywhere I walked. Stinky was putting on a show just for me, pulling up her dress every few minutes to show off the fact that she wasn't wearing a bra or panties.

I let out a wild cheer. I wasn't a lowly hang-around or prospect anymore. I was a full-patch Mongol! A 1 per-center! An outlaw biker! No one could touch me now. I put on my full-patch T-shirt and walked outside, hoping Ciccone would see me in it through his binoculars from his parked Pontiac. I knew he'd be beside himself with pride. No more prospecting. Tonight I'd fire up my hog and ride home a full-fledged outlaw.

At about two in the morning it was time to close the bar and go home. The national president happened to live south of L.A., not far from me, and he and I would be rolling out together. Stinky had started home a couple of minutes before Little Dave and I fired up our bikes. She had walked up the street to the point where she was right beside Ciccone's car when she heard Little Dave and me racing up the hill. Then she turned, bent down, and grabbed the bottom of her dress, pulling it up over her shoulders to expose her completely nude body to Little Dave, me, and the most appreciative backup ATF agent in the country.

Little Dave and I rode to the split in the 2 and 134 freeways, where I broke off and headed east. I was doing ninety miles per hour and feeling sky-high. Red Dog didn't matter now. Nothing else mattered. I'd fucking done it. I was a Mongol.

10

Becoming a full patch was like breaking out of a dark corridor into a field of sunlight. So many things were possible now. I would still have to answer to Domingo, my chapter president, and to all the national officers, but my peer status in the gang opened investigative directions and opportunities we'd never thought possible.

For months Rocky had been telling me about a machine gun that he had at his place. I really wanted to buy that gun from him. Since he was the chapter's sergeant at arms, Rocky had a lot of guns at his disposal, some his own, some the property of the chapter. I'd seen him with a variety of semiautomatics and revolvers, as well as a sawed-off shotgun, an assault rifle, and a machine gun. While I was a prospect and under such heavy scrutiny, I wouldn't have dared offer to buy those guns. Even a dim bulb like Rocky would have seen that as a red flag. But now that I was a patched member of the club, I felt I could pull it off.

Rocky had been out of work for a while, and most of the money he made selling drugs went to fueling his (and his wife, Vicky's) drug habit. He and I were riding in my wired Mustang when he brought up the subject of selling off a few of his guns.

I told Rocky that I wanted the sawed-off shotgun for myself and that I had a friend named Bob who would probably buy everything else. Bob was actually a confidential informant for ATF. As with a lot of CIs, there were times when I think he wasn't sure whose side he wanted to be on. But he had made a couple of other good cases for ATF, and I felt he could help me out.

We had the cash from ATF. I was going to meet Rocky, go by his dad's house, pick up the guns, and meet Bob and another CI named Sergio in the parking lot of Coco's restaurant.

At six that evening I rolled by Rocky's place. His kids were playing out front in the fenced yard, which also contained one of the biggest pit bulls I had ever seen. It had taken me months to make friends with that dog just to feel comfortable entering Rocky's yard. But I never did feel comfortable about seeing Little Rocky, who was only three years old, playing alone with the dog. As a father of two young boys, I found that scary as hell. I could picture the pit locking those powerful jaws onto the little kid's neck.

I walked past the dog, the kids, a busted-up motorcycle, and all the assorted junk. Vicky answered my knock, telling me to come in. Rocky was getting ready. I was carrying a digital wire that evening to get the deal on tape. The wire was concealed in my leather jacket, and I knew better than to take it off. I had carried a miniature tape recorder in my jacket to Rocky's place once before. I'd taken the jacket off, laid it on the couch, and gone into Rocky's bedroom for a few minutes. Sloppy mistake on my part. Vicky, dope fiend that she was, picked up my jacket and started rifling through my pockets, looking for money. I came out from the bedroom and caught her in the act. She just shrugged at me sheepishly. And it was blind luck that she didn't find my hidden recorder.

That damn sure wasn't going to happen again. My leather jacket might as well have been riveted to my back; I sat talking with Vicky while she flicked her lighter, sucking hard on her bong. Rocky walked out of the bedroom.

"Hey, brother," he said, grabbing me with the traditional Mongol handshake and hug. There was such genuine affection in Rocky's embrace, making this another one of those disorienting moments for me; there was no doubt in my mind that Rocky really loved Billy St. John.

Vicky was ignoring the kids, still sucking furiously on her bubbling bong as Rocky and I left the house. We climbed in my Mustang and headed for Rocky's dad's place, only a mile up the road. Rocky was telling me a story about Silent, a Mongol who was featured on *America's Most Wanted* for a vicious murder. I had seen Silent one time drinking in The Place; true to his name, he sat by himself and didn't utter a word the whole night.

This was the essence of my split-screen life. I was pretending to be interested in Rocky's stories about Silent, while all the time I was documenting every detail of our drive for what I knew would ultimately be Rocky's criminal prosecution for this deal.

Rocky's dad's place was a typical low-income Tujunga house. It was locked up and nobody was home.

The guns were hidden inside, Rocky said, but we had no way to get in. So much for our playbook; the whole deal was abruptly put on hold. We headed for The Place to have a beer. I knew that Ciccone would be setting up surveillance for our meeting with Bob and Sergio at Coco's. There was no way for me to get word to him or Bob. I was trying to play it cool, telling myself that the gun deal would still go down as planned. But I knew Rocky's patterns too well. I knew that he operated on impulsive opportunity. If he met some girl at The Place that he wanted to have sex with, the buy would be off.

But Rocky must have really needed the gun money. "Let's go," he barked after we'd finished one beer apiece. "My old man is supposed to be there."

On the drive, Rocky asked me if I thought my friend Bob would be interested in buying some dope.

"Sure, Rock. If the price is right, he'll be into it big-time."

Rocky asked to see my cell phone and then dialed up his meth connection. "Yo, Richie, I'm looking to buy a few OZs. You good for it?"

Ciccone had recently gotten me a RAT phone, an ordinary cellular phone fitted with a sensitive audio bug that could be used for remotely activated surveillance. When I punched a few buttons in the correct order, Ciccone could dial in and listen to conversations from his backup vehicle. The RAT phone isn't a recorder but rather a transmitter that works off cell towers; it's designed to provide an undercover agent with some peace of mind knowing that his backup can hear his "real time" conversations and therefore make a move if things sound like they're going south. But as with any cellular phone, it didn't always work well inside buildings or in bad weather, and whole conversations might be lost to static and dead air. (Eventually I simply stopped carrying it.) The risk of one of the guys "borrowing" it at a drunken Mongol free-for-all and later taking it to a tech expert to be examined outweighed any safety value it provided as a surveillance device.

When we got to Rocky's dad's house, he was sitting out back, rolling a joint. Rocky took a long drag but didn't pass it my way. By this time he knew that I wasn't much into the drug scene. I had transported and sold drugs for Rocky. And after that drug test during the Laughlin run, Rocky was convinced that I'd do a line or smoke a joint if and when I really wanted to. That was good enough for him.

I followed Rocky to the back bedroom, where he bent down and started pulling guns out from under the bed. First the shotgun, followed by a couple of rifles, then an AK-47, but no machine gun. I was disappointed. Rocky handed me the shotgun and a couple of other rifles, then slid the rest of the guns back under the bed. We carried the guns outside and put them in the trunk of my car. Rocky's connection, Richie, called on my cell phone and told Rocky we were good to go on four ounces of crank. Richie said that we should meet with him this evening around ten at the Wed, a bar in Pacoima.

We were late for the meet, but I'd reached Bob on his cell to tell him about the delay. No big deal—Bob operated on drug-dealer time anyway.

I told Rocky that I had to run home and pick up the money for the shotgun. I dropped him off at The Place. Broke as ever, he borrowed a few bucks from me for beer.

I hit Ciccone on his cell phone and told him to meet me just off Lowell Avenue. In a few minutes I was sitting in Ciccone's Pontiac, laying out the details of the gun-and-methamphetamine deal. It was turning into a pretty unusual operation, and we didn't want any unforeseen complications. I was carrying two recording devices just to be sure we got the whole thing on tape. I would be slipping Bob the cash to pay Rocky for the guns, but now I'd have to slip him a few thousand more for the drugs.

I sped back to The Place to pick up Rocky, then on to Coco's. As I pulled into the restaurant parking lot, I spotted Bob and Sergio in their car. In the darkness, it wouldn't be a problem to pull guns out of my trunk and transfer them to Bob's. I reached into the glove compartment and released the trunk. Bob said he was satisfied with the guns as long as they were all in good working order. Rocky guaranteed that they were. All on tape. Sergio had a decoy conversation going with Rocky about the AK-47, and while Rocky was distracted, I slipped the ATF money into Bob's hand. Mission accomplished. Now it was time to finish up the meth deal. We drove to a ratty hole-in-the-wall in Pacoima with an unlit gravel parking lot perfect for an outdoor drug deal. As I pulled in, I caught a glimpse of Ciccone's black Pontiac parked in the rear of a business across the street.

Rocky quickly found his connection at the bar. Richie was in his late thirties, not a biker but rough-looking, heavyset and muscular, with a ponytail that reached three quarters of the way down his back. He wasn't new to this game, and he eyed me with suspicion. Rocky assured Richie that he didn't have to worry about any of us—I was a full-patch Mongol, and Bob and Sergio were friends of mine. Richie nodded. He and Rocky then made a quick run to his house to get the crank. Alone at the bar with Bob and Sergio, I took out a few thousand ATF dollars and passed them to Bob.

"Listen," I said, "when the deal's done, meet me at the intersection near Lowell and the 210. If you get there before me, just wait. I'll drop Rocky off and meet you. We'll voucher the shit then."

When Rocky and Richie returned we all went out to Richie's pickup truck. Richie handed the four ounces of meth to Bob. Bob handed the thick wad of cash to Richie.

My adrenaline was pumping throughout the transaction. I'd been involved in hundreds of similar drug-and-gun deals, and no matter how carefully they're planned, there's always the possibility of a last-minute fuckup. Paranoia runs high among dealers, and a lot of good cops have been shot by some punk who freaks out at the last minute. But this deal went down without a hitch; everybody left the parking lot pleased. As I drove Rocky back to his place on Foothill Boulevard, I nodded to myself. Three guns and four ounces of meth in one smooth deal. ATF and the U.S. Attorney's Office would be beside themselves.

I dropped Rocky off and headed for the meet with Bob and Sergio. Turning off Foothill onto Tujunga Canyon Boulevard, I saw a couple of Los Angeles County Sheriff's deputies sitting in their car at the corner watching traffic.

From a cop's point of view, it was a no-brainer. Ratty-ass Mustang plus dirtbag operator equals one automatic field interrogation. The deputies lit me up before I had made it a quarter mile down Tujunga Canyon.

I didn't have an updated registration sticker for my UC car and could only hope they hadn't caught it. I slid my gun under the seat as their red lights began to glare in my rearview mirror. Clearly, I was in for a hassle, even though I wasn't speeding and I hadn't run any stoplights or signs. I eased over to the side of the road and shut the engine down. I knew the routine and kept my hands on the steering wheel as one of the deputies approached from each side of the car. I had rolled the window down to speak with the deputy when he approached. "Good evening," he said. "May I see your driver's license and registration?"

"Sure," I said, leaning over to open the glove box. I was assisted by the flashlight from the deputy standing on the other side of the car. His hand was gripping his gun. I removed the registration and handed it over with my driver's license. He looked at the license for a couple of seconds without speaking. Then he said, "Would you mind stepping out of the car, Mr. St. John?"

I did as the officer asked.

"Step back to the rear of the car for me."

Again I complied immediately.

Then came the usual questions. "How much you had to drink tonight? Where're you headed? Where're you comin' from? Got anything in the car you shouldn't have?"

Then one officer asked a question that turned the next couple of hours upside down. "Do you mind if we search your car?"

"No, you can't search my car."

I asked him why he stopped me in the first place. He

said that my registration had expired. *Shit*. He asked why I had a problem with him looking in the car. I told him that I just didn't want him looking through my personal things. I told him that he had no right to look in the car and that if he searched it without my permission, anything he found wouldn't be admissible in court anyway. The deputy glared at me and told me to have a seat on the curb. He said it wasn't going to be an illegal search; he was going to legally tow my car in and then do an inventory of it.

I sat down on the curb and started cursing to myself, thinking about Bob and Sergio out there somewhere with four ounces of government-purchased meth and three guns that needed to be vouchered *now* or the whole goddamn deal was going to be inadmissible in court. It was crucial that we preserved the chain of custody for that evidence.

Frustrated, I decided to take a chance. I pulled my RAT phone out of my pocket and dialed up Ciccone. He answered the phone and I had just enough time to blurt out a quick "John, I'm on Tujunga Canyon Road and I need you down here ASAP—" before one of the deputies pulled the phone from my hand and turned it off. I watched the other deputy going through my car. When he got to the driver's side, I saw him bend down as if he was looking under the seat. He'd have had to be blind not to see the handgun.

"Cuff him!"

The deputy's orders were clear.

"Put your hands behind your back."

He put the handcuffs on and locked them in place. Then he asked me about the phone call. "Who the hell were you calling? Who the hell is John?"

"Just a friend of mine."

"If somebody drives by here and cranks off a round at me, you know I'm gonna shoot *you* first and then shoot your friend John."

"That might look kind of bad, you shooting a prisoner in handcuffs."

He told me not to worry. He would take the cuffs off me first. I was hoping that no cars or trucks let off a loud backfire near the area to spook these guys. The deputies had called for backup, which was now arriving on the scene with lights flashing. They were driving a black-and-white four-by-four, and I was promptly tucked away in the back with my hands cuffed behind me. I saw the hook arrive, and they started towing away the Mustang, complete with its expensive ATF surveillance system, which a routine inventory would surely expose.

It looked like I was going to be spending the night in jail. I knew that Bob and Sergio had to be getting anxious waiting for me. If the cops jammed them, they'd have our evidence and we'd *all* be spending the night in jail. Where the hell was Ciccone?

Just before I was driven off to jail, Ciccone pulled up driving his personal BMW. He stopped in the road right beside us. He badged one of the deputies. Two other deputies joined in the conversation. The deputies asked for Ciccone's credentials again as he explained to them that I was a confidential informant for ATF and that I was on a very sensitive assignment. The deputies remained skeptical. As an ex-cop myself, I could see how they might think we were a couple of bad guys trying to run a scam. Ciccone did have what appeared to be legitimate ATF credentials (not a form of identification that patrolmen see often), but he wasn't driving a federal-government car; and I had been so uncooperative, was so unwashed and unkempt and in possession of a handgun, that they had to assume I was probably a wanted criminal and the only prudent course of action was to make the collar and run my fingerprints through the system.

Ciccone said that if they didn't believe his ATF credentials were legit, then they should call Paul,* an L.A. County Sheriff's deputy who would vouch for us. Paul was one of the few law-enforcement people outside ATF who knew about my undercover role. He and his partner, Cleetus,* were deputies who, though not undercover, worked the OMG scene as plainclothesmen, dressed in jeans and motorcycle jackets, riding Harleys. We sometimes crossed paths at various biker bars and parties. Ciccone had let Cleetus and Paul know about my undercover role several months before. In the beginning, I was dead set against it. I didn't trust them, just as I didn't trust anyone outside our tight-knit ATF core. But Cleetus and Paul both proved to be true-blue law-enforcement brothers, and an invaluable intelligence asset to the investigation.

The deputies reached Paul on the phone and asked if he knew about a guy named Billy St. John who was working with ATF. Paul told them that he knew me. They asked him what kind of car Billy St. John drove, and Paul replied that Billy drove a rusted-out red Mustang with a black top.

I could see that the deputies still had no idea what to think of the dirtbag biker they had in the backseat of their black-and-white. It didn't look like anyone was reaching for the handcuff key. They kept grilling Ciccone about the firearm they'd found in my Mustang. "Okay, did you know your informant was carrying a gun?"

It had turned into one of those interagency standoffs that are all too common in the murky world of undercover work. Partly, it's just the nature of the law-enforcement beast: No cop wants to be responsible for a fuckup he'll have to answer for down the line.

Our real quandary stemmed from one of the dirty little secrets of undercover life, a fact that no training program can prepare you for. When you're deep undercover, you

---

*Not their real names.

simply cannot trust your fellow law-enforcement officers. You never know who might blow your cover, and in
order to survive on the street you must live by the rule
that divulging your true identity to a cop—any cop—can
get you killed. Outlaw biker gangs, like the Mafia, have
often bribed cops and developed long-term informants
inside various local and federal law-enforcement agencies. In fact, in the course of our investigation, we discovered that the Mongols had turned a California Highway
Patrol dispatcher into an informant. He was working for
Domingo and the guys in my own San Fernando Valley
Chapter, hanging out at The Place and feeding the Mongols anything they wanted from the highway patrol's
computer system—information on vehicle registrations,
outstanding warrants, and confidential addresses.*

These sheriff's deputies weren't about to uncuff me and
turn me loose with an unlicensed handgun until they'd
checked with a superior officer. More sheriff's department cars pulled up, and out of one stepped a sergeant.
The deputies pulled me from their black-and-white and
took the cuffs off. They wouldn't give me back my gun,
so they handed it to Ciccone—at least he'd shown law-
enforcement credentials.

As they drove away, I reminded Ciccone that Bob and
Sergio were waiting for me with four ounces of meth and
three guns that needed to be vouchered immediately. I
put in a call to Bob and told him to meet us on a side
street just off Tujunga Canyon Boulevard.

A couple of minutes later we were parked next to each
other and Ciccone had vouchered the four ounces of
meth and the three illegal guns. What could have turned

---

*After an investigation, the California Highway Patrol dispatcher,
Bruce Paul Boysen, pled guilty to a felony count of unauthorized computer access. On August 10, 2000, he was sentenced to 180 days in jail
and placed on three years' probation.

into a long night in jail was now looking like one of the better undercover scores in the case.

I was still in my first few weeks as a full patch when Domingo approached me with an unexpected proposition. "Billy, you're gonna be the secretary-treasurer of the chapter."

Rocky had been acting as the chapter's secretary-treasurer, handling the books and dues, when I first started hanging around the club. He wasn't a good choice as anyone's bookkeeper; not only was he functionally illiterate, but he'd regularly allowed money to be taken from the till. Rocky had to answer to the national secretary-treasurer, Leno Luna, patched in with the Mother Chapter down in Commerce. Mother was getting upset with the SFV Chapter's late dues and other missed financial obligations. Domingo was taking constant flak from Mother because of Rocky's irresponsibility, and he wanted someone as secretary-treasurer who could actually handle the job.

I was the most logical candidate. I had a steady job—or so the gang thought—in the avionics industry. They knew I had a military background, which meant I was more disciplined than the typical gangster running on meth. Normally, you had to be in the gang for at least one year before you could become an officer. Domingo said that he would get an exception made from the national officers in Mother.

I had been a full patch for just over a month when the word came from Mother that the secretary-treasurer position was mine. It was unbelievable; not only was I a full patch, but now I was a club officer, which brought a level of prestige and privilege not afforded rank-and-file members. They trusted me with the chapter books—which, of course, would later turn out to be a crucial piece of evidence establishing that the club was an ongoing criminal enterprise.

As secretary-treasurer, I now had access to all the national officers and got a chance to look at Mother's records. I was responsible for taking notes at Church and any other official meetings. I handled all the club's money issues, and when the chapter came into property—usually by extortion or robbery—the secretary-treasurer was responsible for its disposition.

I met with Leno Luna down in Commerce once a week. Luna was a dark-skinned Mexican in his mid-forties who stood about five foot ten and weighed somewhere around 220. An original Mongol who was around during the first war with the Hells Angels, he was a fairly laid-back guy, and I enjoyed being around him. But I could never lose sight of the fact that he was a hard-core Mongol who rode with Red Dog and Diablo, two of the most violent members in the gang.

It didn't take me long to get the SFV Chapter back on good terms with Mother. I made Domingo happy. I made the bosses in ATF happy with the unprecedented access I was getting to the club's inner workings and its most important financial documents, even the gang's official constitution.

But the greatest evidentiary value of the club's books was that it put the gang's hierarchical structure on paper, from the rank-and-file patches to the national president. It wasn't just my word anymore; the books showed the Mongols Motorcycle Club was, as John Ciccone later wrote in his 167-page affidavit in support of our search warrants, a "highly organized criminal enterprise, with a defined, multi-level chain of command." The books showed that the club had between 150 and 200 members in Southern California and some twenty-one chapters across the country, each with a president, vice president, sergeant at arms, and secretary-treasurer, and that the chapters answered and paid a percentage of all income to the Mother Chapter, which was built on the same structure and represented the Mongol Nation as a whole.

This was the hard evidence we needed to prove that the club was a form of organized crime for a prosecution under the Racketeer Influenced and Corrupt Organizations Act.

I made a clear record of the collection of dues from the various chapters, money acquired through gun trafficking, drug dealing, and extortion. I made a record of all money paid out for legal funds and to bail bondsmen. I compiled a list of post office boxes and storage facilities that members of the gang had rented, which would be essential when it came time for us to start preparing search warrants.

Through the national books, I also learned about the war plans for the state of Colorado. There had recently been a showdown between the Mongols and the Sons of Silence Motorcycle Club in Denver. I saw that the Colorado Chapter hadn't been paying its dues recently, and I asked Luna why. He told me that the Colorado Chapter was allowed to keep its dues money in order to purchase firearms for the upcoming war. I also learned that the Mongols were looking to send reinforcements to Colorado to back the Mongols' play against the Sons of Silence.

The Mongols were always looking for ways to make money without anybody going to jail. During Church, I suggested numerous times that the club incorporate, copyright the Mongols name, and trademark the colors. Everyone knew that the Hells Angels were making a fortune legitimately, marketing their famous winged death's head and suing anyone who used the name and logo without permission. Leno Luna and Little Dave, the national president, shot me down whenever I suggested it. Their argument was that if the club did incorporate, we would be inviting government scrutiny.

"We'll have the fuckin' FBI and ATF on our asses," they always said. They wanted nothing to do with anything legitimate. I suggested that we make some aboveboard money selling T-shirts. We could print up a few thousand Mongols shirts, then go to every T-shirt outlet in the L.A. area and leave them there on a consignment basis, tell the shop owners that we'd be back in a week to pick up the money for the shirts. Again, this was too goody-goody for the Mongols. They always needed some other angle, usually one employing their well-developed extortion skill. They suggested that we simply walk in the shops and, just short of armed robbery, demand money for the T-shirts. If the store owner paid up, we'd leave with the money *and* the shirts. My marketing plans never went anywhere after that. Any kind of legitimate business, as far as the gang was concerned, was too much work. It was a lot less complicated to live as a gangster.

During Church one day, Domingo announced that Evel would be transferring from the West Side Chapter to the SFV Chapter. As the secretary-treasurer, I realized that this was good news for the SFV coffers; as an ATF special agent, I recognized it was even better news for our investigation. Evel wielded a lot of influence in the club, and he was a good earner. Unlike guys like Rocky and Rancid, who basically scratched together income from meth deals and extortion jobs, Evel was a professional motorcycle thief. He was one of the Mongols' key players in a massive, multimillion-dollar stolen-vehicle ring that had spread from California throughout the Southwest.

I'd first met Evel back when I was prospecting. He was in his late twenties, with long black hair that he wore in a braided ponytail, a clean-shaven, boyish face, and an array of tattoos on both arms. But he'd been in the club long enough that his colors were attached to a denim vest; only a few Mongols were permitted to sport denim instead of black leather, a kind of grandfather clause among the outlaws. Evel worked as a mechanic and rode the fastest street-legal Harley-Davidson I've ever seen.

We were hauling ass one night on the 210 north of L.A. I was running better than 130 miles per hour when to my astonishment Evel flew past me doing a good 20 miles per hour better. And he had Carrena hanging on the back! He later told me that he still had throttle left when he passed me but had started having visions of teeth, hair, and eyeballs spread all over the concrete.

The first time I saw Evel's bike-thieving skills in action we were in Pasadena, on a sunny afternoon, and the sidewalks were packed with eyewitnesses. There were some sixty Mongols partying that afternoon at a trendy restaurant and bar called Moose McGillycuddy's. There were also four preppy, good-time Harley riders in the restaurant, and they'd left their machines in the parking lot, at the mercy of the Mongol Nation.

I watched as Evel and a few other Mongols walked straight to the chromed-out Harleys in the lot. In a matter of seconds, wires were ripped out from under tanks, engines were roaring, and the four bikes were speeding out of Pasadena, closely followed by a carload of Mongols carrying guns. (John Ciccone, parked a hundred yards away on surveillance duty, managed to capture the whole bike-theft operation with his telephoto lens.)

The Bureau of Alcohol, Tobacco and Firearms had very little experience doing stolen-motorcycle investigations, and Ciccone initially wanted me to stick to guns, drugs, and violence. But assistant United States attorneys Sally Meloch and Jerry Friedberg expressed a strong interest in prosecuting the Mongols in the stolen-bike trade.

Through the Los Angeles Sheriff's Office (LASO), we quickly enlisted the help of Rick Angel from the Progressive Insurance Agency. Progressive Insurance had its own investigative arm, made up largely of retired police detectives, and they said they'd provide us with their intelligence on stolen bikes; more crucially, given the administrative hurdles that Ciccone and I were often running into in the corridors of ATF, Progressive agreed to provide us with the front money with which to purchase stolen motorcycles.

I jumped into the deep end of the business. I started buying stolen Harleys from Evel and his connections. All the while, I was learning how to tear Harleys down, learning which parts had to be destroyed and replaced so the cops would never know that a machine was stolen.

Evel called me to say his connection had a brand-new Softail Springer ready to be delivered whenever I wanted. Our plan with Progressive Insurance was to buy a bike and put it through the complete strip-down and changeover. The intelligence gained from the conversion of my stolen Springer would be a template with which to prosecute all the people involved in the stolen-bike business.

I wanted the bike delivered to my UC place in Diamond Bar. Ciccone and the other backup guys were scurrying around to get people in place who could ID and photograph the bad guys. The deal was set; the guys were supposed to deliver the bike to me at four o'clock that afternoon. I planned to be at my pad waiting with Ciccone and everybody in place. Four rolled around, then four-thirty, and before long it was getting dark outside and I still had no bike. I had given directions to my place, so there shouldn't have been any problem.

I put in a call to Evel. "Yo, brother, I've been waiting for your guys to show up now for going on two hours and ain't nobody showed up yet. What's going on?"

"The guys are still here in the shop," he said. "They're too stupid. They got lost trying to find your place."

"Yo, brother, just how stupid are they? Straight out the 10 to the 57, then take the second exit after they pass the 91?"

Evel said that he'd threaten to beat their asses if they didn't get the bike over to me pretty damn quick. I told Evel that I would meet them right at the off-ramp from the 57. I'd be in my Mustang. Everything was set again.

I was sitting at the Diamond Bar exit off the 57 freeway when a blue van pulled up followed by a guy riding a new Harley-Davidson Softail Springer. I had $2,500 in my pocket to pay for that beautiful $20,000 bike. We rolled into the parking lot of my complex, and I met the main player, a heavyset Hispanic male in his mid-twenties. Once upstairs in my UC pad, I talked with him about supplying more motorcycles. I'd need him to transport them to Las Vegas, I told him, to my stolen-motorcycle partner there. "No problem," he said. I told him I needed to cut Evel out of the business because I needed to make as much as I could and another middleman might just kill my cut. He said he was ready to do business directly with me. I pulled the $2,500 from my pocket and handed it over. He counted the money, then shook my hand. It was now completely dark outside. On the way outside to the van, I made a couple of incriminating statements in front of everyone in the van about what had just happened. I asked about the cops, and two guys spoke up from inside, saying not to worry. They were savvy enough to drive home using a different route just in case the cops had been tailing them.

Now I had the evidence—taped evidence, no less—that everyone in the van was acting in concert with the criminal act that had just gone down. I said adios to my new-found partners and waved as they pulled out into the darkness.

Ciccone was waiting nearby with a team of feds and L.A. County backup. They surveilled the van until it had driven more than ten miles from my place, far enough that a stop by a black-and-white wouldn't look too suspicious. They had the cops in the black-and-white do a standard field interrogation and identified all the participants in the van. While they were making the IDs, I was back at my place locking up my newly acquired Softail Springer, then hitting the computer to type up the details of the transaction in an ROI.

With IDs in hand, Ciccone returned to the scene of the crime. He took down the numbers of the motorcycle and confirmed that it had been recently stolen from an individual south of L.A. The first part of our plan—to show the courts just what was going on in the world of stolen motorcycles—had been accomplished.

Next we went into the "special construction" aspect of the investigation.* My plan was that the SFV guys would help me tear the bike down and get rid of the frame and cases. Buddy from South Pacific Motorcycle would order me a replacement frame and cases. The only thing I didn't account for was how unreliable the Mongols could be.

I rented a storage unit in La Verne, just north of Pomona and about halfway between my real home in Upland and my UC pad in Diamond Bar. We were going to break the bike down there, and I would get rid of the incriminating pieces. ATF would wire the storage unit so that we could get the operation on sound and video. But during the process of wiring the unit, the manager of the storage facility noticed the mysterious-looking ATF van and came down to investigate. The whole operation was compromised in a casual one-minute visit. We couldn't

---

*"Special construction" is the official State of California Department of Motor Vehicles registration designation for a customized motorcycle, as opposed to factory-made bikes by established manufacturers such as Harley-Davidson or Indian.

risk staying and attempting a UC operation; we would have to find another place.

Ciccone and I decided that we'd take the bike back to my UC pad and do the operation right there. The only problem was, my apartment was on the second floor. I'd have to get my Mongol brothers to help me haul the Softail Springer up the stairs. With three or four big guys, it wouldn't be a problem. I went by South Pacific to hook up with Evel, and a new SFV prospect named J. R. Buddy was standing at the door and greeted me. I told him that I had just picked up my new Softail Springer and that I'd have it apart and back together in a week or so. Buddy said that he'd help me as much as he could. Evel asked how everything was going on the new bike.

"I'm gonna have to take my bike to your place and tear it down or get some help hauling it up to my apartment."

Evel said that he would get some help for hauling the bike the next day. I talked with Buddy about ordering a new frame. I told him that I didn't have a lot of money and I wanted to get as far as I could with what little I did have. Since the bike had cost me $2,500, I would need some time to come up with the money for a frame and cases.

"We'll buy a frame with a six-inch stretch and a thirty-six-degree rake on the front," Buddy suggested. "This'll kick out the Springer front and give it a sleeker look. The stretch will set the bike closer to the ground. Yo, Billy, it'll be one badass-lookin' machine."

I told Buddy to order up the frame and that I would bring him the money by the end of the week. He knew I was good for it.

The next morning I was up early waiting for Evel to call. I hadn't slept much the previous night. My girlfriend wanted to do nothing but argue. It was seven in the morning, and instead of a cup of coffee, I reached in the fridge and grabbed a beer. A true Mongol breakfast. I popped the top just when the phone rang. It was Evel. He said that J.R., the new prospect, was on his way over to help get the bike in the apartment. J.R. was a big boy, but two guys wrestling a six-hundred-pound bike up a set of stairs with a ninety-degree turn was going to be a job.

J.R. showed up at about ten. We stripped the gas tank, the fenders, and a few other parts off the bike to make it lighter. Then we rolled the bike to the edge of the stairs and began to push and pull it up. The front wheel was no problem, and the first couple of steps went easy. Then the back wheel hit and everything changed. The bike wasn't built to match the staircase building code. The front wheel was one third of the way up when the back wheel hit. Now we couldn't stop to rest because either the front wheel or the back wheel would always be trying to run back downstairs. Tough going, but we were making progress until we hit the turn. I was huffing and sweating like a bull when I called for a time-out. J.R. was in no better shape. We held on to the bike as we caught our breath. We looked at each other without saying a word, panting away and wondering where the hell all the help from the SFV Chapter was.

I told J.R. that we were going to have to lift the bike up into a wheelie to round the corner. He looked at me with resignation. We gathered all our remaining strength and in one mighty effort pulled the bike up on the rear wheel and swung it around the corner. The front wheel came crashing down, and the bike ran back down the stairs until it smashed into the turn. We rested for a couple of minutes before finally wrestling the bike all the way to the top. To my amazement, no one had seen us.

We pushed the bike through the doorway and into the living room, where I was planning to do the tear-down operation. Exhausted, J.R. and I collapsed on the couch.

I looked at the motorcycle that now adorned the living room floor. Now I truly had a biker pad.

For the next few weeks I spent my time maneuvering around the stolen-motorcycle trade. Evel did most of the work rebuilding my bike on my living room floor and in his garage. Buddy helped by filing off VINs and furnishing parts. Buddy's wife used her name and business to cover the stolen-bike conversion and to get the bike registered. Finally, after about four weeks, the Softail Springer was finished. It turned out to be just about everything I'd ever wanted in a motorcycle. It still couldn't outrun Evel's machine, but then no one's could.

Most important, now we had the hard evidence to back up everything we'd surmised about the "special construction" bikes that were so common among the Mongols and the other OMGs. We no longer had vague theories to take to court about how these bikes were made. We had done it ourselves. We'd documented it all for later prosecution. "Special construction" in the Mongols' world translated to "stolen motorcycle."

11

Living full-time as an outlaw gave me a perspective few law-enforcement officers ever get to experience. I was often more at risk from my supposed brothers in blue than from my adopted brothers in the gang. Just as there were some decent qualities—loyalty, love, respect—among the outlaw bikers, there were some law-enforcement officers who were little more than outlaws with badges.

It first happened on a crystal-clear afternoon in Los Angeles. I'd just paid a visit to Evel down at the South Pacific Motorcycle Shop in El Monte to work on a stolen-motorcycle angle of the investigation. I was on my Harley, ripping up the highway, thinking of slipping away for a few hours to see my kids. We hadn't had any decent father-son time in months. I was gangstered out in Mongol attire: black jeans; long-sleeved, logo-emblazoned black T-shirt; black bandana; Mongol scarf pulled up over my face; and my now well-worn Mongol patch.

I eased my bike onto Lower Azusa Road, cruising eastbound through the city of El Monte. I had gone only a quarter of a mile or so when I pulled up behind an El Monte black-and-white police car. It wasn't a big deal to me; it was broad daylight and I was behind the cops, not in front of them. I eased up to the rear of the patrol car, trying not to bring any undue attention to myself.

I was waiting for the light to change, daydreaming

about my boys, when a screaming voice caught my attention. I looked to both sides, checked my rearview in an attempt to zero in on the disturbance. I didn't see anything to my left, right, or behind. I figured there must be some sort of ruckus going on in front of the police car. Then I realized that it was the officer in the black-and-white, and that he was hollering at me.

This police officer was acting like I'd just run over his firstborn male. His arm was out the window, waving and flailing at me to pass him. "Go around me, you fuckin' piece of shit! Pull around me, you motherfucker!"

The light had turned green, and the cars in front of him proceeded through the intersection. The black-and-white sat stationary at the green light, and the cop kept screaming out the window. I rolled on the throttle, pulled into the lane to the left of the patrol car, and skirted by. The black-and-white dropped in behind me. My mirror was completely filled with the front grille of the police car, inches from my back fender.

I motored on, trying not to make any sudden moves and wondering what the hell this poor excuse for a cop was up to. This wasn't standard police procedure in anyone's handbook. The black-and-white swung over and pulled up alongside me on the right. I glanced over and saw a scarlet-faced cop glaring at me, intense hatred in his eyes. "Get the fuck off my street, you motherfucker. You hear me? Get the fuck outta my town, you sorry piece of shit!"

I was too stunned to respond. And what could I possibly say to this guy that wouldn't get him more fired up? I just moved on toward the next intersection and stopped for the light. When I looked at the black-and-white again, my eyes locked on the barrel of the cop's service gun.

"You see this, you motherfuckin' piece of shit? Get the fuck out of my town. Now."

The light turned green. Getting the fuck out of town now sounded like an outstanding idea to me. I rolled the throttle. The cop car moved with equal haste.

Gathering my wits, I remembered the digital ATF recorder on my belt and reached down to activate it just before having to stop at the next light. I found myself directly next to the black-and-white again. This time I was looking down the barrel not only of the driver's gun but of his partner's also. The cop's red face was turning purple. I looked up from the gun barrel and stared directly into his eyes this time as he screamed, "I'll fuckin' shoot you off that bike, you motherfucker!"

I began to think that he might really do it.

I yelled to the car next to me to look at what these cops were doing to me. The officers reacted by dropping their guns out of sight. The light turned green and I pulled away, making it obvious that I was getting the number on their cruiser.

At the next red light, the black-and-white stopped short of the intersection. I began to walk my bike backward in order to get a better recording. My move was met by an immediate and armed response. "You push that bike back here, and I'll shoot your ass right off of it, you motherfucker!"

It was a credible threat, and I stopped rolling. The light turned green. The cruiser turned right, and I opened up the throttle. With my blood pressure and heart rate going through the roof, I sped on with a mixture of incredulity, anger, and disbelief. I thought of going straight to the El Monte police building and giving it all up—admitting that I was a deep-cover federal agent—just to be able to confront these assholes defaming the reputation of decent cops. I knew that I couldn't do it, but I could fantasize. I rolled on and took some comfort in the fact that it hadn't been nighttime. Under the cover of darkness, in the absence of any witnesses, there was no telling what might have happened. As pissed as I was, we would have to wait to deal with the dirty-cop issue until the undercover investigation was over.

The SFV Chapter was holding Church at Domingo's place, followed by the standard night out barhopping in the San Fernando Valley. I had just gathered some information that a few Mongols had stabbed an individual during a confrontation at a bar in the Hollywood area. I didn't yet know which patches were involved, so I was carrying my NT recorder in my jacket pocket, hoping to capture a conversation about who was responsible for the attempted murder.

I went into my secretary-treasurer mode, taking notes during Church. Domingo, being a savvy criminal, kept the details vague, but he said that the Mongols needed to stay out of the Hollywood area for a while because of something bad that went down at one of the bars. The cops would be looking for any Mongol patches. The victim was too afraid to press charges, but still the Hollywood area would be hot for a while.

After Church, we hit The Place for the usual pool shooting and beer drinking. Everyone was used to me taking off around midnight; they all believed I had to be at my avionics job early in the morning. Rancid asked for a lift home, and like a true Mongol brother, I told him to pack up and we'd roll.

I popped the trunk on the car and put my jacket with the digital recorder in the trunk along with my Mongol colors. Rancid took off his colors, folded them neatly, and threw them in the trunk. In OMG protocol, cars are called "cages," and you never wear your colors while riding in a cage. One of the bullet holes my Mustang had acquired during its earlier undercover life had damaged the locking mechanism in the trunk. Now the only way to pop the trunk was by using the electrical release inside the glove compartment.

Just when we were pulling away from The Place, Rancid said he wanted to stop at the liquor store. I went inside with him to pick up something to eat. Although Rancid had already downed a pint, he grabbed a fifth of JD and opened it in the store. He downed about a quarter of the bottle while standing in the checkout line. I was always astounded by Rancid's ability to drink. We made our way off The Rock to the El Monte area, Rancid continuing to work on that bottle of JD. We were on Lower Azusa Road in El Monte when I passed a black-and-white sitting at an intersection with its headlights off.

The memory of those two El Monte cops leveling their guns at me and threatening to shoot me was fresh in my mind. I damn sure didn't want to see what these cops might do if they saw the likes of a drunken Rancid, who clearly hadn't had a bath or shower in over a month, a guy who at this moment made Charles Manson look like a choirboy.

I mentioned to Rancid what I had just seen.

"Shit," he said, groaning. "I can't take a shakedown, Billy."

A few days earlier Rancid had gotten into a pretty fierce fight with his wife. She'd called the cops, and Rancid had taken off and hadn't seen her since. He knew that the cops had seized a gun from his pad and that they'd been back to his place, and he thought they likely had a warrant out for his arrest. "I know they got paper on me," he said.

I looked up in the mirror and saw headlights come on. The black-and-white pulled out and began tailing me. I wasn't speeding, and I hadn't done anything wrong. "They're right on our tail."

"Man, I can't go to jail right now."

We heard the whooping of the black-and-white as they lit us up.

"Shit," Rancid said. "Don't stop."

I shot him an incredulous glance. "Brother, there's no way we're going to outrun these guys."

Rancid turned and looked out the back window. We were passing by a school that had a large chain-link fence surrounding it. "Pull over, brother, I'm gonna jump out and run."

I stopped the Mustang and looked over at Rancid, who was now clearly wasted. He couldn't even find the door handle. I didn't want to give these trigger-happy boys any excuses. I opened my door and got out, putting my hands over my head. It was two L.A. County deputy sheriffs who had jammed us. With a sudden shudder, I remembered that I still had my switchblade in my pocket. Now I was sure that I was going to jail. One deputy approached me, and the other went to the passenger side of the Mustang. Rancid was still oblivious, drunkenly trying to open the door. No need; the deputy opened it for him.

Just be cool, I kept telling myself. *Just cooperate. They have nothing on us. They'll shake us down and let us go.*

I saw the deputy reach in and remove the open bottle of JD from between Rancid's legs. "What's your name?" he asked.

I almost crapped in my pants when I heard Rancid's response: "Fuck you!"

"Out of the car!"

As Rancid got out, he lost what was left of his balance, falling to one knee and holding on to the car. He pulled himself to his feet but was too drunk to stand straight. The deputy asked Rancid for his identification.

"I don't have any fuckin' identification."

The deputy maintained his professionalism, not losing his cool in spite of the way Rancid was testing him. He took Rancid by the arm and helped him walk to the rear of the car. He told Rancid to sit on the curb. Rancid tried but fell over into the grass. The second deputy asked me to step to the rear of the car, then off the street and onto the grass. "Have you been drinking, sir?"

"I had a few beers earlier in the evening, but none in the last two or three hours."

He proceeded to give me the field sobriety test.

"Sir, stand on one leg. Put your arms out by your side, lean your head back, and close your eyes. With your arms extended, bring your right hand in and touch your nose with your index finger. Now your left . . ."

I wasn't worried about the sobriety test. I wasn't legally drunk, and I was being as cooperative as Rancid was being belligerent. Behind me, I could see Rancid sitting on the curb, spewing profanities, demanding his attorney, even as he began to list twenty degrees to the left, nearly falling into the grass again. The deputy asked for his name. Rancid threw out a bogus one: Richard Clay. I listened intently because I knew they would be asking me to repeat my friend's name. The deputy asked Rancid to repeat his name. This time he answered with a different name: John Martinez.

A backup black-and-white arrived at the scene with two more deputies. One of the deputies went immediately to the Mustang and began to look through it with his flashlight. When he opened the console, he found two 9mm bullets. He came back and showed the bullets to the other deputies, who then asked both of us if we had any weapons on us. I kept thinking about the switchblade in my pocket.

"Fuck you!" Rancid yelled.

Rancid's outburst provided me with a perfect diversion. While the deputies were focused on him, I pulled the knife from my pocket and tossed it silently into the grass. Too late—one eagle-eyed deputy had seen exactly what I'd done. Our eyes met in a moment of silent recognition. I wished more than anything that I could tell this officer who I really was.

He didn't walk over to the switchblade immediately; he began to question me about guns. I swore that I didn't have any on me. He led me to the curb to sit next to Rancid, who was now listing another ten degrees to port. I leaned over to Rancid and whispered in his ear: "What the fuck is wrong with you? You need to cooperate or we're fuckin' going to jail."

"Yeah? Fuck it. I'm going to jail anyway."

Two deputies were now going through the car, asking me how to get into the trunk. I almost visibly shook when I remembered that I had my government NT tape recorder in my jacket pocket. If they pulled that out in front of Rancid, I'd have some serious explaining to do. I told the deputy that the trunk had been damaged some time ago and was permanently shut. He wasn't stupid enough to go for that. Meanwhile, another deputy had opened the glove compartment and was trying to open the trunk with the electronic release button.

The ignition switch had to be on for that release button to work, but soon enough one of the deputies figured this out. He turned the ignition and then hit the trunk release.

The trunk popped open, revealing two carefully folded sets of Mongol colors. The deputies didn't touch a thing in the trunk. They yanked us to our feet, then threw the handcuffs on. I was escorted to the black-and-white parked directly behind my car, and Rancid was taken to the second black-and-white behind that. Deputies now tore apart everything in my bullet-riddled undercover Mustang.

One deputy pulled out my jacket and went through the pockets. In no time, out came the NT recorder. An NT is not some standard tape recorder that Joe Citizen can pick up at the nearest RadioShack. It's a tiny, sophisticated, very expensive digital surveillance device that only a member of law enforcement would use. I was horrified as I watched him toss it roughly on the roof of the Mustang.

I looked back to see if Rancid had observed what just happened. But I couldn't get a good look at his face. As we waited in our cuffs, the deputies continued to tear the car apart. One deputy even took a screwdriver and lifted up the floor panels by the seats. The Mustang had been hardwired by ATF technicians, and these unsuspecting deputies were about to expose an even more expensive and sophisticated recording setup.

I'd been in the back of the black-and-white for about thirty minutes when I was approached by a sergeant for the Los Angeles County Sheriff's Department. He opened the front door and peered at me through the metal separator. "What's with all the recording equipment? You wanna tell me what's going on?"

It was time for me to try some fancy Ciccone-style tap dancing. I told the sergeant that I worked for an avionics company and that we bought and sold high-priced equipment that was all serialized. Any mistakes in model numbers and serial numbers could cost the company tens of thousands of dollars. I told him whenever I bought anything, I put the whole transaction on digital tape. If he wanted, he could even listen to the tapes right now.

The sergeant didn't call my bluff. He didn't say another word to me. He went back and talked with the other deputies.

I'll never know if these cops bought my far-fetched alibi or if they suspected I was an undercover cop and were smart enough to let it alone. They had us stopped for more than two hours when they decided to let us go. One deputy hauled me from the backseat, whirled me around, and unlocked the handcuffs. He told me that he was going to write me a ticket for a taillight being out and that he was going to write my friend up for an open liquor container.

I couldn't believe they were letting us walk, not after all the obscene abuse Rancid had spewed at them. But these officers were the polar opposite of the two goons who'd leveled their service pistols at me.

The deputy told me that he'd put my knife in the trunk of the car and warned me that carrying a switchblade was illegal. I nodded, then went immediately to my car, retrieved the NT tape recorder sitting on the roof, and quickly tucked it away in my pocket, turning to look at Rancid. Fortunately, he was still cuffed inside the other black-and-white and was now practically comatose. Two deputies walked back to the car and opened the back door to let Rancid fall out like a big sack of dirty laundry.

I could hear one of them shouting: "Okay, buddy! Get up! Hey, get up!" They laid him on the ground and then told me to get my buddy on his feet and out of there.

I did my best to lift him. But Rancid weighed a good 220 pounds. There was no way I was going to get him up and into my car. I turned to the deputies. "Can you at least help me get him back to my car?"

They said nothing, but two deputies walked over to Rancid and grabbed him by his arms, pulling him first up to his knees, then to his feet. I thought that Rancid would walk with them to the car, but when they took one step he collapsed on his face again. The deputies held on, dragging him to the car. They tossed him in headfirst and told me again to get him the hell out of there.

I wrestled and shoved Rancid until I got him completely in the car. I couldn't believe we were leaving the scene with only a couple of tickets. We made it to Rancid's place in just a couple of minutes, and I thought that I was going to have to leave him propped up against the apartment-building wall. But much to my surprise, when I hollered for him to wake up, he started blinking at me.

He didn't remember a thing about being stopped by the cops. He didn't even remember leaving The Place. He just thanked me for the ride home and got out of the car.

As I drove home, I put myself in these deputies' shoes and realized that they *must* have known what was going on. I figured that they didn't want to be responsible for blowing some undercover deal.

12

There was one thing I didn't realize when I accepted this undercover assignment: how much it was going to change me. I'd been all fired up to infiltrate the Mongols and do the grueling investigative work; I'd been mentally prepared for the danger, the violence, the guns and drugs, the challenges to my undercover identity.

What I hadn't fully anticipated was the emotional turmoil. I really had to abandon all semblance of my personal life for the duration of the undercover role. The scrutiny was bad enough when I was a lowly prospect, but it got worse once I became a patched-in member and club officer. Before you can become a full patch, they make copies of your picture and distribute it to every other chapter in the club; every patch studies your face closely and considers whether they have a problem with you or may have known you at some point. Every patch stares hard at you and weighs the possibility that you might be a cop trying to infiltrate the club.

There are several hundred Mongols and known associates just in Southern California. So when you're out on the street, there's always a chance of running into them. You realize that even in a state the size of California, you're trapped in a kind of prison of your own making—you can no longer pick up your kids and go to a movie or an amusement park; you can't walk into a restaurant because you might run into some of the most violent criminals in the nation, psychopaths who are supposedly your closest friends.

Now that I was living the life of Billy St. John of the Mongols, my visits with my sons became less and less frequent. Holidays, weekends, birthday parties, baseball games, soccer games, the weekly "Dad time"—I had to give it all up.

As the months of the investigation rolled on, my hair got longer, my beard got longer, my sleepless nights got longer. There was no such thing as downtime or being off-duty. Because of my appearance, I couldn't go anywhere and be considered a member of mainstream America. In my mind, of course, I remained a federal agent, a decorated military veteran, a clean, caring, conscientious parent. But my offensive appearance announced something quite different to the world.

Everywhere I went—shopping for groceries, getting gas—people looked at me with disgust or fear.

My ex-wife, Cari, and our kids were living in a modest suburban Southern California neighborhood. Our boys were attending a good public school. Cari called me one day to see if I could take the boys to parents' night.

"Of course, Cari," I said.

Regardless of everything else that I was pretending to be in my Mongol undercover investigation, I decided I was a parent first. I wanted to look nice for my kids; I still had a closet full of suits, dress shirts, and ties, though I hadn't worn them in several years. But as I looked at myself knotting my tie in the bedroom mirror, it was obvious that I looked more like a homeless person who'd had his first bath in months rather than a conservative, concerned dad. I knew I wouldn't fool anyone in that suit and tie; I took them off and put on my jeans and a white T-shirt.

I told myself that appearances weren't everything; I would speak to my kids' teachers like an educated government agent. I would carry myself with dignity, and people would be as accepting of me as they were of the next parent.

As I parked my car at the school and my sons got out I watched all the other parents and kids recoiling from me with a reaction just short of panic. Before I could even offer a friendly "Good evening," everyone turned away. I wanted to put my arms over my kids' shoulders and walk them into the school, but I was worried that it might not be in their best interest. It took me a moment to gather my composure and remind myself that I was not the scumbag outlaw biker I appeared to be.

The kids and I made our way to my older son's classroom. There were only a couple of parents sitting with the teacher while the kids played together. My kids joined the others as I headed toward the teacher. I moved right up and introduced myself. The other parents were civil but obviously disturbed by my appearance.

The other parents said their good-byes to the teacher, gathered their children, and left without exchanging any pleasantries or making eye contact with me.

There was no one else left in the classroom now. I turned to the teacher. "Listen," I said, "so that you don't get the wrong impression, I want to tell you who I am."

She stared at me with some confusion. I reached into my jacket pocket and produced my ATF credentials. "I'm a special agent for the Bureau of Alcohol, Tobacco and Firearms. I'm forbidden to tell you the details of my job, but I'm working an undercover assignment and that's why I look the way I do. I know my appearance is alarming, but it shouldn't reflect badly on my kids. It's important to me that you know the truth."

I don't think she had any idea how badly I needed to get that off my chest. It was more than just the stigma of being judged at parents' night; I was trying to regain some sense of my *real* self. I could see the immediate relief in her face, but she didn't fully relax. We talked about my older son, then she thanked me for stopping by and ushered me to the door. She looked around for someone else to converse with, for some form of polite escape. She excused herself and hurried off to the room next door.

It was one thing to give my all to an investigation. I had given up plenty of my own life, but my kids' lives were never part of the bargain. They shouldn't have had to sacrifice anything on my behalf. They knew who their father was and loved me in spite of how I looked. But the last thing I wanted was for them to be victims of any ugliness.

I called to my boys and turned to walk away. They ran over to me and asked me if I was going to talk with any of their other teachers. How could I ever explain my twisted emotions, the sense of shame, the need to protect them? It was easier to say that I wouldn't be able to talk to any more teachers that night, that I would call their teachers later.

Standing in the busy school yard, I thought about taking them for ice cream, to a movie, or to their favorite amusement park. Something, anything, to make me feel like a normal dad. I wanted to drop to my knees, close my eyes, and hug them and let them know how dearly I loved them. I didn't want to leave them. I didn't want to have to go back to work.

There were days I was out with the Mongols when I missed those boys so much I wanted to cry. A lot of the Mongols had kids, but the way they treated them often enraged the father in me. Rocky and Vicky lived with their five kids in a rented house a couple of blocks off the main drag in Tujunga. It looked like a homeless shelter, with bodies sleeping everywhere, kids on the floor, kids on the couch, kids in beds, kids crawling on top of kids. It wasn't unusual to find everyone still asleep at noon or even five P.M. on a weekday. The house had a fence around the front yard to keep people out. The fence wasn't much of an obstacle, but the pit bull did keep even the bravest of intruders away. To be on the safe side, I made sure I always had a little treat for the pit.

One day I stopped by at around two P.M. Rocky's two youngest kids—one of whom was called Rocky junior—were playing outside. I knocked on the door, and Vicky started yelling for Rocky, who was still in bed. I stepped inside the living room, which was kept as dark as possible. A couple of kids were still sleeping on the sofa and floor. The TV was on, but the volume was very low so as not to wake anyone. When the front door was shut again, with the curtains drawn, you couldn't tell that it was daylight outside. I looked around, found an unoccupied chair in a corner, and sat down to wait for Rocky.

Vicky came back to the living room, pushing kids' legs out of the way. She had her bong in hand and was ready to get high. She sat on the sofa, staring at me. "This is some good shit, Billy. Wanna hit?"

"Naw. But thanks for asking, Vick. You go right ahead. With these five young'uns, you need it."

"Uh-huh. And today is Little Rocky's birthday, too."

"Oh yeah? You guys gonna have a party?"

She didn't even look up from the bubbling bong. "Naw, maybe next week when I get some money," she said. She took another long hit off the bong and lay back on the couch to enjoy her personal high.

"Yo, Billy," Rocky said as he stumbled into the room, slapping my hand and hugging me tight. He said he needed me to give him a hand on his bike. Translation: Rocky needed me to buy him some parts for his bike.

"Sure, Rock. Go get dressed, and let's go get something to eat."

Glancing around the room, I had to wonder if the five children would get anything to eat today. Vicky was half dozing on the sofa with the bong in her lap. It had been uncomfortable for me sitting there in the dark, and I half-leaped for the door, squinting as I walked back out into the bright sunlit California day. I reached into my jacket pocket for my shades. Rocky's two little ones were still playing and laughing in the front yard.

It always unnerved me to see Rocky's kids playing near that massive pit bull. I knew that if the dog turned on one of them it would surely kill the kid before anyone could do anything about it. I turned to Rocky. "Hey, today is Little Rock's birthday, huh?"

Rocky pushed past me with a rude grunt. "Yup."

I made my way back to my bike, staring at him. *What a piece of shit. Doesn't give a damn about his own son's birthday.* Rocky prepped his bike and began to kick and kick. It usually took at least a dozen kicks before that bike would turn over. Today was no exception. I waited on the street for a few minutes till I heard his bike actually fire up. I knew better than to start my bike before Rocky was under way; I'd burn more gas waiting for him than on a long haul to the desert. He made his way up the sidewalk and through the fence. I fired up and we took off.

After eating lunch and making a quick stop at the auto-parts store for a set of six-banger Chevrolet points that fit a Harley distributor, we were on our way back to Rocky's. I had gotten away with only buying lunch and a set of points. Since the money was coming out of my personal pocket—it was too complicated and slow a process to try to get these petty-cash expenses approved by ATF—I felt good about only having to shell out twenty bucks.

I parked on the street, and Rocky pulled his bike back down to just short of the front porch. As I got off my bike, I bent down to talk with Little Rocky. "Hey, buddy. So today's your birthday, huh?"

He looked up at me with his big brown eyes and said, "Yeah."

"How old are you today?"

He held up four fingers.

Then he looked back down at the broken toy rifle he was carrying. I felt a lump building in my throat, and I could've cried right there. No way this little boy wasn't going to have at least one real birthday present. I turned and made my way back to my bike, then yelled at Rocky, "Be back in a few!"

I rode to the nearby Kmart. I picked up a bright red fire truck and some chocolates and other candy. The more I thought about the situation—missing my own sons something fierce, being unable to spend any quality time with them—the angrier I got. I wanted to call Social Services and have someone come pick up these neglected kids. I wanted to punch Rocky's lights out. I wanted to punch his ol' lady's lights out.

Instead, I'd have to bite my tongue, swallow my anger, and wait for their day to come. I worked to control my rage as I made my way back to Rocky's place. I parked my bike, hid the fire truck and candy behind my back, and strolled up to Little Rocky. "Hey, little guy," I said. "Happy birthday."

His little eyes lit up, and he let out a gasp at the sight of the fire truck. He reached out and took his present. He held the truck in his lap and reached over to give me a hug, and I heard his tiny voice whisper into my ear: "Thank you, Billy."

This time a tear did roll down my cheek but quickly disappeared into my beard and the back of my grease-stained hand.

The Mongols have four required runs each year. The New Year's run is one of them. But the beginning of 2000 wasn't one of my brightest moments. My mood was pretty dark indeed, and the last thing I felt like doing was celebrating.

My aunt, who'd raised me and who'd loved me with a kind of love that I never felt from anyone else in my life, had recently passed away. Her name was Johnnie, and she was the kindest person I have ever known. Simply put, my biological father and mother weren't prepared for the obligations of being parents, and when I was two years old, they left me, my brother, and my older sister with Johnnie, who lived in western North Carolina. At that time my father worked as a police officer in Washington, D.C., and my mother stayed with him there. We didn't see much of our parents for the next four years. When I was six, my father was hired by ATF and stationed in Greensboro, and my parents took Johnnie and us with them. Although we lived under the same roof with our parents for the next fifteen years, it was Johnnie who really raised us. She cooked our meals, took us to church, helped us with our homework, cheered for us at ball games. She was a mother to me, and I grew up calling her Mom. Her passing left a giant hole in what was left of my inner core.

The investigation had mushroomed to the point that I'd lost all touch with my real life. I had spent more time with the Mongols than with my family at Christmas. At the same time, the indifference being shown toward me by ATF brass, as well as our frequent clashes with bureau administrators, had made me start to question my priorities. I hadn't been able to take much personal time in over a year. But Mom's death was different. Here my priorities were completely in focus.

For the first time, I didn't ask my ATF bosses if I could take time off from the Billy St. John role, I told them. I was going back to North Carolina to bury my mother and spend some time mourning with my family. I told the Mongols I wouldn't be around for a while because my mother had died. Then I picked up the pieces of my broken heart and went home to be with my family.

When I returned to Los Angeles, still deeply hurting, I tried to shake off my emotions and get back into the game. I arrived just in time for the Mongols' New Year's run.

It was going to be held at a cheap motel in Cerritos, a middle-class bedroom community on the southeast side of Los Angeles County. The community itself is nice enough, but it has its seedy sections. The fact that the Mongols gravitated to the seediest motel in town came as no surprise.

At about five in the afternoon I motored up to Evel's house, parked my bike in the front yard, and went to the door. Evel immediately gave me a smothering hug. "Sorry about your mom, brother," he said. "I love you."

I thanked him. Evel couldn't see it in my eyes, but I was frozen in space, unable to move as I watched him walk away. He was the first person, other than family, to offer me condolences.

I had been back from the funeral for several days. I had met with several ATF agents, and not one, not even Ciccone, had expressed their sympathy to me. No one from ATF had sent a card or uttered a word. I realized that I was just another number to ATF. I wasn't Bill Queen, a flesh-and-blood man; I was ATF badge number 489. Without warning, I felt some ancient wall crumbling inside me; I wanted to grab Evel and tell him everything— the whole goddamn story. "Look, brother," I wanted to scream, "get your fuckin' shit together—or you're gonna end up in prison!" And at that moment I didn't want to send him to prison. I slumped into his tattered, beer-stained sofa, holding back tears.

I heard another Harley roar up in the front yard. This time it was J.R. He had gone to a fast-food joint to get something to eat. I remember thinking that J.R. needed another fast-food run like he needed a chapped ass. The sound of his bike brought me back to reality, and when he strolled in with his greasy bag of burritos, the first words I heard were "Billy—sorry about your mom." I reached out for the usual Mongol handshake, followed by a sincere hug. "I love you, Billy." I was stunned. The tears welled up again, along with rivers of regret. I sat back down on the couch. *What the fuck are you doin', Billy?* I said to myself. I suddenly felt that Evel and J.R. were the best friends I had in the world. Maybe I could take them both in the back room, beat their asses, straighten them out. Tough love, that's all they needed. My mind was racing and my lips were murmuring wordlessly. I sat in some kind of waking trance, trying hard to hold on to what I knew was right.

Domingo and Rancid rolled in, and the scene played out again and again. By now I was beginning to fantasize about riding off with the Mongols and never returning to ATF. I drank a cold beer with my brothers and wondered if any of them had ever felt such inner turmoil. Did their consciences ever torment them like this?

Several hours later we rolled into a hellhole of a motel in Cerritos, and I remember looking at all the bikes lined up and all the Mongols milling around in the parking lot. I was getting back in the game. I saw Red Dog and a couple of other bad actors that I had a real hard-on for, guys who seriously needed to go to jail. I took a deep breath as I got off the bike. As I looked around, now surrounded by a horde of outlaws, I reminded myself: *I'm a federal agent, and these people would kill me without a second thought if they found that out*. It wasn't what I should've been concentrating on, but at that minute, in that situation, what I needed was a sobering dose of reality.

I pulled off my helmet and tucked it away. I walked toward the motel, shaking hands and greeting Mongols as I went. I made my way to the bar and grabbed a beer.

Everything was going to be okay. As I turned to walk back toward where the SFV Chapter guys were, I was approached by Ray-Ray. He was a huge, bearlike man of Mexican descent, and I had bought enough dope from him to put him in prison until he was a very old man. "Hey, Ray-Ray," I said.

He pulled me to his chest, gripping me in a big Mongol bear hug. "Sorry about your mom, my brother—I love you."

All I could do was stand there. I'd only just gotten my faculties back, and I wasn't prepared for the tumult and internal challenges confronting me. They were trying to pull me to the other side.

One after another, bikers bear-hugged me, expressing their condolences about my mom, telling me they loved me. I couldn't help myself—I felt overwhelmed by a shameful guilt, like lusting after your best friend's wife. I watched the Mongols hugging and high-fiving, laughing and toasting the New Year with beer. They exchanged war stories and put their tattooed arms tightly around one another. They put their arms around me. They freely and sincerely expressed their love for one another and for me. It *was* sincere. I knew that they honestly loved Billy St. John. And at that moment I desperately wanted to *be* Billy St. John.

Yet every time I started to believe the Mongols were truly my friends, every time I'd dream about riding away with them, they'd do something that would snap me back to reality. Their truly criminal, often murderous nature would hit me in the face like a freezing wind, and I'd tell myself, *Okay, now I remember* . . .

Easy was the epitome of the outlaw biker, in serious trouble with the law his entire life. He was unstable and unpredictable. Although he belonged to the Los Angeles Chapter and could most often be found down at Tony's

Hofbrau, he enjoyed hanging out with us at the SFV Chapter. He was inked up heavily with gang and prison tattoos. He shaved his head, and although not much taller than me, he was powerfully muscular. He wore his colors like they were bulletproof and seemed to have no compunction about killing for the club. He often hungered for confrontations, even deadly confrontations. He was truly fearless. Most nights I was glad he was on our side.

When I first met Easy he was dealing with the death of his father. I was hanging out with him one night in an apartment near The Place. We sat in the dimly lit living area, and he talked about his father dying and I talked about losing my mom. Easy said he and his dad were very close and had spent a lot of time together before he died. I thought about my old man and how my relationship with him was quite the opposite. My father was hardly ever around, and when he was, he was usually drunk. But Easy missed his father dearly. He told me straight out that since his father died he didn't care about living anymore. He really didn't give a shit.

I began to realize that Easy was so brave in the face of danger because he wanted to die. Like a terrorist who straps explosives to his own body, Easy had that conflation of suicidal and homicidal impulses. He was ready to die, and he wanted to take whoever was in his way with him. I watched Easy snorting the remainder of his meth and listened to him talk in the most chilling and morbid manner.

I now learned that, prior to becoming a Mongol, Easy had been arrested for child molestation. His own sister had accused him of molesting her two small children. I was surprised to hear this, and surprised that the Mongols let him in the club. Child molesters are not well thought of in any society—including the most hard-core criminal elements. They're the first ones to get stabbed when they get to prison, and often have to do their bids in protective custody.

The room seemed to get even darker when Easy told me how he was going to get revenge. He wanted his sister to really feel some pain, the kind of pain she had inflicted on him. He was going to kill her two children, and then he was going to kill himself. As I watched him talking in the half-lit living room, the hair on the back of my neck stood up.

Easy grew angrier and more animated. I've been around enough bad guys in my career to know that this wasn't just idle talk. He was going to kill his sister's two children slowly in front of her. Beside me, Easy pulled his knife out and gripped it tightly in one hand, saying that he was going to hold the kids by their hair and cut their throats while his sister watched them struggle for their lives.

I sat stone silent, stunned. I didn't know what to say. Easy had worked himself into some kind of a trance while talking about it, and I wasn't about to tell him he was fucking nuts.

I wanted to calm him down, so I told him that it would probably be better to just kill his sister, that the kids didn't do anything to him. No, Easy said. Killing the kids first was the only way he could make his sister suffer enough.

I told Easy that I had plans to meet with someone else that evening and had to leave. As I rolled away, the picture of Easy grasping a small baby girl and cutting her throat kept running through my mind. I had to do something about it immediately. I wasn't going to be able to sleep if I kept this to myself. I grabbed the phone as soon as I got home and dialed up Ciccone.

"Billy Boy, calm down," he said. "What happened tonight?"

I told Ciccone about Easy's plan, making sure that he understood it was not just angry, boastful talk. The next day Ciccone went to work on Easy's background. He found out that Easy had indeed been arrested for child molestation. The question was what to do about his sister and her children. If they were warned about Easy's plan and it got back to Easy, it would be obvious where the information came from and my own life would be in jeopardy. We had no grounds to arrest Easy, so the only solution was to have ATF put a tail on him 24/7 for as long as it took, making sure that he never had a chance to act on his plan to murder his sister and her children.

Rocky wasn't as homicidal as Easy, but like most Mongols, he would gladly kill over money. As it turned out, his wife was a proficient thief. One day Vicky and a girlfriend, Pam, managed to steal a baby grand piano from a storage unit. But they had no one to fence the thing, and it was taking up their whole tiny living room.

I was lying in my bed in the undercover apartment, just starting to doze off, when the phone rang. It was Rocky, sounding upset.

"Yo, Billy, I need your help."

"Sure, Rock. What d'ya need?"

Rocky and another Mongol had pawned their bikes to a drug dealer named Ruben who owned Mo-Hogs Motorcycle Shop in El Sereno. Time was running out for them to come up with the money; Ruben was threatening to sell the bikes if he didn't get two thousand bucks. Rocky started to tell me of his plan to get his Harley back from Ruben.

"This is what we're going to do," he said. "You're going to come over with your car and take me to Ruben's. We'll park in the alley behind his place and wait. I'll go in and tell him that I wanna buy some dope. I'll follow him back to where he keeps it, and when we're back there I'm gonna blow his fuckin' brains out. When the heat cools, we'll go over and get our bikes. Simple as that."

"Rocky, are you fuckin' nuts? We'll get caught. Somebody'll hear the gunshots, go outside, and see you getting in my car. I'll go to jail for murder right along with you."

"That ain't gonna happen. You'll be in the alley. Nobody's gonna see anything. Now get in your fuckin' car and get over here."

"You're gonna dust him for two thousand bucks?"

"Sure, he's a piece of shit anyway."

"Maybe. But he ain't worth spending the rest of your life in prison over."

Rocky was not going to be easily dissuaded. He was sure that we weren't going to get caught, and wanted me to hurry and get over there so we could put the murder plan in motion. I tried to talk him out of it, but he only grew more angry and insistent. Finally, I told Rocky to hold on for a few minutes and I'd call him back.

Ciccone had left for the weekend with his fiancée, so I put in a call to Special Agent John Carr and laid Rocky's crazy story on him.

"Wow, Billy," Carr said. "That's a good one. I don't think ATF's gonna go along with you driving the getaway car on a murder."

I told Carr that Rocky was hell-bent on killing Ruben that night and I was afraid that if I didn't stay on top of him, he would take off and do it without me. From a legal standpoint, acquiescing to a murder was tantamount to participating, and neither was a viable option for a federal agent. Carr and I tried to figure a way out of this one. We could have an LAPD cop waiting in a black-and-white to stop us on the street for some traffic violation, come up with a bogus warrant on some chickenshit charge, and arrest me, Rocky, or both of us. Or maybe I could fake a car crash on the way over.

Then I remembered the grand piano that Rocky's wife had boosted. I knew it wasn't going to be easy to fence a stolen grand piano in outlaw biker circles. I told Carr I'd offer to buy the piano for two thousand dollars so Rocky would have the money to get his bike and the murder would be off. Carr said that it sounded pretty crazy but it was worth a try. I called Rocky back.

"Let's go, Billy!" he said. He was getting impatient, and I'd never heard him sound so intense.

I told Rocky that I'd just talked to Bob, the guy we'd done the guns-and-meth deal with, and that Bob wanted to buy the piano for two grand. "You can take the two grand and get your bike back and you don't have to worry about spending the rest of your life in jail. And neither do I. What d'ya think?"

I was expecting the idea to get shot down immediately, but Rocky was silent for a good ten seconds. Then he said, "See if you can get Bob to give you twenty-five for it."

"Okay, Rock. Get right back to you."

I hung up and tried to catch my breath. Here I was trying to keep both of us out of prison—or so Rocky thought—and he wanted to haggle over stolen-property prices. That's the true criminal mentality.

There was no time to screw around, trying to call the ASAC to see if he'd approve the twenty-five hundred. I would have to foot the bill myself and put the paperwork in later.

"Rocky, brother, it's a go. Bob's sending me the money, and you'll have it tomorrow."

"Yeah, okay, cool. But I still wanna dust Ruben's ass."

"Lighten up, Rock. Ruben'll get his."

He paused to think it over. "Fuck it," he said at last. "You're right. Adios, brother."

I hung up and slumped back into bed, trying to figure out how I was going to write up an ROI explaining that the Bureau of Alcohol, Tobacco and Firearms had come into possession of a natural-wood-finish Wurlitzer baby grand piano.*

In addition to taking the position of secretary-treasurer of the San Fernando Valley Chapter, I also became the club's unofficial doctor. I'd never intended for the gang to learn about my medical training. While serving with the Los Angeles ATF Special Response Team, I'd become a licensed medic and still had a bag with my surgical tools, syringes, and anesthetic.

One night back when I was prospecting, we'd been trying to break into the house of a Mongol associate in order to party with some girls. I was working on the window with Evel when suddenly his knife slipped and sliced my palm deeply, nearly to the bone. I could see that it was going to be good for at least three or four stitches.

The party was off as far as I was concerned. As I fired up the Harley, making a tourniquet of my bloody shirt, I was faced with an undercover dilemma: I could go to the hospital as a Mongol biker, sit there until sunrise, and deal with the no-insurance bullshit. Or I could take the risk and go as an ATF agent and use my government medical insurance. But not only would that be a dangerous security breach, I knew that if the ATF administration ever found out about the injury, the SAC and ASAC would have a pretext to shut the case down. I decided to go home, and sew the wound up myself. I broke out my suture equipment and the lidocaine, gritted my teeth, and pumped up my hand with a syringe big enough to start an IV. When it was numb, I went to work. With only one hand to pull the needle and surgical thread, I did a pretty lousy job, but it was good enough for government work.

---

*The piano was housed as evidence by the LAPD in the Erwin Piper Tech Center in downtown Los Angeles. Vicky Martinez pled guilty to grand larceny and was sentenced to probation.

When Domingo and the rest of the chapter heard how I'd sewn myself up, they all started calling me Dr. St. John. And they didn't hesitate to call me when they needed some emergency medical care. One night, somewhere after four A.M., the phone woke me. I heard Domingo shouting frantically: "Billy, get up and get over here!"

"Over where?"

"Evel's. He beat the shit out of his ol' lady, and we need your help. She's gonna need some stitches."

I shook the sleep from my head and sat up. "Hey, Domingo," I said, "just take her to the emergency room."

"Fuck no, Billy. Evel just got out of the joint for beatin' his ol' lady. If we take her to the emergency room, they'll call the cops and he'll be right back in. Now get over here, brother!"

I told Domingo to hold on, that I would be there as soon as possible.

Four o'clock in the morning. Jesus Christ. I climbed out of bed, threw some water on my face, and got dressed. I called Ciccone and told him that Evel had beaten up his girlfriend and that Domingo wanted me to go over and see what I could do to fix her up. "Good boy," he said. "Lemme know how it goes."

I grabbed my helmet and leathers and headed for the door. I didn't take my medic bag. There was no way I was going to sew up this girl. It was dark, I was tired, and I couldn't believe I was headed back to hook up with the Mongols at this hour. At least I wasn't going to have to deal with any traffic, and there wouldn't be many cops out. I hit the street and hauled ass to Evel's place.

Evel met me at the door, freaking out.

"I fucked up, Billy," he said. "I fucked up bad. I don't even know how it happened, I didn't hit her that hard . . ."

We walked back to the bedroom. I saw his girlfriend lying on the bed. Over and above her upper lip were several small pieces of Scotch tape that were obviously holding that part of her face together. I felt like Marcus Welby making a house call, leaning over her and asking how she was feeling.

She didn't answer. Given that the man who allegedly loved her had just beaten her to a bloody pulp, I don't know what answer I was expecting.

I sat down beside her and began removing the tape. Once I got it all off, it was obvious what had to be done. I had seen the results of Evel beating on his girlfriend before. A few bruises here and there, maybe a fat lip, but this was bad. Evel had opened her up completely, from her lip almost all the way to her nostril. The gash was going to have to be sewn on the inside as well as the outside. I had never done that kind of intricate stitching before.

I told Evel that I couldn't do it, that she would have to go to a doctor.

"No way!" Evel shouted. He made it clear that he wasn't going back to the joint for this one. I told him to make up some story for the emergency-room doctors. Tell them she fell down the stairs. Evel said he'd told them that story the last time, and they didn't go for it. "Just please sew her up!" he implored.

I told him that even if I did sew her up, there was a great likelihood of infection with this kind of wound—an infection that could easily prove fatal. I told him that she would have to go to the doctor for antibiotics anyhow. He said he could handle that, he could get his hands on the drugs, and that I should just go ahead and sew her up. I told him again that I had never sewn up anyone from inside out, that I just couldn't do it. She really needed to go to the doctor. With resignation in his voice, Evel said: "Okay, fuck it, I'll just tape her up."

He began to tape the wound closed again. It was obvious they weren't going to take this poor girl to any hospital. I knew that the time for sewing wounds closed was limited and that if that period ran out, surgery was required. She was a pretty girl, and they were willing to scar her face for life, or let her die of an infection, just to keep Evel out of jail. Knowing that they weren't going to take her to get any medical attention, I relented.

I told Evel that I would have to go back home to get my equipment. I headed for the door, thinking about the consequences of sewing her up. Then about the consequences of not sewing her up. Time was running out. I made up my mind and put my face in the wind.

After a quick round-trip to my UC pad for my medic's gear, I prepped the bed and myself for the job. I had a couple of suture kits that allowed for a combat-acceptable sterile surgery environment. I had the appropriate suture materials for her face and the lidocaine that would make for a relatively painless procedure. I drew the lidocaine into a syringe and looked her in the eyes. I asked her if she was sure she wanted me to do this. She looked at Evel, then back at me, and nodded. She never flinched or blinked. I guess being Evel's ol' lady, she had developed the sort of mettle a lot of soldiers would admire.

I administered the lidocaine and went to work. It took five stitches on the outside and four on the inside to close the wound. When I was through, I looked at my handiwork, and I must say, it looked a hell of a lot better than the one-handed job I had done on myself. Not bad at all. Evel was amazed and kept thanking me emphatically. I told him that we weren't out of the woods yet. She would need to be on Keflex, penicillin, or some other antibiotic for several days. Evel said he could get the drugs from Doc, a Mongol from the Pico Chapter who had some kind of pharmaceutical connection.

Evel hugged me. I turned and told Evel's girl that I would be back in a couple of days to look at her. She didn't open her eyes; she didn't move. "Thanks," she said.

I packed my medic's bag and headed for home.

13

Domingo had come out of prison for his felony-assault conviction shortly before I met him. As a parolee, he couldn't test positive for alcohol, let alone weed, coke, or crank. Any hint of illicit substances in his weekly piss test would send him back to prison immediately; he wouldn't even hang around in a room where others were smoking pot for fear of inhaling enough residual stuff to show up on a test.

I had ridden my president's coattails on the dope issue for a good portion of this investigation. When the drugs started coming out, I ran to find Domingo. As president, he was always offered any hits before I was, and when he turned them down, I was on board quick. "Hell no," I would say. "If my pres ain't doing it, then I ain't doing it. I'm hangin' with you, Pres."

To reward this kind of loyalty, Domingo had entrusted me with a lot of responsibilities within the chapter. In addition to being the secretary-treasurer, I'd also been put in charge of selling off any surplus firearms the chapter had acquired.

When Domingo got off his parole, the level of violence and craziness around me intensified dramatically. I began to worry that the investigation was going to spiral out of control. It started to seem like we couldn't go anywhere without getting into a fight. Domingo was drinking like a man desperate to make up for lost time. I watched his personality change with the alcohol consumption. Once a predictable and reasonably sensible person, he was now turning into an irrational, violent asshole.

It was a Saturday, and we had been invited to party with the Orange County Chapter at the Shack. The Shack was a nice little tavern that had the biker flavor but was still able to maintain a clean enough image to draw a regular, law-abiding crowd. I was hoping to use the party as a chance to pick up some intel on the criminal activities of the Orange County Chapter. I'd told Ciccone I didn't need him to ride backup on this one, as I didn't expect there to be any violent activity. But I hadn't factored in the variable of Domingo's new postparole mood.

With all the administrative headaches in the ATF's L.A. Division, I was looking forward to getting away with my Mongol brothers. In spite of their obvious criminality and character flaws, I'd started to care about them as human beings. It was beginning to pull me apart. I knew, on a conscious level, that I was only doing my job as an ATF agent, but the guilt from knowing I would someday have to testify against guys like Domingo and Evel and Rocky was becoming increasingly disorienting.

We rolled into the Shack, where more than fifty bikes sat in the parking lot. The wind carried the aroma of carne asada. We left the keys in our bikes, knowing they would be safe among our brothers. As we walked to the bar, our Orange County brothers warmly greeted us. Beer was quickly brought by the prospects, and we settled in for a day of partying. I shot pool with the guys and took their money most of the time.

With everyone full of Budweiser, the line at the little one-stall bathroom was deep. I was standing behind Domingo, who became vocally impatient at having to wait.

"Look, I gotta piss," he said, kicking open the door to find a seriously inebriated guy standing at the toilet holding his dick. He wasn't pissing, just standing there staring at the graffiti-covered wall. We looked at him for maybe fifteen seconds, then Domingo snapped. "Dude, other people need to get in here."

Too drunk for his own good, the guy turned and glared at Domingo. "Well, you'll just have to wait, buddy."

Without warning, Domingo charged in like Jack Lambert in the glory days of the Steelers, spearing the dude up against the wall—*thwack!* I charged in behind Domingo, trying to look like I was doing my loyal Mongol duty but in reality wanting to make sure that my president didn't end up killing this drunk fool. I figured if I could maybe pin him against the wall, or put him in a half nelson, I could get him out of the bathroom before Domingo's rage got out of control.

But Domingo was already kicking the guy in the ass and back, and his head had slammed hard against the tiled bathroom wall.

When I loosened my grip on his shirt, the guy lifted his head to reveal a frightening sight. Blood was streaming out of his ear. Had we given him a brain-damaging blow? Thankfully, he wasn't unconscious, just seriously drunk and stunned. Suddenly enraged again, Domingo pinned him against the wall in a choke hold, threatening to finish the job. The guy was given the option of drinking the toilet water or losing his front teeth. But before Domingo could start smashing the guy's head into the toilet bowl, I heard a group of Mongols calling through the bathroom door. "Hey, Domingo, hold it, dude! That's Johnny's brother!"

Domingo was unrelenting, ramming the guy tight against the wall. "You thirsty, motherfucker?"

"Domingo, brother, lighten up!"

Domingo loosened his grip. The guy stood motionless, blood pouring from his ear. I looked into his pupils, searching for further evidence of head trauma. I couldn't

help myself; the medic in me needed to know how badly
he was hurt. I held his face in my hands and turned his
head so I could see exactly where the blood was coming
from. With relief, I saw that it was oozing from a gash in
the top of his ear.

Domingo rammed the guy's head down violently into
the filthy toilet, until his face was half submerged in the
water.

"Domingo!" called one of the Orange County Mongols, pushing his way into the tiny bathroom. "Billy!
That's my brother!"

Domingo eased his grip at last, yanked the drunk's face
out of the toilet. The guy staggered out of the bathroom.
His face was blotchy and bright red, hair standing up in
spikes from the toilet water and blood still pouring from
his ear. He wanted out, but Domingo was determined to
make him work for his freedom. He stayed in the guy's
face all the way to the front door, challenging him to
make a move. The Orange County Mongols continued
their effort to calm Domingo, but he was drunk and beyond talking to. Like a mad dog, he taunted the guy all
the way out into the street, until he was on his bike and
pulling away from the Shack.

Almost every time we went out drinking, Domingo got
into some kind of fight. After about ten nights straight, I
had finally decided to take a night off from the Mongols—I hadn't had a decent father-son night in months.
I'd called both of my "bosses," Ciccone and Domingo,
and told them that I had personal matters I had to take
care of and that I'd be out of the loop for the evening. It
worked fine with Ciccone, but not with Domingo. "Hell
no, Billy," he said. "Crazy Craig's here from Georgia.
We're putting together a little operation."

"What's up, Pres?"

"You need to come over and bring your Mustang and your piece."

"We ridin' sixty-six?"

"Yeah, we ridin' sixty-six."

"Riding sixty-six" was Mongol code for traveling armed in civilian clothes—carrying a firearm while not flying your colors. It was a sign that something serious was going down: a murder, extortion, armed robbery. When engaging in a premeditated violent crime, the club wanted to attract as little attention from law enforcement as possible: no convoy of roaring Harleys, no telltale Mongol patches.

"Okay, bro. See ya in about an hour."

I knew that Ciccone was up to his armpits typing up 3270s, and for a moment I wished I could give him a night off. But I knew I had to get him to rally the troops and have a surveillance team out in front of Domingo's with zoom lenses for the evidence.

I prepped my NT recorder so I could be sure to get everything on tape. I picked up my UC gun, my blue-steel snub-nosed .38-caliber revolver, and opened the cylinder. Six shots. I closed it up and tucked it away under my shirt.

Carrying a gun meant that I didn't just have to worry about what might happen with the Mongols, I also had to worry about getting stopped by the cops and arrested on an illegal gun charge. I considered hiding the .38 in the trunk or under the hood, but then I thought, *So fuckin' what? If I do get popped, it'll be for the club. From the Mongols' point of view, it's just another feather in Billy St. John's cap.*

As I rolled up to Domingo's residence I was greeted by Bucket Head and Crazy Craig lounging in the backyard.

Crazy Craig was a country white boy out of the Georgia Chapter. He had a straight job driving a tractor trailer for Old Dominion and was the proudest brother who had killed for the club. He wore an extra-large set of skull and bones on his colors as testament to that fact. The size of that patch actually rubbed some of the other brothers the wrong way.

Those skull-and-bones patches interested me more than I could safely let on. I was always eager to learn who had been murdered, where, and when the crime had occurred, valuable intel that could be used in an eventual homicide prosecution. But the first thing you learn upon patching into the gang is to not ask questions about matters that don't concern you. Criminal bravado notwithstanding, every member of the Mongols knows that the more people who know about what you've done, the more likely it is that you're going to get caught. They'll brag about their bar fights and other outlaw mayhem, but for the most part they keep their mouths shut about murders. There's no statute of limitations on homicide, and California still has the death penalty on the books. I did once get an older Mongol named Glazer to tell me, in a conversation I secretly recorded, how he'd earned his skull and bones by shooting a Hells Angel during the big war back in the seventies, but that was only because Glazer was too drunk to care about what he was saying.

In the bright sunlight of Domingo's yard, Crazy Craig looked like he was ready to commit another murder, showing off his shiny Smith & Wesson .357 Magnum to Bucket Head. Domingo walked out of the house with his own gun in hand. Rancid came next, tucking his gun under his shirt. Domingo walked up to me with the Mongol handshake and a hug and started laying out the scenario.

The trouble had all started a few months before I began hanging out with the Mongols at The Place. Before Little Dave took over the reins of power in the Mother Chapter, the national president of the Mongols was an old-time biker called Junior. One night at Armond's Tavern in Tujunga, Junior assaulted another patron with a beer bottle and was arrested by the LAPD.

One of the most insidious qualities of the Mongol organization is its willingness to engage in the crime of witness intimidation. No one ever gets away with testifying against a Mongol in open court. As Junior's assault case moved forward on the court calendar, Lud, who had been president of the SFV Chapter before Domingo, and a Mongol named Rodney Hipp were given the assignment of making sure that none of the witnesses against Junior actually made it to court. Although Lud and Hipp had made their best effort at witness tampering, they couldn't locate the victim, who came to court under police protection, testified against Junior, and helped the prosecution send the Mongols' national president to prison for sixteen years.

It was an unpardonable fuckup, and the rage of the Mongol Nation focused on Lud and Hipp. After a hearing they were formally expelled from the club and ordered to surrender their colors. They were also sentenced to take a beating, have any Mongol tattoos burned off their bodies, and give their motorcycles and other valuable personal property to the club. Lud accepted his sentence, but Rodney Hipp fled the state.

The Mongols' national officers decided that if they couldn't find Hipp, they would extort his older brother, Andy, who was not an outlaw biker, merely a regular guy working a mechanic's job.

Domingo had put together a well-coordinated extortion plan. We even had a set of two-way radios, so that Domingo could go in first on a recon mission and then radio us with the okay.

What would be my chances against the four armed Mongols if I had to stop a murder and shoot it out with them? I couldn't let them kill Andy Hipp. But if he resisted—hell, if he so much as talked shit to Domingo—I had little doubt they would beat the shit out of him, if not put a few bullets in his brain. We loaded into two pickup trucks and headed to Andy Hipp's place. I adjusted the snub-nosed .38 in my waistband and smiled. I picked out Crazy Craig, my fellow country white boy, as the first Mongol I'd shoot if things went bad. Then I'd take care of Rancid.

Andy Hipp lived less than two miles from Domingo. I took a deep breath as we stopped a couple of houses away. Domingo tested the two-way radios and handed me one to hold. As Domingo walked up to Hipp's door, I turned to Bucket Head. "What the fuck do we do if we hear a gunshot coming from inside the house?"

Bucket Head didn't hesitate. "What do you think, Billy? We go in and shoot everybody."

The two-way radio in my palm crackled.

"Okay, guys," Domingo said, "come on in."

We loaded into Bucket Head's pickup and backed down the driveway. Domingo and Andy Hipp were standing outside by the garage door. We escorted Hipp inside his garage, out of sight of anyone passing by. It was a perfect place for an execution.

Domingo and Rancid raised their shirts to show the gun butts in their waistbands. They backed Hipp against the wall. I put my hand on my own gun and held my breath, hoping that Hipp had enough sense not to buck any Mongols. Domingo told Hipp that he was being held responsible for his brother's transgressions against the club, that he would have to come up with a thousand dollars immediately or we would take possession of his motorcycle. Hipp's voice trembled as he begged Domingo not to take his bike. He said that he had some money in his savings account and that he would have it for Domingo by tomorrow. Domingo said that we'd be taking anything that we felt was worth taking from Hipp's house, and that it would count toward what the Hipp family owed the Mongols. Hipp begged Domingo not to take any of the tools he needed for his job as a mechanic.

We loaded the pickup truck with electric tools, a Craftsman toolbox, several car jacks, and anything else in the garage that caught Domingo or the other Mongols' fancy. Domingo made it clear that we would be back tomorrow for his bike or the thousand dollars cash.

As we carted away his belongings, I watched Hipp begging, practically in tears. I felt my jaw tighten as I glanced around the garage. But I kept telling myself that they would all pay in due time. When the investigation had run its course, they'd all be hearing the sound of the prison gate slamming shut behind them.

Domingo and Rocky were making both my life as a Mongol and my job as an ATF agent nearly unbearable with their violent and erratic behavior. It was difficult for me to break away from Domingo's orbit for even one night; he always expected me to be partying shoulder-to-shoulder with him. If I said I wanted to leave the party early, Domingo ragged on me and coerced me into staying out until sunrise.

During one standard Saturday-night jam at The Place, I resolved to leave around midnight and to spend some time with my kids in the morning. Domingo could scream till he was blue in the face, but I was giving all day Sunday to my sons. He was sitting near the jukebox with his wife, Terry, and I extended my hand.

"Where the hell do you think you're going, brother?"

"I'm outta here, Pres. I got one bitchin' chick waiting for me." It was the only excuse a Mongol would find acceptable on a Saturday night.

"Yeah, okay, Billy, go get 'em."

Not long after I'd fired up my Softail Springer, a young couple made the mistake of wandering into The Place. They'd never been there before, and didn't know the

1 percenter protocol. The guy was on the big side and looked like he'd seen a few street fights. His girlfriend was in good shape, young and pretty, and unfortunately, Rocky quickly became infatuated with the way she moved. He didn't care that she was with another man. He walked up to her and introduced himself. He flirted with her and pointedly did not say a word to her boyfriend.

"Back off," the insulted boyfriend said finally.

Everybody in The Place knew that you didn't talk to Mongols like that. Rocky invited the newcomer to settle it outside. But once outside, it didn't take Rocky long to realize that he had bitten off more than he could chew. Although Rocky landed a blow or two, the boyfriend was bigger and stronger. The fight went to the ground, and Rocky, now on the bottom, was taking one serious ass whipping.

Domingo caught sight of Rocky getting pounded into the concrete and flew right into action, kicking the guy in the face with his steel-toed boot. The guy wasn't able to recover before Rocky joined Domingo with another boot to the head. Rocky bent down and began delivering blows to his face and head as Domingo kicked him in the back, chest, and stomach. They kicked and stomped until their victim lay completely motionless, barely breathing.

This still wasn't good enough for Rocky. He reached into his pocket and pulled a knife. By this time, several people had walked out of The Place, including the guy's girlfriend. She was terrified and started screaming.

Just before Rocky started to stab the guy, Domingo grabbed him, saying there were too many witnesses. Some sense returned to Rocky, and he put the knife away. He reached into the guy's pants and took his wallet and money.

Meanwhile, the victim's girlfriend had run to the pay phone and called the police. As Rocky tucked away the money and wallet, he heard the sounds of police sirens approaching.

Rocky and Domingo ran back inside The Place and searched out hiding places as the cops pulled up in front. The beaten man lay motionless on the pavement. His lungs, punctured by broken ribs, began to fill with blood. The police called for an ambulance and backup units for what they thought was about to become a murder scene. The victim's girlfriend told the police that Mongols had committed the crime, and gave them a description of the two bikers.

In the confusion, Domingo and Rocky escaped from The Place. Backup units moved in and a manhunt ensued. The paramedics quickly assessed the victim's condition and undertook the painful procedure of administering a chest tube. They worked on him for almost an hour before he was stable enough to transport. It would be more than a week before doctors were certain that he would recover from the beating.

Although there were several eyewitnesses, only one, besides the victim's girlfriend, stepped forward, and she could only identify Rocky. The eyewitness went by the name of Ray Gun. Ray Gun was a big guy, an indigenous Tujunga barroom brawler, who knew better than to try to intervene against the Mongols. But as he stood at the crime scene, watching the paramedics desperately working to save the victim's life, Ray Gun had a crisis of conscience. He listened to the victim's girlfriend begging her boyfriend not to die. It affected Ray Gun to the point that he stepped forward and volunteered to give the police a complete statement of what had happened. He identified Rocky and Domingo as the perpetrators of the assault, giving the police their descriptions and telling them where they lived.

In so doing, Ray Gun guaranteed himself a place on the Mongols' most-wanted list.

* * *

Rocky knew he couldn't go home. He ran to his dad's place, where he hid out for the next couple of weeks. Domingo had no place to hide and was confident no one on The Rock would give him up. But if the victim died, Domingo decided he would go on the lam in Mexico and hang out with the Mongols chapter there. If it looked like he was going down for attempted murder or strong-armed robbery, he would flee to Georgia and hang with Crazy Craig and the Mongols there.

At about four o'clock in the morning Domingo and Terry were awakened by a knock on the front door. "Police! Open up!"

Domingo was still fully dressed. He quietly opened the back door as the police pounded away at the front. Terry was confronted by several cops demanding to speak to Domingo. "He's not home. What do you want to talk with him about?"

"We just want to talk to him," one of the officers told her.

Terry told them that Domingo didn't come home last night and that she didn't know where he was. They wanted to look in the house, and Terry stood aside as they rushed in with guns drawn. They went from room to room and were satisfied that Domingo was in fact not in the house. They told Terry that when she spoke with Domingo, she should tell him to turn himself in.

"Turn himself in for what?" she demanded.

"Just tell him we need to talk to him."

At five o'clock that morning I was asleep in my real home in Upland when my cell phone rang. It was Terry. "Billy, where are you?"

She was frantic, almost in tears, saying the police were after Domingo and that he had been banging on the door of my UC apartment in Diamond Bar trying to get in touch with me. I told Terry that I was at the Chino Airport, only a few miles from my pad. She said that Domingo was at the service station just around the corner and that he needed to hook up with me. I told her I'd get in my car and meet with him in just a few minutes.

Hanging up the phone, I jumped out of bed and threw on my clothes. I gathered up all my Mongol paraphernalia and ran out the door. As I raced toward Diamond Bar, I put in a call to Ciccone. "Dude, something's up. I'm on my way to the UC pad. Domingo's waiting for me. Terry called and said that the cops were looking for Domingo. Hate to do it to you, Johnny, but you better get up and head my way."

"Okay, I'll roll with you."

When I hung up, it hit me hard: My kids were expecting to see me at eight A.M., which was three hours away. Hopefully this bullshit with Domingo wasn't going to take long. I rolled into Diamond Bar in record time, managing somehow to avoid drawing the attention of any cops. Domingo was waiting for me at the service station.

"Where the hell have you been, Billy?" he said angrily.

"Hey, Pres, I had to drop off that equipment at Chino this morning at oh-dark-thirty. What got you up so early this morning?"

"The fuckin' cops," he said. "Let's go to your place and I'll tell you all about it."

There was no handshake, no hug, just one serious meet. I knew some bad shit must have happened the night before. I rolled to the UC pad, followed closely by Domingo. As we parked, I couldn't help but notice that Domingo was behaving in a way I'd never seen before. He was visibly unnerved. I grabbed my keys. On my key ring was a standard car-door security device that in reality controlled the audio-video surveillance equipment in my pad. As we walked in, I hit the remote recording button that turned it all on. Domingo started to talk.

"Billy, me and Rocky beat up a dude at The Place last

night, and I think he might have died." He tried to blame the whole thing on Rocky.

"Rocky was getting his ass beat, and I had to jump in and save him, Billy. I guess we beat the guy a bit too much. Then that dumb-ass Rocky took the guy's wallet and money. Man, I gotta find a place to hide out till I figure out what I'm gonna do."

"Hey, Domingo," I heard myself say, "you know you can stay here as long as you want."

He said he was going to call Terry and have her bring over some clothes and things and he'd stay with me until he decided what to do.

"Cool," I said.

Good thinking, Queen. With Domingo living right on top of me, the UC pad had suddenly turned into an indefinite 24/7 operation. That meant absolutely no downtime. I'd be in full Mongol mode every waking—every sleeping—moment. I walked around my pad making sure there was nothing there that would give me away. Domingo had been up almost all night and was starting to fade. I told him to lie on the couch and try to get some sleep. He did, as I sat back and I regretted missing another outing with my kids. There was no way I could even risk calling them to explain my absence. I sat and wondered how much more of my personal life was going to be permanently swallowed up by the investigation.

Domingo stayed at my pad less than a week. He found out that the victim hadn't died and that the police hadn't been back to his house since that night. What he didn't know was that they had gotten his next-door neighbor to watch for his return. He was home only two days before his place was raided and he was under arrest for assault with a deadly weapon and strong-armed robbery.

While Domingo was hiding out with me, Rocky and his girlfriend had stolen her grandparents' car and run away to Colorado to hide out with the Mongol chapter there. Rocky managed to stay on the lam for several months before he was ultimately tracked down and arrested.

The police report of the assault and robbery clearly listed the name of the eyewitness to the incident. The Mongols are more criminally resourceful than they might appear to outsiders; as I'd seen firsthand during this investigation, the club has its own private eyes and attorneys on the payroll, as well as employees of local police departments and the California Highway Patrol providing them with confidential information. Domingo made bail and was back on the streets of the San Fernando Valley. It didn't take long for the police report of the assault to end up in his hands. Nor did it take long for him to start trying to locate the witness whose name was on that report—Ray Gun.

It was a Saturday night and I was planning to just stop by The Place, have a couple of beers, say hello to the boys, and call it an early night. But somewhere around nine that evening, The Kid and Conan from the RivCo Chapter showed up. Conan had gotten out of prison only a few months earlier but was working hard on a return ticket by selling drugs. He had made use of his time in prison working out, and it showed. He had an intimidating physique and a more intimidating stare.

The Kid, Carrena's ol' man, was another constant headache. I dreaded his coming around because he almost always pushed me to do drugs with him.

But tonight everybody seemed satisfied to drink beer. Somewhere around ten, The Kid, Carrena, and Conan made the suggestion that we all go to the Sundowner for another round.

We rolled into the Sundowner lot and parked in the rear as usual. There were a few cars and no bikes. It had the makings of a trouble-free night. But as soon as we settled in at the bar, Carrena spotted Ray Gun across the room. The Kid, as a chapter president, wielded more power in the club than I did, and he took charge of the situation. He began laying out plans for how we were going to handle Ray Gun. His options ran from murdering him to just beating him senseless.

I told The Kid that it should be Domingo's call. Conan insisted on beating the shit out of him at the very least. By this time, Ray Gun, standing at the far side of the bar with his girlfriend, realized he was in for some trouble. He tried to make his way to the door, but Conan got there first and blocked his escape. Ray Gun's girlfriend shuffled quickly to the bathroom. The Kid sent Carrena to catch her to make sure she didn't call the police on her cell phone. The Kid, Conan, and I converged on Ray Gun.

I kept saying we needed to call Domingo, but Conan shouted that he didn't want to. He felt like taking care of the guy right where he stood. Ray Gun was cornered, clearly shaking. Conan told him that he was going to kill him. Ray Gun began to plead for his life. The Kid grabbed Conan's arm and told him that there were too many witnesses in the bar; we needed to drag him out back and kill him there. Ray Gun begged us to let him go.

No civilians tried to intervene; the bar had gone silent. Ray Gun kept pleading and swearing that he would never testify against Domingo. I tried one more time to reason with The Kid and Conan, saying it was important that we at least get Domingo on the phone and ask what he wanted us to do. All my reasoning fell on deaf ears. They were intent on killing Ray Gun at the Sundowner.

Finally, I told The Kid that if we did kill Ray Gun here in the Sundowner, the crime might come right back on Domingo. He'd be the prime suspect in the cops' eyes, the one guy with a clear-cut motive, and he'd better have an airtight alibi. "Yo, we *really* need to run this past Domingo," I said again.

The Kid finally eased up. He went to the pay phone and called Domingo. Conan was still intent on kicking the shit out of Ray Gun. Ray Gun was trembling and almost in tears when The Kid returned with Domingo's instructions. "He said for us to hold him here. He's coming right over."

While we held Ray Gun in a corner, I assessed my options. If Domingo ordered us to kill him, the case was over tonight, right here in the Sundowner. There was no way I would let the Mongols murder a witness. I'd have to try to stop it. I could try to reason with Domingo, tell him that everyone in the bar had seen us cornering Ray Gun, and if we killed him, we'd all be going down for murder. If Domingo's response was irrational, then I'd have to make a stand. I had no gun, no knife, no weapons other than my two fists and my ability to reason with these killers. If it came down to it, I'd give myself up as an ATF agent in the bar in front of everybody, dial 911, and hope that the cops showed up in time to prevent a murder—Ray Gun's or mine.

Conan stayed in Ray Gun's face telling him how bad he was going to fuck him up. Ray Gun trembled and begged. Now I began to fear that Conan would lose all impulse control, simply stab Ray Gun to death before Domingo showed up. Ray Gun made a pitiful attempt to escape, trying to push past Conan, but Conan knocked him into the wall.

"Try that shit again and we'll dust you," The Kid said.

At last I saw Domingo's powerful, squat figure in the doorway. The expression in his eyes was homicidal, but I waited, wondering what his decision was going to be, what my play would be in response. Domingo was considerably shorter than Ray Gun. He lunged right into Ray Gun's face, gritting his teeth, spit flying—"You'll be lucky if I don't fuckin' kill you!"

"Please, Domingo . . ."

Ray Gun kept begging for his life, swearing he would never testify against a Mongol. He said that he would leave town, that he would do anything Domingo said. Domingo wanted to know why he said anything to the police in the first place. Ray Gun's first response was a denial, and this nearly sent Domingo over the edge. "Your name and your statement's in the goddamn police report, you fuckin' idiot!"

Ray Gun stuttered, apologizing, swearing he would make it up to Domingo. "Please let me go, Domingo. Please, I promise I'll never testify. I swear to God."

"All right," Domingo said finally. "But I want you out of town. And if I even hear a murmur that you might testify, you're a dead man."

Domingo moved to one side of Ray Gun and told him to get the fuck out of there. Ray Gun didn't hesitate; he hit the door, leaving his girlfriend behind.

The victim was so badly beaten that he couldn't identify Domingo, and without Ray Gun's statement, Domingo's prosecution couldn't go forward. But the prosecution didn't need Ray Gun's corroborating statement to make the case stick against Rocky. The victim's ID was enough. When Rocky was extradited from Colorado he found himself up to his ass in indictments and warrants. The State of California had him for assault with a deadly weapon, inflicting serious bodily injury, and robbery. They also had him on grand theft auto. ATF had Rocky for multiple federal drug violations and gun felonies, but in order to protect my UC identity and the integrity of our investigation, we asked the court to seal our indictments until we were prepared to do our final takedown on the Mongols.

I wasn't looking forward to having to testify against Rocky, but as it turned out, he never went to trial on any of his cases. He decided to work out a plea bargain with both the state and the feds.

I never saw Rocky again. When Ciccone called to tell me that Rocky had been sentenced to ten years on one of his state cases, I didn't feel great about it. Rocky had always treated me aboveboard and did his best to look out for me when I was taking all that abuse from Red Dog. I knew that he deserved to go to prison for all the criminal activity he'd been involved in. But I also couldn't forget that had it not been for him, I might well have been stabbed to death in the fight behind the Sundowner. In fact, months later, at his federal sentencing hearing, Rocky's attorney tried to get him some leniency by telling the judge that Rocky had saved the life of a federal agent. I testified that I probably would have been killed if Rocky hadn't intervened.

Rocky was not the hardened career criminal who typically makes up the membership of an outlaw motorcycle gang. He had held down a legit job as a tree trimmer for the City of Los Angeles for thirteen years and could quite easily have stayed straight for his entire life. But he'd fallen for that 1 percenter mirage, been taken in by the tough-guy mystique of the Mongols, and it had cost him big-time.

It was eleven A.M. and I'd just rolled into the South Pacific Motorcycle Shop. As I got off my bike and went inside, I was met by J.R., the hulking prospect who'd helped me carry my Softail Springer up the stairs to my undercover apartment. "Billy, did you hear what happened last night?" J.R. made a slicing motion across his neck.

"What the hell does that mean?"

"We stabbed a dude at Nino's."

Nino's was a popular bar down in Commerce near the Mother Chapter. I'd been down there a few times to meet with Leno Luna.

Evel came out of the back room, taking a break from working on a stolen bike.

"Yeah, Billy, I lost my knife last night," he said, scowling. "Panhead stuck some dude at Nino's with it. Then he tossed it. Somebody owes me forty goddamned bucks for that knife!"

This sounded like more than just a routine bar fight. As nonchalantly as possible, I reached down and activated the digital recording feature in the Motorola pager on my belt. J.R. and Evel proceeded to lay it out for me. I listened, nodding, taking careful mental notes for what might be an impending homicide prosecution.

After leaving South Pacific, I called Ciccone as soon as I could and relayed the information about the incident at Nino's. I told him that not only had the Mongols beaten a civilian, they claimed to have stabbed him to death. Ciccone said he'd look into it with the Commerce cops. He called me back in less than an hour. "Yeah, Billy," he said, with a new urgency in his voice. "Get all you can on that stabbing at Nino's. They're right. The guy they stabbed died."

By the fall of 1999, we'd amassed a long list of federal racketeering crimes against the Mongols—drug dealing, illegal gun trafficking, stolen motorcycles, extortions, assaults—but we couldn't yet make a homicide case. This was frustrating to Ciccone and me—and to the U.S. Attorney's Office—because we *knew* that the Mongols were responsible for a number of unsolved murders in California. But it really came back to that old truism of police work: It's not what you know, but what you can prove.

Now I went to work with renewed vigor, eager to get proof of the homicide in Commerce. As best I could, I established the scenario that had unfolded the previous night, November 25, 1999.

It had begun much like the episode with Rocky and Domingo almost killing their victim at The Place—a routine disagreement over a woman, and a jealous husband who had the temerity to stand up to the Mongols' aggression.

The Mother Chapter had been holding Church at Leno Luna's house in Commerce. When Church broke up they headed to Nino's, the nearest bar. Around nine P.M. a young woman named Sandra Herrera and her girlfriend decided to stop in at Nino's for a drink. Although Sandra had seen the Mongols at the bar on several occasions, she didn't know any of them by name. She had never seen them at their worst and had little insight into their violent nature.

As hard as it is for many people to fathom, there's something about that tattooed, bad-boy biker image that intrigues certain women—even straight, law-abiding women like Sandra.

Some Mongols rolled into Nino's lot, parked their bikes, strolled into the bar, and headed straight for the beer. The music was loud, and the presence of a couple of unescorted women gave them a reason to stay and play. Not that it ever meant much to the Mongols whether a woman was escorted or not.

Panhead didn't have much regard for anyone and needed little provocation to explode into a blur of violence. In his mid-thirties, he sported an array of Mongol tattoos and had the true gangbanger look of East L.A. He often wore a black bandana pulled low over his forehead, so low that he had to cock his head back just to see straight ahead.

Panhead had zeroed in on Sandra and her friend, offering to buy them another round of beer. When they agreed, Pirate, Coyote, and Cowboy joined Panhead at the girls' table, while Little Dave kicked back and watched his boys circling like a flock of vultures.

The possibility of a Mongol gang bang was looming in the air. The Mongols bought beer for the naive young women, who seemed to enjoy the attention. Then Sandra's husband, Daniel, walked in.

Daniel Herrera was a forty-two-year-old working-class guy; he and Sandra had a nice little place in Commerce and a couple of kids. He occasionally stopped in at Nino's to have a beer or two and wind down after work. Though a large man, he wasn't known as a troublemaker.

Daniel wasn't looking for a drink this night, and he wasn't looking for a fight, either. He was just looking for his wife. By this time, however, as far as the Mongols were concerned, Sandra belonged to them.

Daniel was more familiar with the Mongols than Sandra was, and he approached them with caution. In a calm tone of voice, he asked Sandra to come home. His reasonable request hit the Mongols like a brazen insult. He was trying to put an end to their hunt. Everyone waited for Sandra's response. She told Daniel that she wanted to stay and have another drink with her new friends. The Mongols were more than ready to back her play. "It doesn't sound like she wants to go home with you," Panhead said.

Daniel knew better than to tell a Mongol to mind his own business. He ignored Panhead and again looked at Sandra. "You've got two kids at home who need dinner, and we need to get out of here." The Mongols now told Daniel pointedly that perhaps he was the one who needed to get out. He was being offered his last free ticket out, but Daniel stood his ground.

Panhead backed out of the group and hooked up with

J.R., who was holding Evel's eight-inch buck knife. Pan-head ordered J.R. to hand over the blade.

Daniel Herrera wouldn't get a second chance. No one had the power to stop the Mongols now. Daniel had allowed his anger at his wife to get the better of his judgment. "Fuck you then, bitch!" he yelled in her face. "And fuck the Mongols!"

Daniel turned and headed for the door. The blows from fists rained down on him from all directions, but he was still able to make it to the exit. If he could get outside, he might escape with just a few cuts and bruises. He struggled with the Mongols, and he did make it out the door, but the Mongols were now in a frenzy. They kicked and beat Daniel until his face was covered in blood. After a long struggle, he finally managed to get away.

He ran as fast as he could, but the mob of Mongols caught him and resumed the beating. One Mongol fist after another pummeled his face and body until he was nearly unconscious. Then Panhead jumped in and plunged the buck knife deep into his back. The knife pierced his chest; Daniel could no longer fight back. He stumbled a few steps more as blood began to fill his lungs, suffocating him. He fell facedown on the pavement.   •

In the weeks following Herrera's murder in Commerce, I moved carefully among the Mongols, constantly recording my conversations on digital devices. I managed to get dozens of explicit conversations on tape, implicating Panhead and several other Mongols in the murder. I always played dumb with my questions, or tried to sound like I was filled with genuine outlaw awe. I told Panhead that I admired what he did, that I envied the skull-and-crossbones patch he'd earned by killing for the club. Panhead told me that he did what he had to do. In another conversation, at an L.A. muffler shop, I talked to Panhead about "sticking that dude." He was careful not to admit the murder outright, though he didn't deny it.

Finally my interest in the killing got me in hot water with the Mother Chapter. I was at the Easy Rider Convention when several Mongols, including the national sergeant at arms, backed me into a wall and questioned me about why I was talking so much about the murder. They read me the riot act. "Billy, keep your fuckin' mouth shut about Panhead and the dude at Nino's. Do you understand?"

But by that time, I'd captured more than enough on the wire. As a result of those taped conversations and my eyewitness testimony, we were confident that when we closed down the investigation we would bring a murder prosecution and get a conviction in the slaying of Daniel Herrera.

14

By the winter of 2000, as I was nearing the two-year mark with the Mongols, I found myself spending more time at Tony's Hofbrau in East L.A. It was ironic, given the nightmarish impression I'd had the first night I'd ventured down there, how ominous the figures in black had appeared, how much courage I'd had to muster just to back my straight pipes to the curb.

But now Tony's Hofbrau was a kind of oasis within the Mongol Nation. The situation in the San Fernando Valley was too volatile; the brawling and stabbings and drug use in The Place were overwhelming me. For the most part the guys in the SFV Chapter were in their twenties and thirties, and with the constant snorting of crank and coke, they had the stamina to stay up partying and brawling all night for weeks straight.

But the brothers down at Tony's Hofbrau were more laid-back than the typical Mongols. There were several graybeards, guys closer to my own age, some who'd also been in the service during the Vietnam War. The L.A. brothers even listened to better music—soul gems like Marvin Gaye, the Temptations, and classic fifties doo-wop—rather than the heavy-metal shit that was in constant rotation on the jukebox at The Place and that had started to feel like an incessant jackhammering inside my skull. Unlike the SFV Mongols, with these older and mellower L.A. dudes, I didn't have anyone ragging on me for not staying out all night.

I throttled down on Valley Boulevard, and as I rolled up in front of Tony's Hofbrau, a half dozen Mongols from the L.A. Chapter stood outside, watching me back my Harley to the curb. I shut the motor down, took my helmet off, and turned to them with a smile.

"Heya, Billy!"

"It's a black-and-white world, brother!"

As I walked through the doors of Tony's Hofbrau, I felt like a true Mongol and not an ATF special agent. By this time, I felt more welcome in the company of these 1 percenters than I did among my fellow law-enforcement officers. I *wanted* to be at Tony's on this warm night, wanted to have a beer with the L.A. members, and the thought of prosecuting any of them was not in my mind. I sat at the bar and ordered my usual beef sandwich and Bud.

I was especially glad to see Bronson, named for his uncanny resemblance to Charles Bronson and his silent tough-guy bearing. He was an older Mongol who owned and ran a paint shop in L.A. with his dad. I never saw Bronson fighting or doing drugs, but like most of us, he liked his beer.

I had a couple of Buds, talked with Bronson about getting a new paint job for my Softail Springer, and was just getting ready to head home when a new wave of Mongols showed up. Among them I saw Mike Munz, president of the San Diego Chapter. He and I greeted each other with the traditional handshake and hug. Munz was probably the most feared man in the entire Mongol Nation, and for months the San Diego Sheriff's Department had been pushing me to get close to him.

The Southern California area has a good number of cops and investigators working the OMG scene full-time. We call them biker chasers. Billy Guinn from the San

Diego Sheriff's Department was the OMG expert down there, and he wanted a piece of Mike Munz bad. They were looking at Munz for the unsolved murders of two Hells Angels, but they were having a hell of a time coming up with witnesses to testify against him. Munz was a scary guy, heavily into extortion—nothing subtle, just pure fear tactics—and the Mongols had muscled their way into a number of different legitimate bars and strip clubs in the San Diego area. The San Diego Mongols were also suspected of owning an arsenal of high-powered weapons.

Billy Guinn happened to be a friend of John Ciccone's, and they put in a request that I set up an operation down in San Diego. They wanted me to get next to Munz for intel-gathering purposes—any evidence I could find about the open homicides, the extortion, the guns and drugs, which they could then roll into their own prosecution.

Going down to San Diego was a risky proposition. Even hard-core Mongols were terrified of Mike Munz. He was six foot two, better than 250 pounds, rock-solid and evil-eyed. Mongols used to sit around talking about how Munz had done his prison time; whatever joint they sent him to, he would instantly ask the inmates who was in charge of the cell block. And if anyone spoke up, Munz beat his ass to prove that he was now in charge.

In addition to being intimidating, Munz suffered from bipolar disorder and needed lithium just to remain a semifunctional thug. When I first met him, we were all partying at a hotel and I watched him popping lithium from a prescription bottle. He told me that without it, he'd be completely out of control.

After our first few casual encounters, I arranged to meet Munz at a topless club called Pure Platinum near the San Diego airport. Billy Guinn informed me that Pure Platinum was one of the clubs that the Mongols had "taken over." The manager was so afraid of them that he didn't call the police even after a San Diego prospect named Rick Slayton knocked him unconscious in front of a dozen witnesses in his own nightclub. –

I rolled into Pure Platinum at around six-thirty on a Wednesday evening. I saw Munz's hog sitting in the parking lot, but no other bikes were there. I threw my colors on and walked to the front door. A bouncer was waiting to collect the cover charge, but when he saw my colors, he stepped aside. "Welcome. Mike's over at the bar."

Pure Platinum was more upscale than any of the topless joints I was used to going to in L.A.—bigger, cleaner, with a classier clientele. Across the room, Munz gestured for me to come on over. We did the Mongol handshake, and he introduced me to his two stripper girlfriends, sitting on either side of him.

Pure Platinum didn't serve food, so Munz told one of the girls to go out to get me something to eat. Munz then ordered a beer for me and I pulled my money from my pocket. He told me to put my fucking money away. "We don't pay for nothin' here." He called over to the manager, a clean-cut guy in a nice suit and tie.

"This is Billy, my brother from L.A.," Munz said.

"Welcome to Pure Platinum."

"You got a great place here," I said.

"Can I get you guys a bottle of something?"

I could tell the poor guy was completely intimidated but couldn't do a thing about the constant shakedowns from madman Munz and the San Diego crew.

Now Rick Slayton walked in with his girlfriend. A menacing-looking man who rippled with muscles, he had a shaved head, an array of tattoos, and a reputation for loving fights more than he loved riding bikes. He even ended up fighting professionally on the controversial Ultimate Fighting circuit.*

Next to arrive was Jimmy, a Mongol who'd killed a man before I began my undercover role and had managed to convince the court-appointed psychiatrists that he was insane so that he'd done his time in a mental institution.

Everyone continued to drink on the house, and the conversation was progressing smoothly until Munz made an impulsive suggestion—that we all go down to Tijuana, Mexico, that very night.

I didn't mind pushing the envelope on occasion, but a Mexico run would be out of the question. For a United States federal agent, slipping into Mexico unannounced on an undercover deal would be a career-ending mistake. Mexican authorities would go ballistic. Cross-border operations have to be cleared well in advance by both governments. Besides, I'd received intelligence that at least three Mongols in the Mexico Chapter were police officers, one a *federale*.

I made up my mind. This Mexico run wasn't going to happen. But the trouble was, Mike Munz was used to everybody going along with his suggestions. As a chapter president, he outranked me, and turning him down would be a delicate business.

"Come on, Billy. I know this great whorehouse, got the most beautiful chicks in Mexico. For twenty bucks, you can get laid all night long."

"Let's go," Jimmy said, and he even started to get up. I had to come up with something fast.

---

*In March 2002, during one of Slayton's no-holds-barred events at the casino of the Morongo Indian Reservation in Cabazon, California, the Mongols initiated a brawl involving 200 to 300 people when they rushed the ring after Slayton's disqualification from a fight. There were numerous injuries and one stabbing, but no prosecution was ever made, as none of the victims or witnesses were willing to cooperate.

"Look," I said. "I just picked up more than thirty thousand dollars' worth of avionics equipment that I gotta get to Van Nuys by seven in the morning. There ain't no way I'm taking that stuff into Mexico."

"You could leave it at my place," Jimmy said.

"I appreciate the offer, Jimmy, but I came down here tonight just to hook up with you guys. I would love to go to Mexico and get laid, but I just can't do it. I can't risk losing my job. The next time I come down here, I'll be ready for Tijuana, okay?"

Munz stared at me, suddenly intrigued by my job. He asked just what it was that I did for a living. I told him that my company bought and sold the high-tech instruments used in aircraft. He wanted to know if I could get him a job with my company. I told him I'd talk with the owner, though to read Munz's body language it was pretty clear he viewed the word *job* as just another opportunity for a long-term shakedown. "No problem, Billy," he said finally. "We'll do Mexico the next time you make it down here."

Before leaving Pure Platinum, I managed to engage Munz in a conversation about some guns that the SVF Chapter had for sale. I hoped that it would bring a response about the San Diego Chapter's own arsenal. I found out that all their guns were being housed at Jimmy's place. I could hardly keep from smiling when Munz said it. A murderer and an asylum alumnus had been put in charge of the munitions.

When I left Pure Platinum and did the debrief with Ciccone and Guinn, I told them what I'd learned about the San Diego Chapter's firearms, valuable information we needed to prepare the affidavit in order to get search warrants. But I told them I thought it was going to be nearly impossible for me to gather any intel on the homicides of those two Hells Angels in which Munz was the prime suspect. I could feel it in my gut, the undercover instinct telling me to steer clear of this one. Mike Munz was just too violent and unpredictable a character for me to push my luck any further.

I had made the big decision: The Laughlin River Run in April 2000 was going to be the last significant event I would participate in as a Mongol. I'd been riding with the gang for two years and two months, and I'd taken the case further than I'd ever dreamed. I'd patched in and had been performing the duties of secretary-treasurer of the SFV Chapter, and in February I'd been elected chapter vice president. But I had also gone well beyond my personal limit for abuse. My body was breaking down. I was constantly feeling sick, and the years of riding Harleys and hanging out in earsplitting Mongol bars had caused permanent hearing loss.

My personal life was a disaster. I'd lost touch with my own sons. My relationship with my girlfriend was over. I was isolated from my colleagues at ATF, and I knew the administrators in the L.A. Division were wholly indifferent to the sacrifices I'd been making.

As far as the investigation went, I felt like a gambler who'd been letting all his chips ride on the next roll of the dice. At some point the law of averages was going to catch up to me. At some point I would definitely crap out. What I feared most was making a slip, doing something stupid to give myself away. And giving myself away would no doubt cost me my life.

As Laughlin approached, a new wrinkle emerged, stressing me further. We heard that the Hells Angels were spreading a rumor in the biker world that the Mongols had been infiltrated by an undercover cop. Ciccone and I didn't think the rumor referred to me; it was likely just the result of some Angels trying to stir up problems in the Mongols.

But given the suspicion and animosity I'd long been

feeling from guys like Red Dog and The Kid, and given their penchant for crank-induced paranoia, the news wasn't helping me sleep better at night. For several months, I nodded as Mongols discussed the rumor in Church, repeatedly saying that they would murder the undercover if they ever found out who he was.

I had come to dread the moment when I put on my helmet, fired up the Harley, and had to ride in again. I felt like a massive stone wall was about to come crashing down on me at any minute.

Looking for a way to make the trip to Laughlin less onerous, I had been talking with Mongols from the Mother Chapter about riding into Laughlin with them instead of my own fuckup of a chapter. Mother was leaving at a more reasonable hour, and I knew that it would be less of a hassle to ride with a group whose bikes wouldn't be breaking down every twenty miles.

But the more I thought about the run, the less I wanted to make the trip at all. I called Ciccone and told him that I just wasn't up to another six-hour ride with the Mongols, whether it was the Mother Chapter or SFV. Ciccone was frayed to the limit, too, and wasn't thrilled about having to tail us.

So we devised a plan that made our lives easier. We decided to put my bike in the back of a U-Haul trailer and drive it to Needles, California, a small desert community just fifteen minutes from Laughlin proper. Once there, we'd offload my Softail Springer and I'd cross the border into Nevada and on into town. I'd lay some story on the Mongols about having to stop on the way to take care of some business and needing to ride to Laughlin solo. The story wouldn't be a problem. I'd been in long enough now that I could tell them anything.

The day before the run, I went to the U-Haul office in Upland and rented a truck under my Billy St. John name. I drove it home and loaded up my Harley. I noticed that the license tag on the truck was a temporary paper one out of Florida. The tag numbers had been handwritten in with a Magic Marker. The idea that this would be a big problem down the line never crossed my mind.

I had gotten to the point of giving myself a pep talk before every meeting with the Mongols: *Okay, Queen, this is the last time you're gonna have to do this. Nothing's gonna go wrong. It'll be a smooth operation. You can do this, brother.*

To my amazement, Ciccone showed up precisely at ten, as we'd arranged. It was completely unlike him; lack of punctuality was the one thing he had in common with the SFV Chapter. It was great to see him instead of a bunch of Mongols.

We trucked it to Needles without incident. I hunkered down low in the passenger seat to make sure that no Mongols spotted me on the road along the way. After gassing up in Needles we found an out-of-the-way location to offload the bike. Everything went exactly as planned. I threw on my patch, along with my other Mongol regalia, and fired up the bike. The plan was for Ciccone to follow me into Laughlin and break off just before I got to the Riverside Resort Hotel.

We were about five miles out of Laughlin when everything went to shit. First, I felt my bike starting to slow down. Even though I rolled the throttle, it got slower and slower. I began to smell something burning and turned to see that my back brake was seizing up. I pulled off onto the shoulder, and Ciccone stopped behind me in the U-Haul. I told him that I'd have to stay put until the brake caliper cooled or until I could get a pair of pliers to bleed it off.

At that very instant a Las Vegas Metro car rolled up. Las Vegas Metro Police have jurisdiction over the Laughlin municipal area. The cop asked me if I needed help, and I explained to him that my brake had just seized up and that I needed a pair of pliers. He stared at me, then at Ciccone, then back at the U-Haul. Shit. I knew what was coming.

"Who's the guy in the U-Haul?"

"I don't know, I've never seen him before in my life. He just saw me on the side of the road and stopped to see if I needed help."

The cop wasn't biting. I tried to keep his eyes—and my own—on my mechanical problem.

"Got a pair of pliers I can use, Officer?"

The diversionary tactic didn't work.

"Yes, I do, but I want to check some things out first." He backed his patrol car in behind the U-Haul and got out. I muttered under my breath to Ciccone, who had gotten out of the U-Haul, "Don't tell this guy anything." Ciccone nodded his silent acknowledgment.

The cop walked back to my bike. "Got some ID on you?"

I knew the drill; I'd been through this routine more times than I cared to remember. I broke out my undercover license and handed it over.

"This your bike?"

"Yeah, it's mine."

"Where you riding in from?"

"L.A."

Predictable cop questions; predictable Mongol answers. Then the cop asked me once again who Ciccone was.

"I got no idea. The guy just stopped to help me."

He walked over to Ciccone. "Got some ID, bud?"

Ciccone handed over his license. The cop asked Ciccone where he was coming from, and Ciccone's response mirrored mine. "L.A."

Pointing toward me, the cop asked Ciccone if he knew me personally.

"Nope, I just stopped to see if I could help him."

With his clean-shaven face, neatly trimmed hair, flip-flops, and Bermuda shorts, Ciccone didn't look at all like the kind of guy who would risk his neck by stopping to offer assistance to some hard-core outlaw biker on the side of the road. If I'd been in this Metro cop's boots, I wouldn't have believed us either.

The cop took one look at the rinky-dink paper plate on the U-Haul, and it was game over. He picked up his radio and called for a backup unit. I looked at Ciccone and whispered: "Don't tell 'em shit."

"Where you headed?" the cop asked me.

"Laughlin."

Then he looked at Ciccone. "Where you headed?"

"Laughlin." Clearly Ciccone hadn't heard my answer over the traffic, or just didn't expect the cop to keep harassing us.

"What's in the back of the truck?"

"Nothing," Ciccone responded.

We're sitting in the middle of the desert, just outside Laughlin, where thirty thousand bikers of all types are congregating. I'm plainly a 1 percenter in the company of Mr. Clean Jeans, who happens to be driving a very suspicious U-Haul truck, trying to sell this cop a bag of rotten goods he can smell a mile away.

Ciccone had his ATF identification on him, but we had no idea if we could trust these Las Vegas Metro cops with the truth. The Mongols spend a lot of time partying in Laughlin and Vegas, and it wouldn't have surprised me to learn that they had developed informants with access to confidential police information.

The Metro cop turned his attention back to me. "What's in the back of the truck?"

"How should I know? I told you I never seen this guy in my life." I tried to sound like an illiterate punk. The cop looked like he'd heard this line a thousand times before and made no effort to hide his disdain. His backup unit arrived with lights flashing. The cop now told Ciccone and me to assume the position. We placed our hands against the side of the U-Haul, over our heads, legs spread wide. They began to frisk us for weapons.

Both cops went after Ciccone this time. "Sir, where'd you rent this truck?"

"In L.A."

"Let's see the registration and rental papers."

This was a demand, not a request. I could see the cop walking to the cab of the truck. We waited with our hands still overhead. The minute I said I didn't know Ciccone, I knew I'd bet the wrong horse. I was probably too exhausted to think clearly—why hadn't I simply claimed Ciccone was my brother-in-law, helping me move? It's just the nature of undercover work; you're thinking on your feet 24/7, and sometimes you improvise wrong.

The cop, rental agreement in hand, returned to the side of the truck where I was still in the assumed position. He unfolded the agreement, took maybe five seconds to look it over, and discovered that everything he'd heard in the last ten minutes was just so much fabricated bullshit.

Raising his eyes from the rental agreement, he glared at me. "So you've never seen this guy in your life, huh?"

I was off balance, with one foot on the ground and the other in my mouth. I responded like a true Mongol: "No comment."

The two cops decided that the situation demanded a little more backup. One cop got on his radio, while the other decided to take a closer look in the truck.

There were no warrants out for Billy St. John's arrest, and the truck wasn't stolen. So what if I'd been the one who rented the truck and we'd lied to the cops? There was still no justification for an arrest. People lie to cops every day, and cops know it. I figured they'd badger us for a while and then let us go. Standard police procedure. Then I saw the cop who had been looking in the truck jog back to where we were all standing. He grabbed Ciccone and threw him forcefully against the truck. He had him handcuffed in seconds.

What had my little straight-arrow case agent done to deserve such rough treatment?

"Ooh, you musta really fucked up!" I said under my breath.

No sooner had I made my cheap-shot comment than the other cop grabbed me and snapped the cuffs on me. Just then I saw John Carr and Darrin Kozlowski cruising past on Interstate 40—just in time to catch a glimpse of us being cuffed and thrown up against the U-Haul. Seconds later we heard a huge roar and I saw a large group of Mongols on Harleys cruising past and staring at me. Things were going from bad to worse with each passing minute. I'd considered all kinds of things that might go wrong on this last big run with the Mongols, but getting arrested with Ciccone in the desert wasn't one of them.

I saw one of the cops go back to the cab of the truck and return with Ciccone's gun in his hand. "Did you know he had a gun?" the cop asked me.

"No way, man." Like he was going to believe anything I had to say at this point.

The cops were doing everything by the book now. No chances, no mistakes. They demanded to know what was in the back of the truck. When more backup arrived, they opened the U-Haul to find nothing except the elastic tie-downs we'd used to hold my bike.

I saw Ciccone motion to one of the cops, a sergeant, saying that he wanted to talk with him around the back of the truck. The sergeant and another cop led Ciccone off. After about ten minutes they all returned to where I was standing cuffed.

The sergeant made a kind of public statement, as if he

was trying to get it on record for his guys as well as for me. He said that there was no evidence that the gun was unlicensed, and since it had been found in a closed brief-case, they wouldn't be able to charge anyone with its pos-session. He also said that everything else looked in order and that they would be letting both Ciccone and me go on our way.

Free and clear. After taking our pictures and filling out field interrogation cards (standard operating procedure for dealing with known gang members, and my Mongol colors identified me as a real gangster), the cop who'd originally stopped us finally gave me a pair of pliers so I could bleed off the back brake on my bike.

We drove off separately. I was worried about what the passing Mongols might have seen, but it wasn't worth risking another stop to call Ciccone. I had to hurry into Laughlin, show my face at the hotel, and try to pick up my role as Mongol Billy as soon as possible. It wasn't un-til hours later—when I managed to place an inconspicu-ous call to Ciccone—that I learned what had really happened behind that U-Haul. Not relishing the prospect of a few hours in the hoosegow, Ciccone had decided to admit to being an ATF agent while at the same time pre-serving my UC identity.

He told them that he was working undercover on the Mongols and that I was a full-patch member of the club. As a hang-around, he'd been told to drive the truck and follow me to Laughlin, then get lost. Taking into ac-count his straight appearance and my outlaw appear-ance, I knew the cops had to be dubious. But Ciccone had federal credentials, and when they ran a check on his license, it verified that he was a U.S. Treasury De-partment agent.

For these cops to buy the line of crap Ciccone was sell-ing, they would have had to conclude that Ciccone was one of the dumbest people they had ever run into. "If you're an undercover agent, then why the hell are you carrying your ATF credentials?" one of the cops asked. Ciccone explained that the Mongols had told him to follow me out, drop off the truck, and beat it. He didn't think he'd be hanging out with them.

These Las Vegas Metro cops weren't going to risk fucking up a federal investigation, no matter how stupid the undercover agent might be, and risk whatever consequences that might bring down on them from their bosses.

I finally rolled into Laughlin and met up with a group of Mongols standing in the parking lot of the Riverside Hotel. Word had reached them that the Metro cops had Billy St. John hooked up about five miles outside Laughlin. I knew I'd have to come up with yet another story about what had happened on the side of the road—in particular, why I didn't end up behind bars like a good little outlaw.

I had my slightly-resembling-the-truth alibi concocted for them. "Yeah, I can't fuckin' believe it. My back brake locked up on me, and a couple of dudes in a U-Haul stopped to help. The cops swooped in and were on us like stink on shit. Turns out one of the dudes in the U-Haul was wanted for murder up north somewhere. Man, I thought I was going to the gray-bar hotel for sure. They had me hooked for about an hour before they finally let my ass go. Shit, I'm just glad I'm here."

"Brother, you fuckin' lucked out."

"Yeah, I did."

I walked into the Riverside with the Mongols I'd met out front, and we joined about twenty more of our comrades in arms just inside the front doors.

But my luck was about to change. It wasn't going to be a laid-back Laughlin run after all. The Mongols were going into combat mode. There was going to be a showdown with the Hells Angels here in Laughlin.

*　*　*

The state of war between the Hells Angels and the Mongols had never been declared over, and tension between the clubs had been building in the two-plus years I'd been undercover. One night Domingo and I went down to Chatsworth and partied with a group of Angels at the Cowboy Palace. It had been a cool night, Angels buying beer for Mongols, Mongols buying beer for Angels.

But the situation east of L.A., in San Bernardino County, quickly ended any such fraternization. The original chapter of the Hells Angels Motorcycle Club was founded in Fontana, within San Bernardino County, as an offshoot of an older outlaw group known as the Pissed Off Bastards of Bloomington. Consequently, the Angels considered San Bernardino, or "Berdoo," hallowed ground. The Mongols, having won the right to wear the coveted CALIFORNIA lower rocker, agreed not to form a chapter in Berdoo.

The agreement had been honored for decades. But in 1999 a problem arose over a technicality. The agreement stated only that there would be no Mongol chapters established in Berdoo, but it didn't say that there would be no Mongols *living* in Berdoo. And a good number of Mongols did live in Berdoo. Mongols frequented the bars in the area and rode the streets, flying their black-and-white patches with impunity. In time, it started to rub the Berdoo chapter of the Hells Angels raw. The Angels began putting out the word that they were getting fed up with the Mongols invading Berdoo and that they were going to start throwing Mongols out of the bars and shooting them off their bikes if they didn't leave San Bernardino County.

During Church at Evel's place one Thursday night, Domingo announced that the word had come down from Little Dave: Enough was enough; it was time to put the Angels in their fucking place. It was time to show them who really ran the show in Southern California. Little Dave had decided that we were going to go down and make our presence known at the Crossroads, the most popular Hells Angels watering hole in San Bernardino County. We rode out to Berdoo in a Mongol raiding party at least one hundred strong. We only stayed inside the Crossroads for a couple of hours, just long enough to make a point. The Angels weren't going to be kicking any Mongols out of Berdoo anytime soon.

Massing in the lobby of the Riverside, the brothers from Mother now gave me the lowdown on what had happened in Laughlin while Ciccone and I were getting the third degree on the highway. Before I'd arrived, the Mongols had already had a run-in with the Hells Angels inside the casino of the Flamingo. All the months of tension, posturing, and bad blood were coming to a head. Mongols were milling around in the lobby and casino areas waiting for the word on how to deal with the Red and White.

The orders had already come down for a number of Mongols to ride sixty-six, armed but not wearing their colors. This signified seriously bad news; the Mongols are never more dangerous than when massing at a rally like Laughlin, with a cadre of armed "undercovers" ready to kill for the club at a moment's notice. I wondered if Ciccone and the boys had gotten the word, too.

Standard protocol at the Laughlin River Run was for the Mongols to occupy the Riverside Resort Hotel and the Hells Angels to occupy the Flamingo Hilton. It was about nine P.M. when Little Dave and Bobby Loco rallied the troops in front of the Riverside. Bobby Loco addressed the group of Mongols that was now thirty strong and said that there had been a confrontation with the Angels earlier in the day. The plan was for all of us to go to the Flamingo and confront the Hells Angels in the casino, to see what they were made of. There was no way I was going to be able to contact Ciccone to let him know about the impending confrontation. I just hoped he and my backups were out there watching closely.

After Bobby Loco's announcement, we immediately left for the Flamingo. We were being led by Mike Munz, who everyone—Angels, Bandidos, and any other outlaw gangsters—knew to be a human hurricane. Earlier in the evening, in fact, Munz had bumped into a girl, one of the Angels' groupies, in the men's room at the Flamingo and knocked her unconscious. Munz made no distinction between a three-hundred-pound male adversary or a ninety-pound female, especially if she was stumbling into the wrong bathroom and a loudmouth to boot. Even when unarmed, Munz wouldn't hesitate to wade head-long into a gun-and-knife fight or, in this case, into a group of five hundred Hells Angels.

With the precision of an army platoon, we rolled into the Flamingo Hotel, right through hundreds of the Red and White. All around us were those brothers riding sixty-six—a dozen dressed-down Mongols who I knew were all armed to the teeth with clear instructions to take care of business if the shit hit the fan.

The Mongol Nation was stone-faced as we moved through the Flamingo, more than ready to go to war over the day's disrespect. I think the Red and White knew it; the Angel crowd parted wide when the army of Black and White came through. The Mongols strolled around the casino until they found an area in which to circle like a wagon train preparing to stave off an Indian attack. In a defensive maneuver reminiscent of my tour in Vietnam, we stood facing outward, arms crossed, staring out at the crowd from behind dark glasses. There was no doubting the Mongols' mood tonight.

We were substantially outnumbered, and if it went

bad, we might get slaughtered. I looked around for Cleetus and Paul, the two deputies from the Los Angeles County Sheriff's Department who looked and dressed like bikers and were able to mingle freely among the thousands of bikers in Laughlin. I knew that if the bullets started flying in the Flamingo, my only way out alive might be with them. But where the hell were they?

Behind my black shades, I scanned the crowd. I noticed various groups of Angels growing visibly agitated at the Mongol presence. I returned the angry glare of several Angels—what we call the "mad dog"—an outright invitation to confrontation among 1 percenters. While glancing around the casino, I finally spotted Cleetus. He didn't have full-patch status, but he fit right in with any biker crowd. He was able to go places clean-cut John Ciccone—especially in his Bermuda shorts and flip-flops—could only dream of.

Cleetus towered over me at a beefy and muscular six foot four. A gregarious guy with a bellowing laugh, he had a beard longer than mine and wore attire just as offensive to the mainstream as my own. His partner, Paul, tended to stay in Cleetus's shadow but could more than hold his own in any rough situation.

Despite being a cop, Cleetus was something of a Hells Angels aficionado and, truth be told, probably bought into the Red and White hype just a bit. It wasn't that uncommon, even among biker experts, to believe that the Angels were still the gold standard they'd been back in the 1960s. Prominent Hells Angels like Ralph "Sonny" Barger, longtime Oakland Chapter president and considered the founding father, and Chuck Zito, the former New York Chapter president, helped perpetuate the Angels' mystique, keeping the allure of the so-called Big Red Machine in the media spotlight.

We continued mad-dogging the Angels, and in less

than five minutes, the club's upper echelon showed up for a powwow. Even violent criminals are occasionally willing to try a little diplomacy. Little Dave, Bobby Loco, and Mike Munz talked with the Angels' representatives for a few minutes. The Angels assured the Mongols that there would be no further shows of disrespect and apologized for any shown earlier. I was amazed at this act of contrition on the part of the Angels.

Cleetus's black-leather-clad arms were folded across his chest, and his head was shaking in disbelief. He looked at me without saying a word or making a sign, but his eyes spoke volumes. I knew his esteemed Angels had sorely disappointed him.

As we left the Flamingo, various Angels snarled at us under their breath. None dared to make a move on us, though. I read the faces of various Angels' prospects, hang-arounds, and groupies as we rolled out. The followers of what was reputed to be the premier outlaw motorcycle gang in the world were perplexed by what they'd just seen. It was a Black and White world now.

A distinct feeling came over me as I strutted through the Flamingo. I couldn't help myself—I was proud. Proud of my brothers. Proud of myself. I had just stood shoulder-to-shoulder with the Mongols against the notorious Hells Angels. We had backed them down. Right in their own yard, in front of God and every other eyewitness. Without even needing to get physical, we'd given the Angels a lesson in respect.

Having played my part, I marched in lockstep with my Mongol brothers through the flashing lights of the Flamingo casino.

Now it was time for Billy St. John to go home for good.

15

42 Arrested in Motorcycle Gang Raids
BY MITCHELL LANDSBERG, *LOS ANGELES TIMES*

Hundreds of federal agents and Los Angeles County sheriff's deputies fanned out over three states Friday to drop an investigative net over the Mongols motorcycle club, arresting at least 42 people in Southern California and seizing dozens of illegal guns, cocaine and stolen motorcycles, they said.

The crackdown was the culmination of a perilous, 2½-year investigation in which an undercover federal agent joined the club and rose into its executive ranks, an official of the U.S. Bureau of Alcohol, Tobacco and Firearms said.

Authorities described the Mongols as among the most violent of outlaw motorcycle gangs, and said its members were suspected in a wide variety of crimes that included murder, extortion, arson, weapons violations and illegal drug dealing. . . .

The undercover ATF agent, who was not identified, joined the Mongols' San Fernando Valley branch and rose through the ranks to become club treasurer. . . . Before joining, the agent was subjected to a background check by a private investigator working for the Mongols.

How a veteran federal agent managed to pass that check and remain undetected for two years in a reputedly ruthless motorcycle gang was among the tantalizing questions left unanswered by the federal officials, who declined to discuss the operation in any detail. . . .

"Our undercover agent put himself at great and prolonged peril to develop evidence of murder, weapons and narcotics violations, and other serious crimes," Donald Kincaid, the Los Angeles division director of the ATF, said in a written statement. He said the crackdown had "shaken the gang to its core."

It was a harrowing final month, between the last run to Laughlin in April and preparations for the end of my undercover role. Leaving the role meant vanishing at the last possible moment. Adding to my stress level, in the weeks before I was to disappear I had to hang out daily with the gang, while at the same time Ciccone was taking the investigation before a federal grand jury. For hours each day he was laying out the details of our undercover operation for seventeen civilians. We had no idea who some of these men and women might have connections to. Seventeen people who were not in law enforcement now knew of the investigation and could tell their friends and family about a federal undercover agent infiltrating the Mongols.

It took several weeks to complete the operation plan for the final raids. I spent my remaining time with the gang gathering intelligence for Ciccone and the U.S. Attorney's Office for search warrants. I would feed them information about known weapons and narcotics locations for them to write up in the warrants.

On the day of the takedown, May 19, 2000, I vanished forever from my role as Billy St. John. I was relocated to a safe house in downtown Los Angeles. Weeks earlier, my ex-wife and my sons had been moved far from Los Angeles for their safety. Until the investigation was almost over, we'd had no idea they were going to have to move. Although we protested the distant destination chosen by ATF, it was to no avail. We were all very upset.

One week in advance, ATF personnel from bureau headquarters in Washington and from around the United States began to converge on Los Angeles; every ATF Special Response Team from around the country was ordered to participate in the operation. More than 300 ATF agents and 375 Los Angeles County Sheriff's deputies and detectives raided scores of locations, mostly in Southern California but also as far away as Oklahoma, Colorado, and Georgia. The raids netted some seventy illegal firearms, including handguns, machine guns, and assault rifles, as well as explosives; seventeen stolen motorcycles; two kilograms of cocaine; significant quantities of marijuana and methamphetamine; and tens of thousands of dollars in cash. It also led to fifty-four indictments, which, in turn, yielded fifty-three convictions.

(Raids on some of the Mongols' homes turned up frighteningly powerful arsenals. At the residence of Lonnie "Slick" Gallegos, secretary-treasurer of the El Sereno Chapter, Los Angeles County Sheriff's officers and ATF agents found the following: a Beretta shotgun, a Mossberg 12-gauge shotgun, a Glenfield .22 semiautomatic rifle, a Maverick 12-gauge shotgun, a Norinco 84-S assault weapon, a Norinco Mak-90 assault rifle, an Intratec 9mm assault weapon, a Smith & Wesson 9mm pistol, a Jennings .22 semiautomatic pistol, a Charter Arms .44 Special revolver, a .357 Magnum blue-steel revolver, a bulletproof vest, nine plastic bags of marijuana, military and firearms training manuals, $1,400 in cash, and a set of brass knuckles. Though much of the contraband was in plain view, Gallegos's Mongol colors, his most prized possession, were found locked inside a Sentry safe in the garage.)

Throughout the raids, representatives from the United States Attorney's Office, U.S. Customs Service, U.S. Marshals Service, U.S. Immigration and Naturalization Service, the Los Angeles County Sheriff's Department, and the Bureau of Alcohol, Tobacco and Firearms manned a crisis center in downtown L.A.

The crisis center was a buzzing hive of law-enforcement activity. In these cases, no matter how carefully the logistics have been laid out, the facts on the ground invariably change throughout the raids. Some of the gang members can't be easily identified; some lie about their given names and don't have legitimate identification on their persons. I was constantly on the phone helping other agents ID suspects. There were also numerous instances when we had to get "rollback" warrants. In these instances, agents and deputies executing search warrants at dozens of residences and places of business would discover that a location not covered by the original warrant—for example, a detached garage—was actually suspected of housing a stash of firearms or drugs. They would call us at the crisis center, and we'd handle the paperwork of getting a judge to issue a rollback warrant so that we could legally complete the search.

For safety reasons, I could never return to my undercover apartment, and the place was shut down by other ATF agents. I was housed in a downtown Los Angeles hotel and had a Special Response Team assigned to me around the clock for protection. The day of the raids, I reported to the crisis center at four in the morning and began working the phones. It was a surreal feeling: The undercover role was over for me, but what did the future hold? I knew I would be called upon to testify against numerous Mongols and their associates, perhaps for years to come. As I walked around the buzzing crisis center, law-enforcement officers I didn't know kept pointing at me. It made me feel like some kind of sideshow attraction. Other officers were slapping my shoulder, shaking my hand, congratulating me.

After a few hours I felt numb, and deeply conflicted, as I monitored the progress of the raids. I worried about the safety of the agents and officers going into those seventy locations—Mongol residences, clubhouses, and places of business. Hard-core gangsters would be going to jail to-day, but for years I'd been calling these gangsters my brothers. I was both proud of my work as an undercover agent and sad about the ramifications my work would have for some of the men I'd grown close to.

The case was among the most ambitious and logisti-cally complex undercover operations ever undertaken against an outlaw biker organization. In the following months ATF made thirteen more arrests and I began the grueling task of preparing to testify against many of my former Mongol brothers in various federal and state tri-als. Supplementing my eyewitness testimony were hun-dreds of hours of tape recordings I'd made—in my wired Mustang, in my undercover apartment, and using covert ATF digital recorders secreted on my person. I'd gath-ered evidence of major drug dealing, motorcycle theft, extortion, assault, and rape; I'd helped solve the Novem-ber 1999 homicide of Daniel Herrera.

Of the fifty-four people we indicted in the operation, fifty-three were convicted. Most of them opted for guilty pleas when they saw the overwhelming evidence against them. The lone acquittal was the result of one Mongol, Rancid, taking full credit for a firearms violation and ex-onerating his brother outlaw on the witness stand.

The day after the takedown, I was on my way out of Los Angeles with my Special Response Team escort when I received a call on my cell phone. It was Top Hat, a Mon-gol who lived just outside Daytona Beach, Florida. Top Hat had a legitimate job driving a truck long-distance, and throughout the years of the investigation he'd often been out in California. I first met him at Domingo's house during a get-together, and we hit it off immediately. He was an older biker, around my age, and we used to sit around and shoot the shit. During one of these conversations I learned that, prior to patching in with the Mongols, Top Hat had ridden with the Warlocks Motorcycle Club when my ATF buddy Steve Martin went undercover with them. Top Hat rattled off the names of 1 percenters who ended up going to prison because of Martin's undercover work. "No shit, Top?" I said. "Boy, you just never know."

In the frenzy of the previous day's raids, no one in the club was exactly sure what had happened: Had the Mongol leadership been infiltrated by a federal agent or a cop? Had one of the patches been cooperating? Had the gang simply been targeted in a conventional surveillance and wiretap case?

From the backseat of the SRT's Chevrolet Suburban, I gestured for all the other agents to keep silent. Top Hat had just gotten word of the California raids and wanted to make sure I was okay.

"Yeah, Top. I'm okay. Can you believe this shit?"

"I been through this before, Billy. I can't believe it's happening again." He got quiet for a second, then said: "Look, we know who rolled on us."

I prepared for him to unload on me, but what he said next threw me completely off-guard. "It's that big fat fucker in the South Bay Chapter." I knew who he was referring to—a new patch we called Preacher. I knew that many of the Mongols had never trusted Preacher, partly because he had "patched over" from another outlaw club, partly because his attitude was far too laid-back for most of the boys.

But Preacher was going to be dealt with very shortly, Top Hat assured me. The Mongols had dispatched four guys to his home to kill him *today*. "They're on their way now," he said.

"They sure it's him, Top? 'Cause I don't think so."

"Yeah, Billy, they know it's him. That fucker's gonna be dead in short order."

I made the kind of snap decision that had become second nature to me during my years of undercover life: I was going to tell Top Hat who I really was, let the entire Mongol Nation know the truth about Billy St. John. I had no other choice; as a law-enforcement officer, my first sworn duty was to protect an innocent life. And if the hit team was already in motion, then it was only about an hour before they'd be at Preacher's place. There was no way I could stall and bullshit Top Hat, dilly-dally with excuses, try to get Ciccone on the phone and put together an ATF operation to stop the murder. The only guy who could save Preacher now was Billy St. John.

I took a deep breath and glanced out the tinted window of the SUV as the freeway flew past. "Top, that South Bay Mongol didn't roll," I said.

"Yeah, he did, Billy. Now it's just a matter of taking him out."

"Listen to me carefully, Top. He didn't roll. You know how I know he didn't roll? 'Cause it was me, Top Hat. I'm an agent for ATF. You hear me? So you need to call whoever's in charge of that murder detail and tell 'em the truth. Billy St. John rolled. If they kill that dude, they'll be killing the wrong guy, and I'll make sure they spend a long fuckin' time in prison for it."

Top Hat didn't say another word. I heard his breathing for a few seconds, then he hung up.

I called Ciccone to tell him that the Mongols now knew the truth about me. He immediately dispatched ATF agents to make certain that Preacher wasn't harmed.

As we drove out of Los Angeles, I didn't know just how to feel. My world seemed to be crashing down on me.

* * *

My testimony against the Mongols stretched on for two more years, through more than two dozen hearings and trials in different jurisdictions. Long before my first court appearance, I was permanently relocated to a safe house in Plano, Texas. As I was driven to my new temporary home by a Special Response Team, the reality hit me: I was leaving my whole life behind. My ex-wife and my sons had been moved to Florida, set up under new legal names. It was now going to be nearly impossible for me to spend any regular time with my children. The nighttimes in Texas were the worst. I missed my kids, missed Southern California, missed my friends. I had thousands of hours of undercover taped conversations to be transcribed, and although I was assigned to the Dallas Field Division, I had little to no contact with them. The only people I saw on occasion were members of the Dallas ATF SRT charged with my security.

The first time I flew back to L.A. to testify was in the prosecution of Junior, who'd been the national president of the Mongols before Little Dave. When I had left California, I was still in Billy St. John mode, with my stringy hair hanging down my back, my beard long and straggly and turning white. Everyone in ATF had gotten used to that version of me.

When I landed at LAX for Junior's trial, I was clean-cut, clean-shaven, and looked like any other cop. I could see Special Agent John Jacques, in the company of several heavily armed Special Response Team agents, waiting to meet me as I got off the plane. Jacques and I had gone through several ATF medic schools together and even administered IVs to each other in training. I waved to him, but he just stared past me. "Hey!" I yelled. "Are you guys looking for me, or are you here to pick up somebody else?"

Jacques let out a huge laugh when he finally recognized

me. "Jesus," he said. "I was looking for Billy the Biker."

I shook hands with Jacques and the members of my protection detail, and they hustled me out of LAX to a clandestine hotel in the Covina area. I had worked on a lot of ATF protection details throughout my career, guarding the president of the United States and various dignitaries from around the world. I knew the procedures, but it was odd to be the one protected.

I knew there was good reason for the protection. If the Mongols could get away with it, I knew they would try to kill me. I'd heard them talk about it in Church; I'd heard proven murderers talking matter-of-factly about cop killing. I remembered the night when Domingo had told me that he'd like to go out in a blaze of glory, killing a bunch of cops. He'd go down in Mongol legend as a great hero, the biggest murderer in a club filled with murderers. I thought about the gang members who had military backgrounds and the possibility of a sniper shot outside the courthouse.

I tried to calm myself down as we rode to the courthouse in the San Fernando Valley. I had ATF agents in front of me and behind me. Deputies from the Los Angeles County Sheriff's Department, charged with security at all Los Angeles courthouses, had a massive presence there that day. If the Mongols wanted to take a shot at me, they would have their work cut out for them. We pulled into the back of the courthouse near a loading dock. ATF agents checked and double-checked the area for suspicious vehicles and people. Several deputies waited at the back door as I was escorted up the loading ramp. The hallways were carefully cleared and secured as I entered them. I was quickly rushed to a secure room, where I waited to be escorted by agents into the courtroom.

Early on in my undercover role, Junior had been convicted of assault with a deadly weapon and sentenced to sixteen years in state prison. But his attorneys managed to get his conviction overturned on a technicality and win him a new trial. I was being called as an expert witness to demonstrate that the Mongols had been engaged in the crime of witness tampering. I had been privy to a number of conversations with Domingo and Red Dog that involved the gang's intimidating the witnesses scheduled to testify against Junior as well as trying to find other witnesses willing to falsely testify on his behalf.

The psychological ordeal of looking a Mongol in the eye for the first time since I emerged from the undercover role was tempered by the fact that I hardly knew Junior. I had only met him once during my first Laughlin River Run with the gang, so there weren't many personal feelings between us. Junior was a very violent man and a lifelong criminal, and I knew that he needed to be in prison.

Mongols who wanted to be in the courtroom while I gave my testimony were being strip-searched. There were several in attendance. But the Los Angeles County Sheriff's Department was taking no chances, and they weren't going to let any intimidation tactics by Mongols go unchallenged.

Over the years, testifying against my former Mongol brothers became a kind of personal purgatory. I came to dread those court dates almost as much as I dreaded my time as a Mongol prospect. Red Dog, much to my relief, pleaded guilty to a federal firearms violation, and was sentenced to three years in prison without my having to give eyewitness testimony against him in open court.

I hated the anticipation of making eye contact with the Mongols I had come to know well in my years undercover. My mind would play tricks on me as I sat in my Texas house, playing with Winchester, my golden retriever, and reviewing my tape transcripts before each court date. I was their friend. I was their brother. I drank with them. I partied with them. I rode with them and fought for them. I knew their kids' names and they told me they loved me. Jesus, I had no doubt that guys like Domingo, Rocky, and Evel would have died for me.

I knew that going eyeball to eyeball with Evel in court was going to be painful. (Domingo had pled guilty, so I never had to testify against him.) In February 2001 I was subpoenaed to testify against Evel. Once again, on a bright Monday morning I found myself staring anxiously out the window of a Boeing 777 on my way to Los Angeles. My protection detail was there to meet me, and the trip from LAX to a hideout hotel went smoothly. I had a few days in which to sit down with the prosecuting attorney whittling out a strategy. It was no big deal, as far as trials go, except that I really did not want to see Evel get hammered again. He had already taken a couple of hits—convicted in separate assault and theft cases—and now he was looking at spending more years in the penitentiary.

He was on trial for his role in the Mongols' stolen-motorcycle ring, but I just didn't see the benefit of adding another dozen years to Evel's prison time. But it wasn't my call to make. I was just a small cog in a much larger machine. Besides, I said to myself, Evel had no one to blame but himself. I kept telling myself that I was on the right side here, that I was doing what needed to be done.

But I'd been in the law-enforcement business for a long time, and I'd seen the outrageous occur in court. I'd seen the most vicious criminals, murderers who should be doing life in prison, walk away scot-free. I had to tell myself over and over that it wasn't *me* that Evel loved; it wasn't *me* that Evel would have given his life for. Evel loved my persona; he loved a shadow I'd created in his mind: Billy St. John, the hard-core Mongol outlaw. Evel wouldn't have hesitated to kill Special Agent William Queen.

Wednesday rolled around, and I found myself sitting

outside the courtroom in that horrible limbo, waiting to testify, to face Evel. Ciccone was already inside the courtroom sitting next to the assistant United States attorney.

I was trying to calm my nerves by making small talk with Zack from the Los Angeles County Sheriff's Department, who was a friend as well as a member of my protection detail. I kept drifting back and forth between the present and the past. I could see myself laughing and drinking beer with Evel up in my undercover apartment as we broke down that stolen Softail Springer. I could see myself doing better than 130 miles per hour on the 210 freeway as Evel blew past me with plenty of throttle to spare. Then I remembered the awful scene in his house when he'd split his wife's face wide open and I'd done my damnedest to stitch her back up.

God, I wished I could be a regular cop like Zack. It was all black and white to him. There were no personal issues; it was simply a matter of right or wrong.

But things weren't so clear-cut to me. The cop in me knew that the Mongols were serious bad guys who needed to be prosecuted and put away. But there was another factor that cops like Zack and Ciccone could never understand. I'd not only witnessed it and lived it—I had *felt* it.

When my mom died and no one from ATF had so much as offered their condolences, but the whole of the Mongol Nation embraced me, and guys like Evel had hugged me and told me, "I love you, Billy," I felt and understood the bond holding together these outlaw motorcycle gangs.

We could take down their gun-trafficking networks, bust their drug-dealing operations, prosecute them for extortion and armed robbery and rape and homicide. The thing we could never attack was the love these guys felt for their brothers; in many cases it was a love stronger than for their blood relations. It was stronger than the most addictive narcotic.

The door swung open suddenly. It was Ciccone, and his expression was resolute. "Billy, you're up," he said.

I walked into the courtroom and caught a quick glimpse of Evel as I made my way to the witness stand, stopping short to be sworn in by the clerk.

"Do you solemnly swear that the testimony you are about to give will be the truth, the whole truth, and nothing but the truth, so help you God?"

The whole *truth?* I thought. The court was in no way interested in hearing the whole truth. "I do," I said, then took the witness stand.

At first I tried not to look at Evel, but it was like some invisible force, some gravitational pull, wrenching my eyes toward him. I glanced over to see him staring right at me. He wasn't mad-dogging me. He wasn't giving me that Mongol murder glare like we'd given the Angels in Laughlin. If anything, Evel's eyes looked hurt and plaintive. *Billy, what the hell are you doing? Can't you see it's me? It's Evel!*

Just then I heard the judge's voice echoing in the hollow-sounding courtroom. "Would you state your full name for the court, and spell the last name, please?"

It took me a moment to regain my composure. "Yes, Your Honor. It's William Queen. Q-U-E-E-N. Special agent with the Bureau of Alcohol, Tobacco and Firearms."

Epilogue

Our undercover investigation was a massive blow to the Mongols Motorcycle Club, but the gang was by no means decimated. Exactly two years after my last day with them, a large convoy of Mongols rolled into Laughlin, Nevada, for an annual show of strength at River Run 2002. And just as I'd seen in the Flamingo casino, the Mongols went prepared for anything the Hells Angels might try.

This time the showdown went beyond posturing.

On April 27, 2002, just after two A.M., a group of about thirty-five Hells Angels left the Flamingo Hotel and cruised on their Harleys to nearby Harrah's Casino to back fifty Angels who were already there. On the casino floor they squared off against about forty Mongols. An Angel delivered a karate kick to the chest of a Mongol. Then all hell broke loose, with fists flying, and a blur of wrenches and hammers and knives. In the mêlée, one Mongol pulled a semiautomatic and shot an Angel point-blank in the belly.

When the battle was over, three bikers lay dead—two Angels and one Mongol. Dozens of innocent bystanders had been hurt in the rioting. A third Angel was later found shot to death on the highway in San Bernardino County. He had been on his way home from the Laughlin run.

The Mongol who was stabbed to death inside Harrah's

was my friend Bronson, the mellow, older brother from the L.A. Chapter who had helped me paint my Softail Springer. I'd imagined many of the Mongols I knew dying in battle with the Hells Angels, but Bronson wasn't one of them. I was very sorry it had to be him.

But it's the nature of the 1 percenter world. Motorcycle gangs like the Mongols, for all the terror and violence they inspire in law-abiding citizens, wreak their most complete devastation on their own. Prison, drug addiction, or violent death is the expected end for any man willing to wear that black-and-white patch.

Mongols Motorcycle Club Defendants' Court Proceedings

DEFENDANTS WHO PLED GUILTY

1. AFANESKO, James "Jimmy": Pled guilty to a violation of the Federal Firearms Laws (Title 18, U.S. Code, sec. 922[g]1). Sentenced to federal prison.

2. ALARCON, Phillip "Evel": Pled guilty to Interstate Transfer of Stolen Motorcycles (RICO Predicate Act). Sentenced to federal prison.

3. McDONALD, Jeremy "J.R.": Pled guilty to Interstate Transfer of Stolen Motorcycles (RICO Predicate Act). Sentenced to federal prison.

4. CHAVEZ, Raymond "Ray-Ray": Pled guilty to a violation of the Federal Firearms Laws (Title 18, U.S. Code, sec. 922[g]1) and violations of the Federal Narcotics Laws (Title 21, U.S. Code, sec. 841[a]1). Sentenced to federal prison.

5. JARVIS, Donald "Red Dog": Pled guilty to a violation of the Federal Firearms Laws (Title 18, U.S. Code, sec. 922[g]1). Sentenced to federal prison.

6. LUNA, Thomas "Tommy T": Pled guilty to a violation of the Federal Narcotics Laws (Title 21, U.S. Code, sec. 841[a]1). Sentenced to federal prison.

7. BERRARA, Carrena: Pled guilty to a violation of the Federal Narcotics Laws (Title 21, U.S. Code, sec. 841[a]1). Sentenced to federal prison.

8. BOYSON, Bruce: Pled guilty to unauthorized use of a law-enforcement computer. Boyson was a dispatcher for the California Highway Patrol who accessed law-enforcement computers on behalf of the Mongols. Boyson was fired from the CHP, received a felony conviction, and served a short jail term. After serving the term, Boyson was placed on probation for three years.

9. VEGA, Johnny "Cowboy": Pled guilty to a violation of the Federal Firearms Laws (Title 18, U.S. Code, sec. 922[g]1). Sentenced to federal prison.

MURDER CASES

1. GUTIERREZ, Adrian "Panhead": Gutierrez was tried in Superior Court of Los Angeles and found guilty of murder with a "gang allegation enhancement" and sentenced to state prison.

2. HANNA, David: Murder charges are still under investigation.

MACHINE-GUN CASES

The following five defendants pled guilty in the Central Judicial District of California to trafficking in machine guns and were sentenced to federal prison:

1. ALVAREZ, Timothy "Domingo"
2. GARCIA, Robert "Bobby Loco"
3. JIMENEZ, Ernest "AK"
4. LUJAN, Michael "Mansion Mike"
5. VOGEL, Richard "Shaggy"

The following two defendants pled guilty in the Central Judicial District of California to possession of a machine gun and were sentenced to federal prison:

1. JIMENEZ, Ernest "AK"
2. VEGA, Johnny "Cowboy"

FIREARMS CASES

With the one exception noted (Cardenas; see below), all of the following defendants were convicted in the U.S. District Court or Los Angeles County Superior Court of various firearms-related charges and were sentenced to federal or state prison:

1. CASTILLO, Christopher "Recon"
2. CLAYTON, Richard "Rancid"
3. CRAMER, Douglas "Bucket Head"
4. GALLEGOS, Lonnie "Slick"
5. GONZALEZ, Joe "Lil Joe"
6. GUEVARA, Martin "Largo"
7. HOWARD, Joseph "The Kid"
8. VALLES, Leonard "Lenny"
9. CARDENAS, Manuel "Woody" (trial, found not guilty)*

---

*Defense witness, a Mongol, testified firearm was his. This witness's testimony resulted in an indictment charging him with this offense.

NARCOTICS CASES

The following defendants were convicted in U.S. District Court or Los Angeles County Superior Court of various narcotics-related charges and were sentenced to federal or state prison:

1. FRANCHINA, Richard "Richie"
2. MARTINEZ, Rudy "Rocky"
3. NELSON, Donald "Hobbit"
4. RAMIREZ, Giovonni "Geo"
5. PANACCIA, Michael "Casper"
6. GARCIA, Robert "Bobby Loco"

INTERSTATE THEFTS OF STOLEN MOTORCYCLES

The following two defendants were convicted in U.S. District Court for removing vehicle-identification numbers (VINs) on motorcycles and submitting fraudulent motorcycle-registration documents and sentenced to federal prison:

1. MGRDICHIAN, Gerard "Buddy"
2. MGRDICHIAN, Joanne

STOLEN-PROPERTY CASES

The following two defendants were convicted in Los Angeles County Superior Court of possessing known stolen property and sentenced to state prison:

1. MARTINEZ, Vicky
2. Pam LAST NAME UNK

ASSAULT CASES

The following defendant was found guilty in state court, County of San Diego, for assault with a deadly weapon and was sentenced to state prison:

1. SLAYTON, Richard

STOLEN MOTORCYCLES

The following defendants were convicted in Los Angeles County Superior Court of motorcycle thefts:

1. GOMEZ, Felipe
2. MARTINEZ, Francisco
3. PIZANO, Jose

RICO

RICO charges against the Mongols Motorcycle Club and its members are still pending.

CASE AGENT: Special Agent John Ciccone—L.A. Group II

UNDERCOVER AGENT: Special Agent William Queen—L.A. Group II

Acknowledgments

I would like to thank my beautiful wife, Allysson, for lighting the fire that truly got things rolling on this book. Your love and encouragement kept it together. I love you.

To my children, who lost their dad for years. If I could trade the Mongol investigation for what we lost, I would. I love you.

To Carolyn, Jimmy, Gene, and Debbie, we lost that time too. I love you.

Thanks to Doug Century, my book doctor, who deserves a great deal of credit for the success of this book.

Thanks to Lee Boudreaux, my book editor, and the rest of the Random House team who contributed to the book.

To all those who made up the team that brought the Mongols to justice.

Thanks to John Ciccone, Darrin Kozlowski, John Carr, Eric Harden, Cleetus, and Paul.

Thanks to Tom Brandon, the Group II supervisor who stood up for John Ciccone and me.

Thanks to Sally Meloch, the assistant United States attorney in charge of this investigation.

Thanks to Jerry Friedberg, the assistant United States attorney who kept order when things got disorderly.

Thanks to John Cooper, for his support at bureau headquarters.

Thanks to Al Phoenix, for everything he did for me both in bureau headquarters and out in the field.

Thanks to George Bernard, Steve Campbell, and John Tailor, for backing me and making things safer.

Thanks to Steve Trethewy, for the support in Phoenix and for the support in writing this book.

Thanks to Howard Levine, for being there for me when times got tough.

Thanks to Steve Martin, for propping me up as only he could.

During my career as an ATF agent, I was privileged to work for a few supervisors who went out of their way to back me and support me when it was unpopular with other administrators. They were the kind of people who would stand up for what is right no matter who it concerned or what perils it might bring them. They made decisions based on right and wrong with no regard for political or other self-serving interests. They are the kind of people who make our country great and who I sincerely admire. Thanks to Lanny Royer, Tony Ferguson, and Larry Cornelison.